Jossey-Bass Teacher

Jossey-Bass Teacher provides educators with practical knowledge and tools to create a positive and lifelong impact on student learning. We offer classroom-tested and research-based teaching resources for a variety of grade levels and subject areas. Whether you are an aspiring, new, or veteran teacher, we want to help you make every teaching day your best.

From ready-to-use classroom activities to the latest teaching framework, our value-packed books provide insightful, practical, and comprehensive materials on the topics that matter most to K–12 teachers. We hope to become your trusted source for the best ideas from the most experienced and respected experts in the field.

JB JOSSEY-BASS

· Got ·
Grammar?

Ready-to-Use Lessons & Activities
That Make Grammar Fun

Jack Umstatter

BICENTENNIAL
1807
WILEY
2007
BICENTENNIAL

John Wiley & Sons, Inc.

Published by Jossey-Bass
A Wiley Imprint
989 Market Street, San Francisco, CA 94103-1741 www.josseybass.com

Wiley Bicentennial Logo: Richard J. Pacifico

Jossey-Bass books and products are available through most bookstores. To contact Jossey-Bass directly call our Customer Care Department within the U.S. at 800-956-7739, outside the U.S. at 317-572-3986, or fax 317-572-4002.

Jossey-Bass also publishes its books in a variety of electronic formats. Some content that appears in print may not be available in electronic books.

ISBN: 978−0−7879−9387−0

Printed in the United States of America
FIRST EDITION
PB PRINTING 10 9 8 7 6 5 4 3 2 1

About This Book

Got Grammar? Ready-to-Use Lessons and Activities That Make Grammar Fun was created for you, the busy English language arts teacher, and your students who need to know grammar as well as any other generation of students before them. Divided into six sections—Parts of Speech, Parts of a Sentence, Sentences, Usage, Mechanics, and Meeting the Tests Head-On. This comprehensive instruction, activity, and test resource contains over 60 reproducible, ready-to-use grammar lessons, along with many ready-to-use activities that include 15 diagnostic tests, 15 section review activities, 18 final tests, and over 100 other creative, reinforcement activities. Your students will also benefit from the Writing Tip at the end of each instructional lesson, and you will benefit from the time saved in preparing these lessons, activities, tests, and answer keys.

    Got Grammar? is an entire course of grammar, with ready-to-use, reproducible lessons, diagnostic and final tests, and reinforcement and review activities all in one book. Crosswords, magic squares, matching columns, riddles, find the words and phrases, and other fun activities will engage your students and create enthusiasm for learning grammar. Whether these lessons and activities are used sequentially or as needed, your classroom will come alive as your students enjoy working their way through this classroom-tested, user-friendly way to learn grammar. Enjoy!

About the Author

Jack Umstatter has taught English on both the junior high school and senior high school levels since 1972. He has also taught education at Dowling College in Oakdale, New York, for the past fifteen years, and writing and literature at Suffolk County Community College for the past four years. He recently retired from the Cold Spring Harbor School District, where he taught English and co-chaired the department.

    Mr. Umstatter graduated from Manhattan College with a B.A. in English and completed his M.A. degree in English at Stony Brook University. He earned his educational administration degree at Long Island University.

    Selected Teacher of the Year several times, Mr. Umstatter was elected to *Who's Who Among America's Teachers,* and has appeared in *Contemporary Authors.* He has taught all levels of secondary English classes, including honors and Advanced Placement classes. As coach of the high school's academic team, the Brainstormers, he led the West Islip High School team in capturing the Long Island and New York State championships in Lake Forest, Illinois. His teams at Cold Spring Harbor High School also competed in the Questions Unlimited National Academic Championships in New Orleans and Los Angeles.

    Mr. Umstatter's publications include *Hooked on Literature* (1994), *201 Ready-to-Use Word Games for the English Classroom* (1994), *Brain Games!* (1996), *Hooked on English!* (1997), the six-volume *Writing Skills Curriculum Library* (1999), *Grammar Grabbers!* (2000), *English Brainstormers!* (2002), *Words, Words, Words* (2003), and *Readers at Risk* (2005), all published by Jossey-Bass.

Dedication

To my good friend and English department companion,
Jim Pryal, for his guidance, care, humor, and love of grammar.
Our years together were both fun and memorable.
Thanks for the memories.

Acknowledgments

My special thanks to my wife, Chris, for always being ready to assist in this project whenever needed.

I also thank my daughters, Kate and Maureen, for their inspiring work as teachers of young children. Your students are so fortunate to be in your classrooms!

Many thanks to Margie McAneny, my editor, for her care, guidance, and insightful suggestions along the way. I have truly enjoyed working with you.

Thanks as well to Paul Foster, my publisher, for his unwavering support of this and other educational resources I have been honored to write for Jossey-Bass.

Once again, my thanks and appreciation to Diane Turso for her keen eye and outstanding efforts in proofreading this book.

Contents

How This Book Maps to Education Standards

Below are nationally accepted standards for teaching Language Arts/Writing from Mid-continent Research for Education and Learning (McREL), along with references to material in this book that helps teachers to meet the standards. For more on McREL standards, go to www.mcrel.org.

Standards Grid

	Sec. 1	Sec. 2	Sec. 3	Sec. 4	Sec. 5	Sec. 6
USES THE GENERAL SKILLS AND STRATEGIES OF THE WRITING PROCESS						
5. Uses content, style, and structure appropriate for specific audiences and purposes	X	X	X	X	X	X
USES THE STYLISTIC AND RHETORICAL ASPECTS OF WRITING						
3. Uses a variety of sentence structures and lengths (e.g., complex and compound-complex sentences; parallel or repetitive sentence structure)		X	X	X	X	X
USES GRAMMATICAL AND MECHANICAL CONVENTIONS IN WRITTEN COMPOSITION						
1. Uses pronouns in written compositions	X	X		X		X
2. Uses nouns in written compositions	X	X		X		X
3. Uses verbs in written compositions	X	X	X	X		X
4. Uses adjectives in written compositions	X	X		X		X
5. Uses adverbs in written compositions	X	X		X		X
8. Uses conventions of spelling in written compositions				X	X	X
9. Uses conventions of capitalization in written compositions		X	X	X	X	X
10. Uses conventions of punctuation in written compositions		X	X	X	X	X

Introduction

Grammar is a piano I play by ear. All I know about grammar is its power.
　　　　　　　—Joan Didion, acclaimed writer and Pulitzer Prize finalist

Grammar is back! Actually, it never went away, but grammar in many educational settings seemed to have been on the back burner for a time. Now grammar has made its resurgence, and as Joan Didion points out, grammar has power. Certainly the local, state, and national standardized tests have given grammar more prominence. In addition, the college admissions examinations have given new life to grammar's importance. Today's students are held more accountable for grammar than their more recent predecessors were, and as a result, the same holds true for you as a teacher of the English language and its many fascinating components. Understandably, the word *grammar* now appears more often on the pages of curriculum guides and important examinations, as well as on the lips of concerned parents eager to know that grammar is being taught and learned.

Adhering closely to the standards, benchmarks, and practices established by the National Council of Teachers of English, the International Reading Association, and Mid-Continent Research for Education and Learning, *Got Grammar? Ready-to-Use Lessons and Activities That Make Grammar Fun* contains a unique combination of practical and reproducible grammar instruction lessons, activities, diagnostic tests, and final tests to ensure that your middle school, junior high school, and high school students have learned the necessary grammar skills. The lessons are instructive and user friendly, the activities are fun and engaging, and the diagnostic and final tests are informative and practical. Divided into six units, this resource features many ready-to-use activities: 15 diagnostic tests, 15 section review activities, 18 final tests, and numerous other creative, reinforcement activities that make learning grammar enjoyable. Answer keys accompany these tests and activities. Each lesson includes a special segment entitled Writing Tip that will help your students to recognize and use that specific grammar component's usage and strength as they become more skillful and confident writers. Puzzles, such as crosswords, find the words or phrases, magic squares, matching columns, and riddles and the self-check components of these and other activities, will interest and motivate your students. These activities, tests, and answer keys are ready to use, so you will save preparation time and be able to devote your energies to some of your other teaching responsibilities. You and your students can use these lessons and activities sequentially or select them as needed.

Section One, "Parts of Speech," familiarizes students with the eight parts of speech. The fifteen activities, two diagnostic tests, and two final tests will give students a firm grasp of the basic units of the English language.

The twenty-one lessons and twenty-three activities found in Section Two, "Parts of a Sentence," cover sentence subjects; predicates; prepositional phrases; verbal phrases; appositive phrases; direct and indirect objects; and adverb, adjective, and noun clauses. Three review activities and five final tests on these topics areas reinforce these essential grammar aspects.

Section Three, "Sentences," covers complete and incomplete sentences, types of sentences by purpose and structure, and sentence starters. Twelve activities accompany these eleven lessons. A combination of seven diagnostic and final tests provides students with ample opportunities to understand these skills so necessary for effective writing.

Section Four, "Usage," includes subject and verb agreement; indefinite pronoun agreement; irregular verbs; verb tense; nominative, objective, and possessive cases; objects of the preposition; modifiers; and many words often confused. Four diagnostic tests and five final tests emphasize the materials studied in the twenty-one lessons and their accompanying twenty-three activities.

Section Five, "Mechanics," focuses on capitalization, spelling, and punctuation. Special emphasis is placed on the comma, one of the most challenging marks of punctuation for young writers. The two final tests examine students' knowledge of the grammar topics covered in the eight lessons and their twenty-one complementary activities.

The sixteen activities in Section Six, "Meeting the Tests Head-On," will prepare students for testing situations that will check their grammar proficiencies. The types of questions here are similar to those found on standardized examinations. Practice will prepare students thoroughly for these important examinations. In many cases, the answer keys explain why the choices are correct or incorrect.

Artemus Ward, a nineteenth-century satirist, once proclaimed, "Why care for grammar as long as we are good?" Although Ward may have echoed the thoughts of those who are not rabid (or even less fanatical) advocates of the study of grammar, students in today's grammar-conscious educational community do not have that choice. Grammar is on the front burner once again, and test constructionists expect students to know grammar. The price of not knowing grammar can be costly, academically and socially. *Got Grammar?* will allow your students to know grammar's powers, as Joan Didion does, and to use their grammatical skills not only in their academic testing situations but also in their daily writings and conversations. What a terrific combination!

Jack Umstatter

Section One
Parts of Speech

Diagnostic Tests

DIAGNOSTIC TEST 1   PARTS OF SPEECH

For each underlined word in the following sentences, identify and then write the part of speech on the line next to the number. Each part of speech is used at least once. Each correct answer earns 5 points. Use the following abbreviations:

noun—N	adverb—ADV
pronoun—PRO	preposition—PREP
verb—V	conjunction—CONJ
adjective—ADJ	interjection—INT

1. _____ They <u>attended</u> the concert last weekend.

2. _____ Several cats ran <u>into</u> Rob's garage.

3. _____ The truck driver delivered the packages <u>quickly</u>.

4. _____ <u>Fast</u> runners won all the awards at the track meet.

5. _____ My friends and I walked home <u>after</u> school.

6. _____ I wanted a peanut butter <u>and</u> jelly sandwich for lunch yesterday.

7. _____ <u>She</u> was counting the ballots during social studies class.

8. _____ <u>Hey</u>! That is my seat.

9. _____ Will <u>they</u> finish the test on time?

10. _____ The <u>diagram</u> was pretty complicated for us.

11. _____ He will practice his musical piece <u>soon</u>.

12. _____ Reggie saw the <u>awesome</u> sight from the air.

13. _____ Her sister is the oldest member of the <u>group</u>.

14. _____ <u>Check</u> the score, Tom.

15. _____ Will the students be able to find the answer by <u>themselves</u>?

16. _____ Are you sure of <u>yourself</u>?

17. _____ They <u>slowly</u> carried the couch down the stairs.

18. _____ Can you see beyond the hills <u>from</u> the top of the tower?

19. _____ <u>Hurray</u>! Our team has finally scored a touchdown.

20. _____ The troop had been scattered throughout the <u>woods</u>.

Number correct _____ × 5 = _____%

DIAGNOSTIC TEST 2 PARTS OF SPEECH

On the line next to the number, write the first letter of the word indicated by the part of speech in the parentheses. Underline the indicated word within the sentence. If your consecutive letters are correct, you will spell out the names of four trees in items 1 through 12 and four first names in items 13 to 25. Write these six names on the lines below the last numbered item. Each correct answer is worth 4 points.

1. _____ **(preposition)** He walked around the corner.

2. _____ **(pronoun)** Paul hopes that she will sing with the choir.

3. _____ **(pronoun)** Can Jerry help him with the science project?

4. _____ **(noun)** Have you seen the eraser?

5. _____ **(noun)** The lock was stuck.

6. _____ **(noun)** She purchased the margarine with him.

7. _____ **(adjective)** Older people tire more easily.

8. _____ **(adjective)** He is agile.

9. _____ **(adjective)** Kind people are often rewarded.

10. _____ **(adverb)** The police officer ran fast.

11. _____ **(adverb)** My sister answered the question intelligently.

12. _____ **(adverb)** You really should see this art exhibit, Kenny.

13. _____ **(preposition)** Reggie fell by the stairs.

14. _____ **(preposition)** Can you jump over the hurdle?

15. _____ **(preposition)** May I sit between you two?

DIAGNOSTIC TEST 2   PARTS OF SPEECH *(Continued)*

16. _____ **(verb)** Joke about it now.

17. _____ **(verb)** They overcharged me.

18. _____ **(verb)** Ozzie, eat up.

19. _____ **(conjunction)** I cannot go, for I have much to do.

20. _____ **(conjunction)** I like peanuts and potato chips.

21. _____ **(conjunction)** He wants to buy the house, yet he knows it is too expensive.

22. _____ **(interjection)** Jeepers! This is a great deal.

23. _____ **(interjection)** Ah! The sun is so warm.

24. _____ **(interjection)** No! I will never try that.

25. _____ **(adverb)** Georgette eventually walked her brother to the station.

The four trees are _____, _____, _____, and _____.

The four first names are _____, _____, _____, and _____.

Number correct _____ × 4 = _____%

Lessons and Activities

(1.1) Nouns

A **noun** is the name of a person, place, thing, or idea:

People	farmer, mechanic, father, Professor Haskins, editors, Marcia
Places	ocean, Canada, porch, Spain, classroom
Things	scissors, giraffe, pen, smiles, tugboat, skateboard, braces, drill
Ideas	love, inspiration, courage, anxiety, eagerness, happiness

All nouns are either common or proper nouns:

A **common noun** names any person, place, or thing. Examples are *basketball, video, wizard, coin, woman,* and *coach.*

A **proper noun** names a particular person, place, or thing and begins with a capital letter. Examples are *Winston Churchill, Babe Ruth, Mr. Richard Turner,* and *Chicago.*

Know the difference between a common and a proper noun:

Common Nouns	Proper Nouns
hospital	Mercy General Hospital
woman	Martha Washington
school	Sayville Middle School
newspaper	*The New York Times*

Here are some specific types of nouns:

A **collective noun** names a group of people or things. Examples of collective nouns are *jury, herd, flock, family, fleet, club, class,* and *group.*

A **compound noun** is a noun consisting of more than a single word. It could be separate words such as *social studies, physical education,* and *dining room.* It could be two words joined by a hyphen such as *merry-go-round, thirty-three, sister-in-law,* and *great-grandmother.* It could be a combined word such as *schoolteacher, bookkeeper, landlord,* and *headmaster.*

📖 **WRITING TIP** *Use a dictionary or a thesaurus for help in choosing the most precise noun for your purpose.*

(1.1A) Plus a Quotation (Nouns)

Underline each noun in the following sentences. Then write the first letter of each noun on the line next to the sentence. If your answers are correct, you will spell out the words of a quotation and the name of the famous American who said the quotation. Write the quotation and its author's name on the lines below sentence 15.

1. _____ Wendy located her housekeeper.

2. _____ Some answers on this test are about electricity.

3. _____ Her violin and easel were missing.

4. _____ Their rabbit that left the yard was returned by the officer.

5. _____ He used this umbrella in Alabama.

6. _____ After the rain, the electrician checked the box.

7. _____ The end of the afternoon arrived quickly.

8. _____ This group is funny.

9. _____ The ostrich and the orangutan are interesting.

10. _____ My doctor and my orthodontist are neighbors.

11. _____ In the evening, Archie likes to go boating.

12. _____ Unfortunately, he had a rash and an allergy.

13. _____ Her height and agility helped her win the match.

14. _____ Linda cared for the infant throughout the night.

15. _____ The garbage carton near the oven had licorice and noodles in it.

The quotation and its author:

_____

_____

_____

_____

(1.1B) Nouns Abound in the Classroom

Twenty common nouns of people and things found in a classroom are hidden in this puzzle. Words are placed backward, forward, diagonally, up, and down. Circle the hidden nouns, and write those nouns on the lines below.

w	h	g	f	c	b	b	v	l	j	y	y	w	s	b	f	t	b	j	x
n	d	f	s	h	b	t	l	j	w	v	v	k	h	o	f	x	r	y	d
s	j	m	p	f	z	l	g	v	y	l	c	j	a	o	j	v	x	q	l
d	x	s	m	b	y	s	g	n	m	a	s	b	r	k	p	h	y	g	v
p	j	r	y	t	k	f	r	q	p	q	f	x	p	s	e	k	n	v	v
a	r	u	m	k	n	e	j	k	y	d	f	c	e	h	n	j	v	m	c
p	o	l	y	e	h	l	c	z	b	n	h	c	n	e	c	n	n	g	k
e	o	e	e	c	f	a	d	r	z	a	k	k	e	l	i	j	j	w	y
r	d	r	a	o	b	k	c	a	l	b	s	t	r	f	l	r	n	w	s
t	c	e	k	f	p	o	n	k	x	e	e	t	l	k	e	e	o	k	r
s	t	l	p	c	c	j	o	f	d	s	h	a	u	l	p	d	g	h	c
e	r	a	s	e	r	w	c	k	o	k	g	x	p	d	n	t	m	t	w
s	m	x	l	d	f	k	t	l	n	h	y	a	m	i	e	f	y	r	j
l	r	h	k	l	v	y	c	f	q	d	t	s	w	p	b	n	r	d	s
k	y	l	m	d	v	n	b	h	g	s	n	b	d	t	q	r	t	z	q

The nouns:

_____   _____

_____   _____

_____   _____

_____   _____

_____   _____

_____   _____

_____   _____

_____   _____

_____   _____

_____   _____

(1.2) Pronouns

A **pronoun** is a word used in place of one or more nouns.

We use pronouns to:

▸ Refer to a noun (called its antecedent) that usually comes before the pronoun

▸ Make our writing clearer, smoother, and less awkward

In the sentence, "Roberto feels that he can win the race," *he* is the pronoun, and *Roberto* is the antecedent.

In the sentence, "Terry and Jim know that they are best friends," *they* is the pronoun, and *Terry* and *Jim* are the noun antecedents.

There are several types of pronouns.

Personal pronouns refer to people and things. They are divided into three categories called *first person* (referring to the person who is speaking: *I* went to the mall), *second person* (referring to the person spoken to: Joey, can *you* see the bus?), and *third person* (referring to anyone or anything else: Bob saw *us* do this assignment). The pronouns in the two example sentences above are personal pronouns.

The following list shows these three categories of personal pronouns:

	Singular	**Plural**
First person (the person speaking)	I, my, mine, me	we, our, ours, us
Second person (the person spoken to)	you, your, yours	you, your, yours
Third person (some other person or thing)	he, his, him, she, her, hers, it, its	they, their, theirs, them

(1.2) Pronouns *(Continued)*

In addition to personal pronouns, there are several other types of pronouns: *reflexive pronouns, relative pronouns, interrogative pronouns, demonstrative pronouns,* and *indefinite pronouns.*

A **reflexive pronoun** is formed by adding *-self* or *-selves* to certain personal pronouns. Examples of reflexive pronouns are *myself, himself, herself, itself, ourselves, themselves, yourself,* and *yourselves.* The sentence, "I found it myself," contains the personal pronoun *I* and the reflexive pronoun *myself.*

Hisself and *theirselves* are NOT real words.

An **interrogative pronoun** is used to ask a question. These pronouns are *which, who, whom,* and *whose.*

A **demonstrative pronoun** is used to point out a specific person or thing. These pronouns include *this, that, these,* and *those.* In the sentence, "Theresa, is this yours?" *this* is the demonstrative pronoun, and *yours* is the personal pronoun.

An **indefinite pronoun** often does not refer to a specific or definite person or thing. It usually does not have a definite or specific antecedent as a personal pronoun does. In the sentence, *"Everybody* will select *another* to help with *everything,"* the three italicized words are all indefinite pronouns since they take the place of a noun and do not refer to a specific or definite person or thing.

These are all indefinite pronouns:

all	each	more	one
another	either	most	other
any	everybody	much	several
anybody	everyone	neither	some
anyone	everything	nobody	somebody
anything	few	none	someone
both	many	no one	

📖 **WRITING TIP** *Make sure that your pronouns are clear so that readers will not be confused. In the sentence, "John told Fred that he had been invited to Lucy's party," do we know who he is? Not really! Set up the situation preceding that sentence so that it is clear who he is.*

(1.2A) Two at a Time (Pronouns)

Underline the two pronouns found in each sentence. Above each pronoun label its type using these abbreviations: personal (PER), reflexive (REF), demonstrative (DEM), interrogative (INT), or indefinite (IND) pronoun.

1. This is the way to do it.

2. He hurt himself during gym class.

3. Can you and they finish the cleaning by three o'clock?

4. Who is the person with her?

5. I held the door for them.

6. Please tell him that we said hello.

7. Ours is older than theirs.

8. Neither of them is the clear winner of the race as of now.

9. Will she watch someone while Sarah goes shopping?

10. Those are the best ones to buy.

11. Please bring yours to us.

12. After Jerry spotted the giraffe, he photographed it.

13. Everything has gone well for us.

14. Will they be able to move the belongings by themselves?

15. All of the students know both.

(1.2B) Naming the Pronouns

1. Name four three-letter pronouns:

_____ _____ _____ _____

2. Name four pronouns that start with the letter *t:*

_____ _____ _____ _____

3. Name six indefinite pronouns:

_____ _____ _____

_____ _____ _____

4. Name three pronouns that end with *-elves:*

_____ _____ _____

5. Name four pronouns that end with *-self:*

_____ _____ _____

_____

6. Name four interrogative pronouns:

_____ _____ _____ _____

7. Circle ten different pronouns in this paragraph. For the total of ten pronouns, if a pronoun appears more than once within the paragraph, count it only once.

I could not fall asleep last night. It felt as if somebody kept knocking on the window keeping me up most of the night. This is pretty unusual. So I tried to calm myself down and think about other things besides being unable to sleep. All of my work paid off when I finally fell asleep.

(1.3) Adjectives

An **adjective** modifies (qualifies or limits the meaning of) a noun or a pronoun. It answers the questions, *What kind? Which one(s)? How many? How much?*

> Carrie read an **interesting** story. (*What kind* of story?)
>
> The **recent** article has that information. (*Which* article?)
>
> Kent owns **those** surfboards. (*Which* surfboards?)
>
> Wendy paid **fifty** dollars for the jacket. (*How many* dollars?)
>
> **Much** space was devoted to her artwork. (*How much* space?)

The words *a, an,* and *the* are the most frequently used adjectives. Although they are sometimes referred to as articles or noun markers, they are really adjectives, plain and simple. Use *a* before words that start with a consonant sound (*a* joking man or *a* lucky lottery player) and *an* before words that start with a vowel sound (*an* hour's wait or *an* interesting story).

An adjective can come before or after the noun or pronoun it describes:

> **Older** cards are found on the table. (*Which* cards?)
>
> **Tall** players and **intelligent** coaches were interviewed by the **interested** reporter. (*Which* players? *Which* coaches? *Which* reporter?)
>
> **Tired** and **hungry**, the campers reached the lodge. (*What kind* of campers?)
>
> The campers, **tired** and **hungry**, reached the lodge. (*What kind* of campers?)

There are several types of adjectives:

A **proper adjective** is formed from a proper noun.

> Italian bread   Herculean strength   Midas touch   Canadian sunset

A **compound adjective** is a word composed of two or more words. Sometimes these words are hyphenated.

> landmark decision   black-and-blue mark   hometown hero

Do not use a hyphen after an adverb ending in *-ly*.

> newly painted mural   sickly sweet odor   recently purchased

1.3 Adjectives *(Continued)*

People sometimes confuse adjectives with nouns or with pronouns. Here are some points to remember.

QUESTION 1: *When is a word a noun? When is a word an adjective?*

The **magazine** article applauded the students' efforts in the charity drive. (*Magazine* is an adjective that describes *which* article.)

The article about the students' efforts in the charity drive was in the **magazine.** (Here *magazine* is a noun since it is the name of a thing and does not describe anything.)

Our **Thanksgiving** celebration was fun. (*Thanksgiving* is an adjective describing *which* celebration.)

We celebrated **Thanksgiving.** (*Thanksgiving* is the name of the holiday that was celebrated.)

QUESTION 2: *When is a word a pronoun? When is a word an adjective?*

These **demonstrative pronouns** can be used as adjectives: *that, these, this,* and *those.*

These **interrogative pronouns** can be used as adjectives: *what* and *which.*

These **indefinite pronouns** can be used as adjectives: *all, another, any, both, each, either, few, many, more, most, neither, other, several,* and *some.*

This problem is difficult. (*This* is an **adjective** since it answers the question, *Which problem?*)

This is difficult. (*This* is a **pronoun** since it takes the place of a noun and does not modify a noun or a pronoun.)

Some people are very funny. (*Some* is an **adjective** since it answers the question, *Which people?*)

Some are funny. (*Some* is a **pronoun** since it takes the place of a noun and does not modify a noun or a pronoun.)

WRITING TIP *Adjectives tell more and help your reader know more about people, places, and things. Select the precise word to describe people, places, and things. Which is the most accurate adjective to describe the student:* smart, brilliant, insightful, clever, brainy, *or* bright? *Decide. Use a dictionary to find the subtle difference in adjectives that are closely related in meaning.*

(1.3A) And a Trip to the Zoo (Adjectives)

Sixteen of the words in this activity are not adjectives. Twenty-four are adjectives. On the line after each question number, write the first letter of the twenty-four adjectives in this list below. Then write these twenty-four letters (consecutively) on the lines below Zoo Animals. These twenty-four consecutive letters spell out the names of five animals found in a zoo.

1. _____ nothing
2. _____ pretty
3. _____ crust
4. _____ faith
5. _____ attractive
6. _____ grabbed
7. _____ nice
8. _____ America
9. _____ dainty
10. _____ agile
11. _____ mechanic
12. _____ mean
13. _____ they
14. _____ odd
15. _____ noisy
16. _____ nor
17. _____ kind
18. _____ neither
19. _____ easy
20. _____ young

21. _____ plumber
22. _____ brave
23. _____ interesting
24. _____ marry
25. _____ smart
26. _____ old
27. _____ solitude
28. _____ nasty
29. _____ beautifully
30. _____ proud
31. _____ infantile
32. _____ earn
33. _____ great
34. _____ forget
35. _____ zany
36. _____ elegant
37. _____ boastful
38. _____ rigid
39. _____ decide
40. _____ average

Zoo Animals:

_____

_____

(1.3B) Listing Three Adjectives

1. Name three complimentary adjectives that describe one of your friends:

_____   _____   _____

2. Name three adjectives that describe the beach on a summer's day:

_____   _____   _____

3. Name three adjectives that describe a Super Bowl crowd:

_____   _____   _____

4. Name three adjectives that describe one of your Halloween costumes:

_____   _____   _____

5. Name three adjectives that describe a famous actor or actress:

_____   _____   _____

6. Name three adjectives that describe a book or magazine article that you recently read:

_____   _____   _____

7. Name three adjectives that describe a typical spring day where you live:

_____   _____   _____

8. Name three adjectives that describe your favorite song:

_____   _____   _____

9. Name three adjectives that describe one of your recent math tests:

_____   _____   _____

10. Name three adjectives that describe one of your most difficult experiences:

_____   _____   _____

(1.4) Verbs

There are several types of **verbs** to be studied: the action verb, the linking verb, and the helping verb.

⊠ Action Verbs

An **action verb** tells what action (often a physical action) a subject is performing, has performed, or will perform.

> My father *delivers* packages to department stores each day.
>
> Louie *bowled* a perfect game last night.
>
> Suzanne *skated* across the rink in Central Park.
>
> *Turn* at the next corner, Noel.
>
> Oscar will *help* Petra with the project.

⊠ Linking Verbs

A **linking verb** connects (or links) a subject to a noun or an adjective in the predicate. The most common linking verbs are the forms of the verb "to be" (*is, are, was, were, been, being, am*) and *appear, become, feel, grow, look, remain, seem, smell, sound, stay, taste,* and *turn.*

> **My sister *is* a doctor.** (The linking verb, *is,* connects the subject, *sister,* with the predicate nominative, *doctor.*)
>
> **My sister *is* studying to become a doctor.** (In this sentence the word *is* is a helping verb for the main verb, *studying. Is* does not function as a linking verb.)
>
> **He *appeared* tired.** (The linking verb, *appeared,* links the subject, *He,* with the predicate adjective, *tired.*)
>
> **He *appeared* at the game.** (In this sentence the verb, *appeared,* is an action verb, not a linking verb.)

In the following group of sentences, the odd-numbered sentences exemplify the linking verb and the even-numbered sentences show the same verb used as either an action verb or a helping verb. Discuss why each verb functions as it does.

1. Reggie *looked* confused.
2. Reggie *looked* for his missing wallet.
3. Tammy *grew* tired during the long concert.
4. Tammy *grew* tomatoes in her garden this year.
5. I *feel* confused in math class.
6. I *feel* the penny at the bottom of this pool.

(1.4) Verbs *(Continued)*

⊠ Helping Verbs

A **helping verb** assists the main verb in a sentence. There can be more than one helping verb in each sentence. In a questioning (interrogative) sentence, the helping verb is usually separated from the main verb.

The common helping verbs are *am, is, are, was, were, be, been, being, has, had, have, do, does, did, may, might, must, can, could, shall, should, will,* and *would.*

The *italicized* word in each sentence below is the helping verb. The underlined word is the main verb.

The members *are* <u>going</u> to the city tomorrow evening.

Are the members <u>going</u> to the city tomorrow evening?

That joke *has been* <u>heard</u> around the office.

Has that joke *been* <u>heard</u> around the office?

Her brothers *are* <u>leaving</u> for the train.

Are her brothers <u>leaving</u> for the train?

Think you know your verbs? On the lines below, write a verb that starts with the letter *a,* and then one that starts with the letter *b,* and so forth until you have written a verb for each of the twenty-six letters of the alphabet. These verbs can be action, linking, or helping verbs.

_____

_____

_____

_____

_____

_____

_____

✍ **WRITING TIP** *Use the precise verb for each situation.* Walk *might not suit the situation as well as* stroll, pace, totter, *or* saunter. *Use a dictionary or a thesaurus to help you along.*

(1.4A) Where the Boys Are (Verbs)

Underline the verb in each of the following sentences. Then on the line before each sentence, write the first letter of the verb found in that sentence. Finally, write the twenty consecutive letters on the lines below the last numbered item to identify the names of five boys.

1. _____ Will he remember the name of the boys?

2. _____ Yes, she understands your explanation.

3. _____ Please shuffle the cards now.

4. _____ Send the messenger to the principal's office.

5. _____ Juan jokes around most of the time.

6. _____ You omitted several names of tonight's program.

7. _____ The scientists simulated the rocket's path.

8. _____ Mrs. Simmons, our teacher, erased the board quickly.

9. _____ The plant withered last week.

10. _____ Coach Albers inspired us before the big football game last week.

11. _____ The runner leaped with enthusiasm after her record-breaking performance.

12. _____ They loved last night's dance recital.

13. _____ The cyclists pedaled through the mountains during the grueling segment of the Tour de France.

14. _____ He envies the other players.

15. _____ I told you that earlier.

16. _____ The artist etched the rough outline.

17. _____ I forgot my jacket in the music room.

18. _____ They easily recalled the unforgettable incident.

19. _____ That game ended his hopes for a professional career.

20. _____ Her parents decided that long ago.

The names of the five boys are _____, _____,

_____, _____, and _____.

1.4B Connecting Verbs and Vocabulary

Thirty verbs are listed alphabetically in the box below. Show your vocabulary knowledge by placing each specific verb in its proper space underneath one of the five less specific general verbs that follow. Each less specific general verb should have six specific verbs below it. Use each specific verb only once.

accomplish	achieve	apprehend	chatter	chuckle
claw	collar	confess	conquer	corral
giggle	gossip	guffaw	howl	meander
overcome	parade	plod	pronounce	roar
score	shuffle	snare	snicker	soliloquize
stride	trap	trek	triumph	verbalize

Walk:

_____

_____

Talk:

_____

_____

Laugh:

_____

_____

Succeed:

_____

_____

Catch:

_____

_____

(1.4C) You Will Not Need Help Here (Verbs)

Fill in the blanks in each sentence with a helping verb or a main verb.

1. We should _____ _____ by tomorrow afternoon.

2. Joey would _____ _____ your phone number anyway.

3. None of us _____ _____ that you remembered his locker combination.

4. The president _____ _____ many television appearances.

5. They had _____ in the fifty-mile run.

6. Our friends have _____ several wild animals.

7. She is _____ a great time at the dance.

8. You _____ _____ the election by many votes, Teresa.

9. I am _____ to the rodeo with Todd and Frank tomorrow.

10. Roberto and Herm are _____ the float for the homecoming parade.

11. All of us can _____ to your interesting story.

12. He will probably _____ your help installing the air-conditioner.

13. I _____ be _____ with you if I need a ride tonight.

14. Most of the actors were certainly _____ to the Academy Awards that evening.

15. The passengers _____ being _____ at the airport gate.

(1.5) Adverbs

An **adverb** is a word that modifies (qualifies or limits) a verb, an adjective, or another adverb.

- ▸ Many adverbs end in -ly.
- ▸ Adverbs answer any of these four questions: *Where? When? How? To what extent?*
- ▸ Adverbs make writing more specific and more exact.
- ▸ Here are some adverbs that do not end in -ly:

again	almost	alone	already	also
always	away	even	ever	here
just	later	never	not	now
nowhere	often	perhaps	quite	rather
seldom	so	sometimes	somewhat	somewhere
soon	then	there	today	too
very	yesterday	yet		

Adverbs modify verbs:

John ate *quickly*. (*How* did he eat?)

I walk *there*. (*Where* did I walk?)

Ashleigh will eat *soon*. (*When* will Ashleigh eat?)

Adverbs modify adjectives:

Rex is *very* happy. (*Very* modifies the adjective *happy* and answers the question, *To what extent?*)

The program was *too* unrealistic. (*Too* modifies the adjective *unrealistic* and answers the question, *To what extent?*)

Adverbs modify other adverbs:

Warren walks *too* quickly. (*Too* modifies the adverb *quickly* and answers the question, *How quickly?*)

He moved *rather* recently. (*Rather* modifies the adverb *recently* and answers the question, *How recently?*)

(1.5) Adverbs *(Continued)*

When is a word an adjective, and when is it an adjective? Adjectives describe nouns and pronouns. Adverbs do not. Adverbs describe verbs, adjectives, and other adverbs. Adjectives do not.

Helen has a *yearly* membership at the local health club. (*Yearly* is an adjective since it modifies the noun *membership* and tells *which* membership.)

Helen contributes *yearly*. (*Yearly* is an adverb since it modifies the verb *contributes* and answers the question, *When does Helen contribute?*)

Mike arrived *late*. (*Late* is an adverb since it tells *when* Mike arrived.)

The *late* delivery cut down on sales in the supermarket. (*Late* is an adjective because it tells *which* delivery.)

WRITING TIP *Adverbs help readers visualize actions better. Select the precise adverb to help your reader see more clearly.* Slowly *might not be as accurate as* gradually, leisurely, *or* unhurriedly. *Use a dictionary or thesaurus for help.*

Name _____   Date _____   Period _____

1.5A **Scrambled Up for You! (Adverbs)**

In each sentence, the letters of the underlined adverb are scrambled. Unscramble the letters, and write the word on the line provided before the sentence.

1. _____ He walks <u>tsaf</u>.

2. _____ Do you want to stop <u>ehre</u>?

3. _____ He visits his grandmother <u>ywlkee</u>.

4. _____ Do you feel <u>lewl</u> enough to go on the trip?

5. _____ Have you <u>erve</u> been to Mexico City?

6. _____ I <u>wasaly</u> run errands for her.

7. _____ Have I met you <u>foebre</u>?

8. _____ I would <u>raerht</u> drive to your house tonight.

9. _____ Are you <u>ilslt</u> going to go to summer school?

10. _____ I am <u>tno</u> trying to insult you, Nick.

11. _____ Will you bat <u>frsit</u> tonight?

12. _____ Are you <u>ftneo</u> at this location, Mitch?

13. _____ Let's start the performance <u>onw</u>.

14. _____ May I <u>aosl</u> assist you, Helene?

15. _____ Thank you <u>nlidyk</u>.

© 2007 by John Wiley & Sons, Inc.

28

1.5B **Dressing Up (Adverbs)**

On the line next to the sentence number, tell whether the underlined adverb modifies a verb, an adjective, or another adverb by writing the correct answer's corresponding letter. Then fill in the spaces within the three sentences after sentence 15. If your answers are correct, you will understand this activity's title.

1. _____ Patricia slept <u>peacefully</u>. **(b)** verb **(c)** adjective **(d)** adverb

2. _____ Our teachers are <u>very</u> happy with the results. **(t)** verb **(s)** adjective **(l)** adverb

3. _____ Larry's <u>unusually</u> good cooking skills came in handy last weekend. **(b)** verb **(h)** adjective **(o)** adverb

4. _____ He ran <u>swiftly</u> away from the tackler. **(e)** verb **(a)** adjective **(i)** adverb

5. _____ She danced <u>so</u> gracefully in the competition. **(d)** verb **(m)** adjective **(p)** adverb

6. _____ They sang <u>beautifully</u> during the entire winter concert. **(l)** verb **(n)** adjective **(p)** adverb

7. _____ My aunt was <u>extremely</u> hungry after we completed the three-hour hike. **(r)** verb **(o)** adjective **(d)** adverb

8. _____ We had met <u>somewhat</u> earlier than you think. **(v)** verb **(n)** adjective **(a)** adverb

9. _____ Are they going <u>away</u>? **(t)** verb **(e)** adjective **(r)** adverb

10. _____ His <u>rather</u> clever remarks were not appreciated. **(g)** verb **(e)** adjective **(u)** adverb

11. _____ These stories seem <u>strangely</u> familiar to me. **(x)** verb **(s)** adjective **(o)** adverb

12. _____ They will <u>hardly</u> try to win. **(n)** verb **(r)** adjective **(s)** adverb

13. _____ Francine earns high grades <u>quite</u> often. **(t)** verb **(e)** adjective **(t)** adverb

14. _____ Do not walk <u>alone</u> in the forest. **(s)** verb **(u)** adjective **(f)** adverb

15. _____ We met <u>only</u> recently. **(g)** verb **(h)** adjective **(s)** adverb

The five sentences that illustrate an adverb modifying a verb are numbers _____, _____, _____, _____, and _____. Their corresponding letters spell the word

_____.

The five sentences that illustrate an adverb modifying an adjective are numbers _____, _____, _____, _____, and _____. Their corresponding letters spell the word

_____.

The five sentences that illustrate an adverb modifying another adverb are numbers _____, _____, _____, _____, and _____. Their corresponding letters spell the word

_____.

(1.6) Prepositions

A **common preposition** is a word that shows the relationship between a noun or a pronoun and another word in the sentence.

The man swam *under* the bridge. (*Under* connects the idea of *swam* and *bridge*.)

She walked *down* the aisle. (*Down* connects *walked* and *aisle*.)

Julie walked *around* the campus and *toward* town. (*Around* connects *walked* and *campus*. *Toward* connects *walked* and *town*.)

Here are the most commonly used prepositions:

aboard	about	above	across
after	against	along	among
around	as	at	before
behind	below	beneath	beside
besides	between	beyond	but
by	concerning	despite	down
during	except	for	from
in	inside	into	like
near	of	off	on
onto	opposite	out	outside
over	past	since	through
throughout	till	to	toward
under	underneath	until	up
upon	with	within	without

But is a preposition only when it can be replaced by the word *except*. So in the sentence, "All *but* Teddy went inside," *but* is a preposition since it connects *All* and *Teddy* and can be replaced by the word *except*.

A way to get to know these fifty-six prepositions is to remember this sentence: *The plane, Prepi I, flew _____ the clouds.* Any single word that can logically be placed into this space is a preposition, so the only words that you would still have to memorize are those that do not logically fit into this space. Compose the list of these words, memorize the Prepi I sentence, and you will know your prepositions!

(1.6) Prepositions *(Continued)*

Another type of preposition is the **compound preposition.** It does the same as a common preposition but is composed of two or more words. Here are the most common compound prepositions:

according to	ahead of	apart from	as of
aside from	because of	by means of	in addition to
in back of	in front of	in place of	in spite of
instead of	in view of	next to	on account of
out of	prior to		

Adverb or preposition? The difference between a preposition and an adverb is that an adverb answers the questions, *Where? When? How? To what extent?* by itself. Both common and compound prepositions need more than just themselves to answer the same questions:

He fell *down.* (*Down* is an *adverb* because it takes only one word to tell where he fell.)

He fell *down* the stairs. (*Down* is a *preposition* because it takes more than a single word to tell where he fell.)

Trey walked *aboard.* (*Aboard* is an adverb because it takes only one word needed to tell where Trey walked.)

Trey walked *aboard* the ship. (*Aboard* is a preposition because it takes more than one word to tell where Trey walked.)

 WRITING TIP *Know when a word is a preposition and when it is an adverb. In the sentence "The captain walked aboard," aboard is an adverb because it does not start a prepositional phrase. In the sentence "The captain walked aboard the ship," aboard is a preposition that begins the prepositional phrase, aboard the ship. Look for the prepositional phrase to check that the word is a preposition and not an adverb.*

(1.6A) Finding the Four Words (Prepositions)

Underline the preposition in each of the following sentences. Then write the first letter of the preposition on the line before the sentence. Transfer the fifteen consecutive letters to the lines below the last numbered sentence to form four words.

1. _____ The teammates walked beyond the bleachers.

2. _____ The track team ran into the hills.

3. _____ The temperature is several degrees below zero.

4. _____ Call me around four o'clock.

5. _____ It is a matter concerning bad behavior.

6. _____ The parents joined in the conversation.

7. _____ Ronnie fell asleep during the professor's lecture.

8. _____ We found the sleeping cat underneath the blanket.

9. _____ The couple walked near the bridge.

10. _____ The children slid down the slide yesterday.

11. _____ We lost contact over time.

12. _____ This letter is addressed to your sister.

13. _____ The strong man swam across the wide lake.

14. _____ This group is under great suspicion.

15. _____ I pointed toward the tall building.

The four words are _____, _____, _____,
and _____.

(1.7) Conjunctions

A **conjunction** connects words or group of words. There are three types of conjunctions: **coordinating conjunctions, correlative conjunctions,** and **subordinating conjunctions.** The first two types of conjunctions are discussed below, and the third type is discussed in lesson 2.19.

A **coordinating conjunction** is a single connecting word. These seven words are *for, and, nor, but, or, yet,* and *so.*

The boys *and* girls worked at the fair. (*And* joins the names *boys* and *girls*.)

Paula *or* Jeannine can go with you tonight. (*Or* joins the names *Paula* and *Jeannine*.)

I would like to help you, *but* I will be busy tonight. (*But* joins two sentences or complete ideas.)

We must leave early *so* we can get to the wedding reception on time. (*So* joins two sentences or two complete ideas.)

Remember the made-up word FANBOYS when you memorize the coordinating conjunctions. Each letter in this word (**F**or, **A**nd, **N**or, **B**ut, **O**r, **Y**et, **S**o) stands for a coordinating conjunction.

Correlative conjunctions are pairs of connecting words. These five pairs of words are *both/and, either/or, neither/nor, not only/but also,* and *whether/or.*

Both Henry *and* Henrietta are leaving the dance now. (The correlative conjunctions join two names.)

Not only will they leave now, *but* they will *also* not be here to help clean up. (The correlative conjunctions join two sentences or complete ideas.)

Either go with them *or* stay here and help. (The correlative conjunctions illustrate a choice.)

He went *neither* to the stadium *nor* to the concert hall during this vacation. (The correlative conjunctions join two prepositional phrases.)

 WRITING TIP *Using conjunctions adds sophistication to sentences. Rather than using two very simple sentences such as, "The monkey climbed the tree," and "The monkey threw down a banana," combine them by using the conjunction* and: *"The monkey climbed the tree and threw down a banana" is a more sophisticated sentence. Make good use of the conjunctions for combining ideas.*

(1.7A) Appropriately Chosen! (Conjunctions)

Circle the conjunction or pair of conjunctions in each sentence:

1. Lyle chose both steak and salad for his dinner.
2. I chose neither steak nor salad for my dinner.
3. Either you or he can drive Dad to the train station tomorrow morning.
4. The panda wanted to eat, for he was hungry.
5. Peanut butter and jelly is Rex's favorite sandwich.
6. Not only the girls but also the boys will be invited to the assembly.
7. Sara did not know whether to swing at the ball or take the pitch.
8. Mark would like to go, but he cannot.
9. Rich likes the food at this restaurant, yet he seldom eats here.
10. Run with him or her.

Use these coordinating and correlative conjunctions in your own sentences:

11. Use *neither ... nor:*

_____

_____

12. Use *but:*

_____

_____

13. Use *for:*

_____

_____

14. Use *or:*

_____

_____

15. Use *either ... or:*

_____

_____

(1.8) Interjections

An **interjection** is a word that expresses strong feeling or emotion:

▶ An interjection usually comes at the beginning of the sentence.

▶ An interjection is often followed by an exclamation point (!) when the emotion is strong or a comma (,) when the emotion is mild.

▶ Do not overuse interjections. Include one when you want to make your point. If you use too many interjections, your writing loses its power and effectiveness.

▶ Here are some common interjections:

Aw	Bravo	Darn	Dear me
Eek	Eh	Gee	Golly
Goodness gracious	Gosh	Hallelujah	Hey
Horrors	Hurrah	Hurray	Mmm
Oh	Oh no	Oops	Ouch
Phew	Rats	Really	Ugh
Well	Whoa	Whoops	Wow
Yea	Yeh	Yes	Yippee

 WRITING TIP *Interjections express emotion. Do not overuse this part of speech, which generally is found in dialogue.*

(1.8A) **With Great Feeling!!! (Interjections)**

Write an appropriate interjection for each of the following sentences in the space provided. There may be more than one answer for each space.

1. _____! I smashed my finger with the hammer.

2. _____, all right, Nick.

3. _____! We have finally beaten that team!

4. _____, take it easy, Reggie!

5. _____, I think we better look over this paper immediately.

6. _____, I forgot to take out the garbage this morning.

7. _____! The tickets for his concert are incredibly expensive!

8. _____! You did so well in tonight's school play!

9. _____! You have no right to say that to him!

10. _____, now I see what you are trying to say.

11. _____. I am not very keen on that idea.

12. _____, what did Mike say about his tryout?

13. _____! Does your hand still hurt from the accident?

14. _____! Get away from my new car, kid!

15. _____, this food is absolutely delicious!

Review Activities

REVIEW ACTIVITY 1   O WHAT AN ACTIVITY!
(PARTS OF SPEECH)

Every word in Group One begins with the letter *o*. Match each with its description found in Group Two. Each item in both groups is used only once. Write the correct number in the appropriate box of the magic square. If your answers are correct, each row, each column, and each diagonal will add up to the same number.

Group One

A. our

B. outside

C. Ohio

D. or

E. one

F. ours

G. Oh

H. oafish

I. own

J. off

K. ordered

L. only

M. owl

N. oneself

O. owners

P. originally

Group Two

1. possessive pronoun

2. present tense verb

3. plural noun

4. conjunction

5. singular noun

6. adverb and preposition

7. adjective

8. past tense verb

9. proper noun

10. adverb only

11. adverb, adjective, noun, and preposition

12. adjective, pronoun, and noun

13. adjective, conjunction, and adverb

14. interjection

15. pronoun and adjective

16. reflexive pronoun

A =	B =	C =	D =
E =	F =	G =	H =
I =	J =	K =	L =
M =	N =	O =	P =

REVIEW ACTIVITY 2   FINDING THE MISSING LINK (PARTS OF SPEECH)

Fill in each sentence's blank with an appropriate word. Reread the sentence to ensure that the sentence makes sense with the new word in it. Then, on the line next to the sentence's number, write the part of speech (use the key below) of the word that you used to fill in that particular blank. Then you have found the missing link!

adjective = ADJ	interjection = I	pronoun = PN
adverb = ADVB	noun = N	verb = V
conjunction = C	preposition = P	

_____ 1. _____ the answer is correct, circle the letter.

_____ 2. They _____ had time to down their meal before the taxi arrived.

_____ 3. These _____ flowers make such a beautiful sight in our backyard.

_____ 4. _____! I could not believe how much his crushing tackle hurt me.

_____ 5. Dwayne carried the five gifts _____ the room.

_____ 6. _____ of these towels could be folded more neatly.

_____ 7. My sister's _____ had to be towed to the body shop yesterday.

_____ 8. The older computer was _____ by my neighbor in just over an hour.

_____ 9. We _____ a colorful poster from the local car salesman.

_____ 10. Tall, dark, and _____, my sister's boyfriend makes his presence known immediately.

_____ 11. I have not spoken to the principal _____ this important issue yet.

_____ 12. Neither of _____ had been invited to the retirement party.

_____ 13. Yes, I would love to be there, _____ I have already made other plans.

_____ 14. Rita was selected as our next _____.

_____ 15. The police officers had trouble catching up to the _____ car.

_____ 16. All of the invitees _____ approached the host and hostess.

_____ 17. I could _____ do much with that intricate design.

_____ 18. Lonnie thanked the _____ for all that they had done for him.

_____ 19. Most of the restaurant patrons wanted to see the _____ who had just entered the building.

_____ 20. The truck was carefully _____ by the experienced driver.

REVIEW ACTIVITY 3   CHECKING OUT THE TWO SENTENCES (PARTS OF SPEECH)

Fill in the correct letters within the crossword puzzle. Here are the two sentences that you will use to do so.

Sentence 1: They waited patiently inside the arena to meet the star of the game, but she went out the other door.

Sentence 2: You can help these older people with the heavy packages and then report to me again, Rich.

Across

2. the last adverb in the second sentence

5. the first verb in the first sentence

6. the second pronoun in the first sentence

8. the helping verb in the second sentence

10. the first pronoun in the first sentence

11. the pronoun-adjective in the first sentence

13. the only proper noun in either sentence

14. the number of nouns in the first sentence

16. the part of speech of *people* in the second sentence

17. the last pronoun in the second sentence

Down

1. the conjunction in the first sentence

2. the conjunction in the second sentence

3. the first preposition in the first sentence

4. the first main verb in the second sentence

5. the first preposition in the second sentence

7. the adverb in the first sentence

9. the number of prepositions in the first sentence

10. the number of articles in the first sentence

12. the last verb in the second sentence

15. the adjective describing *people* in the second sentence

REVIEW ACTIVITY 3   CHECKING OUT THE TWO SENTENCES
(PARTS OF SPEECH) (*Continued*)

Final Tests

FINAL TEST 1   PARTS OF SPEECH

Decide whether each underlined word is a noun (N), pronoun (PN), verb (V), adjective (ADJ), adverb (ADVB), conjunction (C), preposition (P), or interjection (I). Then write its abbreviation on the line before the sentence. Each correct answer scores 5 points.

1. _____ <u>Slow</u> down.

2. _____ I would like to go, <u>but</u> I have to help my sister.

3. _____ Can you please drive more <u>slowly</u>?

4. _____ <u>He</u> is our legislator.

5. _____ The captain looked for a better <u>route</u>.

6. _____ <u>Wow</u>! Are we there already?

7. _____ The pictures fell <u>from</u> the table.

8. _____ I can certainly use your help <u>during</u> the ordeal.

9. _____ This <u>extravagant</u> home is overpriced even for today's market.

10. _____ Mom <u>and</u> Dad just returned from Charlotte, North Carolina.

11. _____ <u>Diplomacy</u> is the best tactic.

12. _____ They think that their dog will like <u>it</u>.

13. _____ Some of these stories are discussed <u>often</u>.

14. _____ Either the giraffe <u>or</u> the monkey will be fed now.

15. _____ We will probably <u>hinder</u> the process if we try to help them.

16. _____ Helene <u>cautiously</u> approached the dog.

17. _____ <u>Can</u> you help with the moving?

18. _____ They will do most of the moving <u>themselves</u>.

19. _____ I am <u>not</u> hungry.

20. _____ This is a very <u>pretty</u> necklace.

Number correct _____ × 5 = _____%

FINAL TEST 2   PARTS OF SPEECH

How well do you know the eight parts of speech? This activity will test your mettle! Write ten sentences using the parts of speech in the order specified. If the abbreviations are capitalized, the word in the sentence should be capitalized as well.

Here is the abbreviation code: n = noun; pro = pronoun; adj = adjective; v = verb; advb = adverb; c = conjunction; prep = preposition; hv = helping verb; mv = main verb; pro-adj = pronoun-adjective (such as *these*); art = article (*a, an,* or *the*).

1. Pro / hv / mv / art / n / prep / pro.

   _____

2. Pro / prep / pro-adj / n / v / adj.

   _____

3. MV / pro-adj / n / advb.

   _____

4. N / conj / N / hv / mv / prep / N.

   _____

5. Pro-adj / n / hv / conj / hv / mv / prep / pro-adj / n.

   _____

6. HV / pro / mv / art / adj / n / prep / art / adj / n?

   _____

7. Pro / hv / mv /, conj / pro / v / n.

   _____

8. N / v / pro / advb / advb.

   _____

9. Art / n / advb / v / pro-adj / n / advb / prep / art / n.

   _____

10. Prep / pro-adj / noun, art / n / v / prep / art / n.

    _____

Section Two
Parts of a Sentence

Diagnostic Tests

DIAGNOSTIC TEST 1   THE PARTS OF A SENTENCE

This is a practice test. It will never be scored. Use it as an indication of what you know and what you need to know.

Circle the simple subject, and underline the complete subject in each of these five sentences:

1. The musicians in the orchestra are paid well.

2. Some books in the library need to be restocked.

3. My friends in Nebraska should be coming here this summer.

4. The colors of the mural are exhilarating.

5. Each of the gymnasts will perform this evening.

Circle the simple predicate, and underline the complete predicate in each of these next five sentences:

6. He helps with the shopping.

7. The singers performed last night.

8. The message tells much.

9. Our new director hosted a meeting at his house.

10. Several fish swam toward the boat.

Underline the verb phrase in each of these sentences:

11. The bed will be shipped tomorrow.

12. Our friends are traveling in Europe.

13. Will you help with the packages?

14. David and Fran were stopping at the store.

15. We had heard the beautiful music.

Underline the compound subjects in these sentences:

16. The boss and her workers will meet in Boston next week.

17. You and I can handle this problem, Nera.

18. The cat and the mouse watched for each other.

19. Windows and walls need to be cleaned tomorrow.

20. There are Bob and Hank.

DIAGNOSTIC TEST 2   PREPOSITIONAL AND VERBAL PHRASES

Each of these answers earns 5 points. Underline the prepositional phrase in each of these five sentences:

1. Mom cooked the meal within an hour.

2. He broke the record by three seconds.

3. In a minute I can help you.

4. Some of the pretzels are stale.

5. Will you go to the game tonight?

Underline the appositive phrase in each sentence:

6. Gary Thomas, our professor, is extremely intelligent.

7. Chicago, the Windy City, is in Illinois.

8. My cousin, a broadcaster, is quote well spoken.

9. The heart of the book, the eighth chapter, is touching.

10. Manhattan College, the home of the Jaspers, is a great school.

Underline the misplaced or dangling modifier in each of these five sentences:

11. Following the path, the flower was spotted by the hikers.

12. At the age of nine, my grandmother taught me how to sew.

13. While drinking the water, the bottle was dropped by the spectator.

14. After winning the contest, the ticket was turned in by the happy family.

15. We saw the flowers walking to the library.

Underline the verbal phrase in each of these five sentences. Then write G for gerund, I for infinitive, or P for participle on the line before the sentence:

16. _____ To win the contest was her goal.

17. _____ Collecting stamps is a good hobby for older people as well.

18. _____ Seeing the stray cat, the police officer stopped the oncoming traffic.

19. _____ Ted needed to finish his essay.

20. _____ The worker wiping his brow is my neighbor.

Number correct _____ × 5 = _____%

DIAGNOSTIC TEST 3   COMPLEMENTS

There are five direct objects (DO), five indirect objects (IO), five predicate nominatives (PN), and five predicate adjectives (PA) underlined in the following twenty sentences. Write the appropriate two-letter abbreviation on the line next to the sentence's number. Each answer is worth 5 points.

1. _____ She is our <u>sister</u>.

2. _____ We gave the <u>presents</u> to the children.

3. _____ He is <u>handsome</u>.

4. _____ The principal paid <u>Veronica</u> a compliment.

5. _____ Ms. Higgins is the <u>mayor</u> of our town.

6. _____ The quarterback handed the <u>referee</u> the ball.

7. _____ The store manager told <u>Gina</u> about the sale.

8. _____ He presented the <u>award</u> at the assembly.

9. _____ The documentary is very <u>interesting</u>.

10. _____ Henry Treeble is the <u>boy</u> in the picture.

11. _____ Lend the <u>money</u> to them soon.

12. _____ My cousin is quite <u>bashful</u>.

13. _____ The master of ceremonies presented <u>Roberta</u> a plaque for her volunteer work.

14. _____ The best painter is <u>Ursula</u>.

15. _____ The group donated <u>goods</u> to the poor.

16. _____ He is <u>confident</u>.

17. _____ Chris told her <u>dad</u> about the effects of the new medicine.

18. _____ Our favorite former president is <u>she</u>.

19. _____ The television producers expected better <u>work</u> from their workers.

20. _____ The New England hills are <u>picturesque</u>.

Number correct _____ × 5 = _____%

DIAGNOSTIC TEST 4   SUBORDINATE CLAUSES

Identify the type of underlined subordinate clause by writing ADV for adverb, ADJ for adjective, and N for noun clause on the line before each sentence. Each answer is worth 5 points.

1. _____ The man who helped you is my dad.

2. _____ Few understood what he was saying.

3. _____ After he watched his younger sister, he came out with us.

4. _____ I can appreciate what you are going through these days.

5. _____ These pictures, which I bought last week, are funny.

6. _____ Whenever I start to feel tired, I take a brisk walk.

7. _____ The market is more crowded than it was yesterday.

8. _____ What he believes is not understood by those close to him.

9. _____ Unless you hear from us, go right to the station after work.

10. _____ She is the cheerleader whom I saw last night.

11. _____ We can go there if it is not out of the way.

12. _____ I thought that you would be the next representative.

13. _____ Who my best friends are is quite obvious.

14. _____ Evening is the time when he becomes fatigued.

15. _____ Rosemary has a tennis racket that is very expensive.

Number correct _____ × 5 = _____%

Lessons and Activities

Name _____ Date _____ Period _____

 2.1 Simple Subjects

The **simple subject** is the main word in the complete subject. In the sentence, "Our boss helped with the difficult work assignment," *boss* is the simple subject. The same holds true for *Georgia* in the sentence, "*Georgia* is our computer systems director."

The **simple subject** is italicized in each sentence below:

> My *aunt* drove us to the museum.
>
> *You* can make the drawing more realistic.
>
> A talented, versatile *musician* joined our orchestra last week.
>
> The first *batter* in the lineup is Tammy.
>
> The *stack* of papers is near the sofa.
>
> *Someone* in this row dropped a wallet.
>
> Near the fence is my *car*.

Insert a simple subject in each group of words that follows. Then you will have a complete sentence.

1. _____ is cutting wood outside his garage.

2. Can _____ take this home with you?

3. This _____ is very beautiful.

4. _____ will be trying out his new guitar soon.

5. _____ read all the assigned pages twice last night.

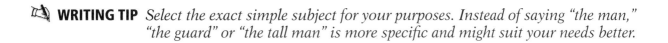

WRITING TIP *Select the exact simple subject for your purposes. Instead of saying "the man," "the guard" or "the tall man" is more specific and might suit your needs better.*

(2.1A) Look for Something Easy (Simple Subjects)

Underline the simple subject in each sentence. Then write the first letter of each simple subject in consecutive order on the line below the last numbered sentence. If your answers are correct, you will compose a sentence that might be what this activity is for you!

1. _____ Tennis is an exciting sport to watch on television.

2. _____ Halloween is always interesting in our neighborhood.

3. _____ The Incas lived in Peru.

4. _____ Solitude is important to Ken's stress level.

5. _____ His chances of winning the debate are very good.

6. _____ Asteroids were discussed at the science convention.

7. _____ Newfoundland can be cold in the winter months.

8. _____ New beginnings are a luxury for teachers each new school year.

9. _____ There are many elements in the world.

10. _____ Strong shoulders have helped him to avoid injuries during his hockey career.

11. _____ Olives were served with the delicious sandwich.

12. _____ Eavesdropping was one of Hank's favorite activities.

13. _____ His arm was twisted in the tackle on the thirty-yard line.

14. _____ My sousaphone was quite expensive to rent last term.

15. _____ Several considerate youngsters helped the man out of the room.

The sentence is:

_____

_____.

2.2 Complete Subjects

A **complete subject** contains all the words that help to identify the main person, place, thing, or idea of the sentence. In the sentence, "The women on the planning committee agreed to this change in plans," the simple subject is *women,* and the complete subject is *the women on the planning committee.*

The **complete subject** in each of the following sentences is italicized. The **simple subject** is underlined.

The <u>stack</u> *of papers* is near the sofa.

<u>*Someone*</u> *in this row* is sitting in the wrong seat.

A wonderful, exciting <u>event</u> is planned.

A wonderful and exciting <u>display</u> is planned.

In the back of the room was *our* <u>display</u>.

Fill in the blanks in the following list with a complete subject to compose a complete sentence:

_____

was cheering for her favorite team.

_____

could not see the bicyclist making the turn.

In the middle of the crowd was _____

_____.

Can _____

help move this heavy piece of furniture?

Without a decent plan, _____

will not succeed in this endeavor.

 WRITING TIP *Be specific in your word choices to give your readers a better picture of what you are trying to show them. A simple subject such as "those women" is not as specific and explicit as "the women on the planning committee." The complete subject, "Those women on the planning committee," is more specific and clearer.*

(2.2A) Healthy Advice (Complete Subjects)

Match the complete subject in Column A with its sentence's second part in Column B. Write the answer's two-letter combination on the line next to the corresponding number and then again (in order) on the lines after the columns. Each is used only once. If your answers are correct, you will spell out a familiar proverb.

Column A

1. _____ The flock of birds
2. _____ The all-star player
3. _____ Our trip to the West Coast
4. _____ A fool and his money
5. _____ Too many cooks
6. _____ Last week's hurricane
7. _____ Grandpa's silly stories
8. _____ My little sister's crayons
9. _____ Antique cars
10. _____ My favorite rock group
11. _____ Honesty
12. _____ Jessica's parents
13. _____ His meticulous wife
14. _____ The milk
15. _____ The Marines

Column B

(an) flew over us.

(ap) trains hard during the winter months.

(da) spoil the soup.

(ea) are soon parted.

(ed) will be performing in Denver.

(ee) are often retold at gatherings.

(oc) is the best policy.

(pl) was filled with many great memories.

(ps) were scattered about her room.

(ra) likes to keep her house spotlessly clean.

(th) are featured in our town's parade each year.

(to) renewed their wedding vows at church today.

(wa) was left out all night and turned sour.

(y!) are a rugged group of soldiers.

(yk) caused damage to the farmer's crops.

The familiar proverb is:

_____

_____.

2.3 Subjects in Unusual Positions

Sometimes the subject of a sentence is not in the usual position. Most often, the subject is found near the beginning of a sentence. In the sentence, "The ventriloquist performed many tricks," the subject, *ventriloquist*, is near the start of the sentence. In an inverted sentence, the subject can appear in several different positions within a sentence.

Check the examples of inverted subjects in the following sentences. The subject of each sentence is italicized, and the position of the subject is explained in parentheses after the sentence.

Can *they* succeed at this task? (between the helping and main verbs)

There are fifty *states*. (at the sentence's end)

Under my uncle's shed is a buried *treasure*. (at the sentence's end)

When did the *roofers* arrive at the job? (between the helping and main verbs)

Why do *all* of the participants believe that story? (between the helping and main verbs)

How were the *guests* last night? (after the main verb)

Over the river and through the woods is Grandmother's *house*. (at the sentence's end)

 HELPFUL HINT *When you are trying to find the subject of a sentence that asks a question, answer the question. Most of the time, the subject will appear readily to you. As an example, in the sentence, "When will the programs air?" you can turn the question into an answer by saying, "The programs will air this Friday night." Now the subject,* programs, *is more readily seen and understood.*

 WRITING TIP *When you write, you do not have to place your sentence's subject near the beginning of the sentence. Vary the position of your subjects. "Behind the red barn on our farm was a stray dog" is a sentence that employs its simple subject,* dog, *in a rather different position. Use your creativity to place the subjects in different positions within your paragraphs.*

You Name Them (Subjects in Unusual Positions)

Circle the simple subject in each of the following sentences. Then write the first two letters of the subject on the line next to the sentence number. Finally, write the thirty letters consecutively on the lines below the last numbered item. If your answers are correct, you will spell out six first names. Have fun!

1. _____ How old is Rudy?

2. _____ There are many states in our country.

3. _____ Will you be leaving home soon?

4. _____ Has the liver been examined yet?

5. _____ How important is velocity in this experiment?

6. _____ What does this signify?

7. _____ Why must the election be reviewed?

8. _____ Can the margin be widened?

9. _____ There is loneliness as well.

10. _____ In our city, larceny is a major concern.

11. _____ Where is the mirror that needs to be thrown in the garbage?

12. _____ Was the kerchief returned?

13. _____ Now can the registrants move to another line?

14. _____ There are many giants in those fairy tales.

15. _____ Will nature often soothe your worries?

The six names are _____, _____, _____,

_____, _____, and _____.

(2.4) Simple Predicates

A **simple predicate** (verb) is the main word or phrase in the complete predicate. In the sentence, "My music teacher taught me a complicated piece yesterday," the simple predicate is *taught*. Verbs that show action are relatively easy to detect. These verbs include *am, are, be, been, being, is, was,* and *were*. Thus, in the sentence, "My uncle is a mechanic," the verb of statement, *is,* does not necessarily show action. It makes a statement.

The verb in each sentence below is italicized:

> Veronica *completed* the puzzle in record time.
>
> One of Joanna's favorite card games *is* Spades.
>
> My friend *borrowed* my social studies book.
>
> The summers in Maine *are* fantastic.
>
> Hector *is* here with us.
>
> They *received* mixed messages from her.
>
> All of the hair stylists *are* happy at their job.

Insert a simple predicate in each blank to complete the sentence:

The O'Connors _____ on vacation with their relatives each July.

They _____ their exercise routine early today.

_____ the soccer ball into the net.

He _____ on the boat's top level.

The wind _____ during the hurricane.

🖎 **WRITING TIP** *Devote time to vocabulary study to learn more words. Why? You will increase your ability to select the precise words to meet your writing needs. This works well when you are looking for the best action words. Perhaps you can become your own thesaurus!*

(2.4A) Matching Them Up (Simple Predicates)

Underline the simple predicate in each of the sentences in Group One. Then match the predicate with its synonym from Group Two's list of predicates. Write the synonym's corresponding letter on the line next to the matching predicate's sentence.

Group One	*Group Two*
1. _____ He permitted us to send out the invitations.	a. allowed
2. _____ Maurice fondly recalled his childhood days in Missouri.	b. carefully examine
3. _____ The train conductor assisted the passengers with their concerns.	c. chose
4. _____ All the runners sprinted toward the finish line.	d. commenced
5. _____ Several of the campers vacated the area immediately.	e. discussed
6. _____ The class officers debated the merits of the request.	f. helped
7. _____ We guffawed at many of the comedian's one-liners.	g. laughed loudly
8. _____ The strong worker hurled the bricks across the yard.	h. left
9. _____ A few of the musicians started to warm up for the performance.	i. moved around
10. _____ They selected Roberto as their club's new president.	j. practice
11. _____ The confident young man strutted into the dance club.	k. ran quickly
12. _____ The editors peruse all of the articles each day.	l. remembered
13. _____ The proctors circulated about the room during the two-hour examination.	m. threw
14. _____ At the last moment, the limo driver veered to the right to avoid hitting the car.	n. turned sharply
15. _____ The actors rehearse their lines before every performance.	o. walked confidently

(2.5) Compound Verbs

A **compound verb** (predicate) is two or more verbs in a single sentence. These verbs, joined by a conjunction, have the same subject. In the sentence, "The older dog generally just ate his food and slept each day," the compound verbs are *ate* and *slept,* and the conjunction is *and*. In the sentence, "The older dog just ate his food, and he slept most of the day," there is no compound verb since the subject of the first main clause, *dog*, has only one verb, *ate*, and the subject of the second main clause, *he*, has only one verb, *slept*. Remember that the verbs in a compound verb must have the same subject.

The compound verbs are in italics in these sentences:

> Tito *sings* and *dances* well.
>
> You can either *stop* here or *proceed* onward with caution.
>
> They *dragged* the heavy cartons into the garage and *opened* them.
>
> Our professor *lectured, read,* and *discussed* the topic.
>
> Marcia *bought* and *signed* the get-well card.
>
> Will the director *announce* the actors' names or *post* the list?
>
> Joe's neighbor can neither *speak* French nor *read* Spanish.
>
> The waitress *welcomed* us, *brought* us some water, and then *took* our order.

Insert a verb in each of the following spaces so that each sentence has a compound verb in it:

Will the quiz show host _____ and _____ the questions?

Geraldine has _____ and _____ the mile race at our school the past three years.

_____, _____, and _____ if you want to be safe on the roads.

The detective _____ the plot and _____ the alleged criminal.

Our relatives _____ the wedding and _____ at our house for the next few days.

 WRITING TIP *Compound verbs help make writing more concise. You can include several actions in just one sentence with compound verbs. Writing that the woman "talked, laughed, and relaxed" allows you as a writer to cluster several ideas in a single group of words.*

(2.5A) A Walk in the Park (Compound Verbs)

Some sentences contain compound verbs (predicates), and some do not. Circle the compound verbs in the following sentences. Underline the single verb in the other sentences; then you do not need to do anything else with these single verbs. Then write the first letter of each compound verb on the line next to the sentence number. Finally, write those letters in consecutive order below the final numbered item. If your answers are correct, you will spell out the names of four parks found in New York City. Enjoy the trip!

1. _____ They chatted with one another and then exchanged e-mail addresses.

2. _____ *Monica* and *Ross* are the characters' names.

3. _____ We can either nail or tack this board to the wall.

4. _____ As a student, you should always read, ask, and listen.

5. _____ Yvonne pleases and respects her elders.

6. _____ Can you remember my birthday?

7. _____ Bob offers or suggests new ideas judiciously.

8. _____ Prepare, execute, and control this important assignment, Rena.

9. _____ The linebacker tackled the fullback and broke the other team's momentum.

10. _____ The victorious boxer raised her arms and yelled at the other fighter.

11. _____ Our debater argued the point, negated his opponent's points, and triumphed.

12. _____ Neither the musician nor the conductor recognized the former orchestra member.

13. _____ Read, investigate, validate, and explore your points of defense.

14. _____ Roll over, and then sit up straight.

15. _____ The teacher imparted knowledge, defied the normal teaching procedures, and exposed her students to exciting ways of thinking.

The letters spell out the names of these four New York City parks: _____,

_____, _____, and _____.

(2.6) Complete Predicates

A **complete predicate** is the main verb along with all of its modifiers. In the sentence, "The violinist received an award this evening," the simple predicate is *received* and the complete predicate is *received an award this evening*. The complete predicates are italicized in these sentences:

The firefighter *carried the heavy package from the garage.*

Some of the old magazines *were thrown into the recycling bin.*

Each pile of leaves *was removed by noon.*

The grand prize winner *is Kayla's father-in-law.*

Insert a complete predicate on the following lines to make each group of words a complete sentence:

The two pilots _____

_____.

Some of the directions _____

_____.

They _____

_____.

Later in the movie the protagonist _____

_____.

These orphans _____

_____.

 WRITING TIP *Use accurate and the most telling verbs in your writings. The word* walk *is not as detailed as* saunter, stroll, amble, *or* totter. *The same holds true for phrases that you include in your complete predicate. Strive for accuracy and detail when selecting verbs and phrases.*

(2.6A) Yours to Complete (Complete Predicates)

Make each group of words a sentence by adding a complete predicate. Share your sentences with your classmates.

1. At the beginning of the show, the host _____

   _____

   _____.

2. The magician _____

   _____

   _____.

3. Several balloons _____

   _____

   _____.

4. Our trip to Texas _____

   _____

   _____.

5. Last week Grandfather _____

   _____

   _____.

6. My favorite singer _____

   _____

   _____.

7. Tuesday_____

   _____

   _____.

Yours to Complete *(Continued)*

8. Zoo visitors _____

_____

_____ .

9. Her favorite television program _____

_____

_____ .

10. Ms. Thompson, our English teacher, _____

_____

_____ .

11. Some of these artifacts _____

_____

_____ .

12. Midway, an airport in Chicago, _____

_____

_____ .

13. Our four new puppies _____

_____

_____ .

14. The eye doctor _____

_____

_____ .

15. All of the Halloween candies _____

_____

_____ .

(2.7) Verb Phrases

A **verb phrase** is a main verb plus one or more helping verbs. A verb phrase may contain more than one helping verb. In the sentence, "Adella will help with the shopping," the verb phrase is *will help*. In the sentence, "Adella should be helping with the shopping," the verb phrase is *should be helping*. The verb phrase is italicized in each of these sentences:

> The military officer *will be returning* home soon.
>
> You *might have forgotten* your wallet.
>
> *Have* any of these plans for the new auditorium *been presented* to you yet?
>
> *Can* they *recall* that uneventful occurrence?
>
> The expert *has priced* some of the valuable antiques.
>
> We *were retelling* the funny stories about our camping trip.
>
> *Are* you *helping* the minister tomorrow?
>
> Never *shall* we *forget* this moment.

Complete each sentence by inserting a verb phrase:

Jasmine _____ _____ _____ good grades in her social studies class.

_____ he _____ his win streak at the tournament?

Our local pharmacist _____ _____ our family for many years.

There _____ _____ more than one answer.

_____ the librarian _____ you the book's location?

✍ **WRITING TIP** *Be sure that you use phrases that are in the correct verb tense when writing stories and essays. Study the verb tenses to ensure accuracy. Examine the other sentences within your paragraph to check that your verb phrase is in the correct tense.*

(2.7A) Phasing In Verb Phrases (Verb Phrases)

Underline the verb phrase in each of the following sentences. Some verb phrases have two words, and some have three words. Do not underline any other parts of speech except the verbs.

1. They were running for the city bus.

2. She had been sewing for over an hour.

3. I will be moving to Oklahoma this fall.

4. Do you remember your first bicycle?

5. This sign may appear on several papers.

6. Several people had really enjoyed your presentation.

7. My neighbor will probably help with the chores.

8. We had been previewing the movie before lunch.

9. The director has helped with the rehearsal.

10. The workers will make several changes today.

11. Coach Mathers will not tolerate such poor effort from you.

12. Are you going to school now, Michael?

13. Can you find the missing piece of the puzzle?

14. The painters had resurfaced the wall during the weekend.

15. Will you soon begin the festivities, Priya?

(2.8) Prepositional Phrases

A **prepositional phrase** begins with a preposition and usually ends with a noun or pronoun. Examples of prepositional phrases are *near the sink, by the mansion, around the corner,* and *concerning this item.* The noun or pronoun that ends the prepositional phrase is called the **object of the preposition.** A prepositional phrase can function as either an adjective phrase or an adverb phrase.

The prepositional phrase is italicized in each sentence below. A sentence can have more than one prepositional phrase, as the last sentence in this list shows.

The new show will air *in October.*

At this moment, I do not want any more calls.

Some *of the merchandise* will be sold tomorrow.

You are just *like me!*

Throughout the day, we will be watching you work.

Please line up *between these two cadets.*

Before breakfast, Mom attends exercise class.

Everybody *from our group* will attend the meeting *in the cafeteria.*

Complete each sentence by inserting a prepositional phrase.

She ran _____.

Cathy sang quite beautifully _____.

Please take this carton _____.

Listen _____.

The birds usually fly south _____.

✍ **WRITING TIP** *Depending on whether the prepositional phrase is used as an adjective or adverb, the phrase can modify a noun, pronoun, verb, adjective, or another adverb. The most important aspect of the prepositional phrase for you as a writer is that you use it for descriptive purposes to add greater clarity to your sentences.*

Hidden Prepositional Phrases

The fourteen prepositional phrases listed below are hidden in this grid. The phrases can be found horizontally, vertically, diagonally, backward, or forward. Circle these fourteen phrases, and then on another sheet of paper, use each phrase in a separate sentence. If you would like to include two or more phrases in a single sentence, do so.

i	h	b	k	a	m	u	y	q	r	k	n	r	p	v	v	b	a	t	d
n	l	y	a	s	l	p	p	v	x	l	z	a	v	j	y	e	p	b	b
t	b	h	o	r	b	o	v	o	r	f	s	h	z	d	s	f	c	q	w
h	x	i	m	n	o	j	n	i	n	t	o	t	h	e	w	o	o	d	s
e	c	m	y	p	t	u	r	g	t	t	y	q	h	q	m	r	w	w	g
m	q	s	n	b	x	h	n	h	t	f	h	t	n	z	l	e	r	j	q
e	m	e	k	i	l	j	e	d	m	h	d	e	m	n	p	n	p	q	f
a	y	l	f	g	m	s	d	s	t	n	e	x	p	m	g	o	m	h	q
n	r	f	b	g	t	r	s	x	o	h	v	s	c	i	x	o	x	b	j
t	r	w	y	a	b	y	m	y	m	f	e	c	h	b	l	n	s	m	f
i	b	g	n	y	p	s	e	w	m	b	a	t	p	o	s	l	s	w	z
m	x	d	l	h	d	b	f	r	z	f	h	n	r	r	r	c	o	j	w
e	s	d	o	w	n	t	h	e	h	a	l	l	w	a	y	e	t	w	w
l	j	h	c	b	f	o	r	t	h	e	b	l	e	a	c	h	e	r	s
s	i	n	c	e	y	e	s	t	e	r	d	a	y	x	c	k	y	n	x

along the shore   in the meantime

around the track   into the woods

before noon   like me

beyond the sea   on the sofa

by himself   past the stands

down the hallway   since yesterday

for the bleachers   upon the pillow

(2.8B) One to a Sentence (Prepositional Phrases)

Each of the following sentences contains one prepositional phrase. Underline the phrase. Then circle the preposition that begins the phrase.

1. The esteemed orchestra conductor was irritated by the backstage noise.

2. Our team scored three runs in the last inning.

3. Those women under the large beach umbrella did not get sunburned.

4. Many ducks wading in the pond seemed content.

5. A windy road beyond the mountain will lead us there.

6. A member of the police force arrested the bank robber.

7. Two rooms within the castle contain valuable documents.

8. The excitement during the wrestling match was quite evident.

9. Marisa asked her mother for a favor.

10. The question concerning your eligibility will be addressed next week.

11. The chatty youngster remained quiet for only a few minutes.

12. The parking lots near Fenway Park are full.

13. I do like to exercise in the morning.

14. The homesick sailor aboard the ship cannot wait to be home again.

15. Unfortunately, the executive left her briefcase at the office.

(2.9) Adjective Phrases

An **adjective phrase** is a prepositional phrase that acts as an adjective since the phrase modifies a noun or a pronoun. An adjective phrase begins with a preposition and usually ends with a noun or pronoun. It answers the question, "Which one?"

The italicized words in the following sentences are adjective phrases. The question that each answers is in parentheses.

> The tent *in our backyard* is getting old. (Which tent?)
>
> This food *for my dog* is not cheap! (Which food?)
>
> These maps *on my desk* belong to someone else. (Which maps?)
>
> Directions *to the festival* will be mailed soon. (Which directions?)
>
> Have you read this book *by Toni Morrison*? (Which book?)

Complete each sentence by adding an adjective phrase in the blank:

The pretty picture _____
is right here.

Some_____
have already been printed.

The key _____
is under the mat.

Bob's talent _____
has been recognized before.

These roads _____
need to be repaved soon.

🖎 **WRITING TIP** *Generally, adjective phrases are not movable within a sentence. They follow the nouns that they modify. In the sentence, "The officer near the door is my father's friend," the phrase* near the door *is an adjective phrase since it modifies the noun* officer *and answers the question,* Which one? *If you move that phrase away from the word it modifies, you will probably make it an adverb phrase.*

(2.9A) Making Sense of the Adjective Phrase

Compose sentences using the following prepositional phrases as adjective phrases. Thus, the phrase should follow directly after the noun that it modifies or describes.

1. with the stack of books

_____

_____

_____

2. under the bed

_____

_____

_____

3. along the river

_____

_____

_____

4. by the new stadium

_____

_____

_____

5. during our family party

_____

_____

_____

(2.9A) Making Sense of the Adjective Phrase *(Continued)*

6. with my best friends

_____

_____

_____

7. of her favorite songs

_____

_____

_____

8. into the next room

_____

_____

_____

9. aboard the ocean liner

_____

_____

_____

10. for the concert

_____

_____

_____

(2.10) Adverb Phrases

An **adverb phrase** is a prepositional phrase that acts as an adverb. The phrase begins with a preposition and usually ends with a noun or pronoun. This phrase modifies an adjective, a verb, or another adverb. It answers one of these questions: *When? Where? How? Why? Under what conditions? To what degree?*

Here are some examples of adverb phrases, which are italicized, with the question that the adverb phrase answers in parentheses:

The book was found *beneath the newspapers.* (Where?)

After school the children walked home. (When?)

Many spectators left the stadium *in a hurry.* (How?)

The party ended *because of the rain.* (Why?)

Kim won the race *by two feet.* (To what degree?)

Situated *near the river,* the museum attracted many visitors. (Where?)

The movers delivered our furniture *around four o'clock* yesterday afternoon. (When?)

Complete these sentences by adding an adverb phrase to each one:

The famous author was signing his books _____.

Most adults enjoy walking _____.

They should win this election _____.

Larry hailed the cab _____.

_____ Kerry heard her mother call her name.

WRITING TIP *If you can move a phrase within a sentence, it is usually an adverb phrase rather than an adjective phrase. The prepositional phrase* in a pinch *can be moved, as shown in these two sentences:* In a pinch, *you can call on me.* You can call on me *in a pinch.*

(2.10A) Traveling the World (Adverb Phrases)

Each of the following sentences contains a prepositional phrase used as an adverb phrase. Underline those fifteen phrases. Then write the first letter of the last word in each phrase (consecutively) on the lines below the last numbered sentence. If your answers are correct, you will spell out the names of three countries.

1. When she walked near the podium, we all stood up.

2. My brother provides instruments for that orchestra.

3. He believes that it is bad luck to walk under a ladder.

4. The trucker could not make a delivery to the arena yesterday.

5. My dad and I jogged around the neighborhood last night.

6. Near the daffodils is my baseball.

7. Harry brought new spirit into the election.

8. We thought that we left the tire near the garage.

9. The youngsters were playing with their yo-yos.

10. We drove past the playground last Tuesday evening.

11. She was riding in the truck.

12. How many times has she now walked around that lake?

13. My sister talked to her accountant.

14. On that occasion I would like to address the officials.

15. We had not seen each other since last semester.

The three countries are _____, _____, and

_____.

2.11 Appositives

An **appositive** is a noun or pronoun, often with modifiers, placed beside another noun or pronoun to explain or identify it. It is another way of telling who or what the noun or pronoun is. The appositive can either precede or follow the word it modifies. There are no verbs in an appositive phrase.

Here are some examples of appositives. The italicized words in each sentence form the appositive phrase. The underlined word is the simple appositive.

My dad, *a retired <u>chauffeur</u>,* always enjoys his free time now.

The final tennis match, *a three-hour <u>classic</u>,* was a thriller.

A *spectacular <u>shortstop</u>,* Derek Jeter is the captain of the New York Yankees.

Mrs. Brennan, *my daughters' piano <u>teacher</u>,* has moved to another state.

New York, *the Empire <u>State</u>,* is quite populated.

Mr. Hall, *our <u>principal</u>,* spoke eloquently about the event.

F. Scott Fitzgerald, *the <u>author</u> of many fine novels and short stories,* led an interesting life.

"Laura Lee," *the charter fishing <u>boat</u>,* has left the dock.

Complete each sentence by inserting an appositive word or phrase:

_____, our neighbor, is a funny person.

Lydia's best tennis shot, _____, helped her in her match against Tanya.

_____, the newest street in our town, has six new homes on it already.

My family's new car, _____, is parked next door tonight.

Princeton University, _____, is located in New Jersey.

✍ **WRITING TIP** *An appositive adds information about a person, place, or thing. It is not an adjective. Instead, it is another name for that person, place, or thing. Do not include a verb in an appositive phrase. Here are two examples:*

Reggie White, a former football player, *was an outstanding player. (The words "a former football player" form an appositive phrase. There is no verb within the appositive phrase.)*

Reggie White, who was a former football player, *was an outstanding player. (The words "who was a former football player" are a subordinate or dependent clause, and not an appositive phrase. There is a verb within the subordinate or dependent clause.)*

(2.11A) Be Positive About Appositives

Match the fifteen appositives in Group B with their appropriate sentences in Group A. Then write the corresponding two-letter code in Group B on the line next to the appropriate sentence. If your answers are correct, you will spell out a useful piece of advice. Write that sentence in its designated place at the end of this activity.

Group A

1. _____ The woods of Connecticut, _____, are beautiful.

2. _____ Lou Gehrig, _____, wore number four.

3. _____ We studied the Nile, _____.

4. _____ E, _____, appears in many, many words.

5. _____ Alpha, _____, is a word that appears often in crossword puzzles.

6. _____ Asia, _____, is quite expansive.

7. _____ The cheetah, _____, can outrun many of it enemies.

8. _____ Queens, _____, abuts Nassau County.

9. _____ Maine, _____, is the only monosyllabic state.

10. _____ In biology class we studied the ulna, _____.

11. _____ Pele, _____, made soccer popular in our country.

12. _____ The Executive, _____, is headed by the president.

13. _____ The incisors, _____, are used primarily for cutting and chewing food.

14. _____ Many automobile experts thought that the Edsel, _____, would be a big-selling car.

15. _____ Bill and Melinda Gates, _____, have given away millions of dollars.

(2.11A) Be Positive About Appositives *(Continued)*

Group B

an. a soccer legend

ap. the Nutmeg State

ce. a bone in the arm

ea. the eye teeth

ei. a very fast animal

id. one of the three branches of the U.S. government

ll. well-known philanthropists

nf. the most populated New York City borough

or. one of the fifty states

po. the Pride of the Yankees

si. the world's longest river

sr. the world's largest continent

ti. the English language's most-often-used letter

ve. the Greek alphabet's first letter

we. a disappointing model

The useful piece of advice is:

_____

_____.

© 2007 by John Wiley & Sons, Inc.

(2.12) Misplaced Prepositional Phrases

A **prepositional phrase** should clearly indicate the word that it modifies. If it is misplaced, it should be moved to its proper position within the sentence. Often the phrase is quite close to the noun that it modifies.

Here are examples of misplaced prepositional phrases and how they can be corrected:

***Beneath the pile of wood,* John found the missing hammers.** (Was John beneath the pile of wood? No! The missing hammers were beneath the pile of wood.) The correct wording of this sentence is, "John found the missing hammers beneath the pile of wood."

The car transported the celebrity *with squeaky wheels.* (Did the celebrity have squeaky wheels? No! The car had squeaky wheels.) The correct wording of this sentence is, "The car with squeaky wheels transported the celebrity."

A vampire chased the girl *with frightening fangs.* (Did the girl have the frightening fangs? No! The vampire had frightening fangs.) The correct wording of this sentence is, "A vampire with frightening fangs chased the girl."

***At the bottom of the glass,* we saw the olive.** (Were we at the bottom of the glass? No! The olive was at the bottom of the glass.) The correct wording of this sentence is, "We saw the olive at the bottom of the glass."

***Inside the computer,* I looked for the defective part.** (Were you inside the computer? No! The defective part was inside the computer.) The correct wording of this sentence is, "I looked for the defective part inside the computer."

 WRITING TIP *Check that you have correctly placed prepositional phrases in your sentences. Read the sentences several times to ensure that prepositional phrases are in the proper modifying position. Otherwise, the reader may get a good laugh out of the misplaced prepositional phrase, as you did with the misplaced prepositional phrases in this lesson!*

(2.12A) Misplaced Information (Prepositional Phrases)

Each of the following sentences contains a misplaced prepositional phrase. Circle the misplaced prepositional phrase. Then, on a separate sheet of paper, write each sentence, placing the misplaced phrase in its proper position within the sentence.

1. Under the bed the guests beckoned to the disobedient dog.

2. My dad in the oven turned over the steak.

3. In the trunk of my car, we moved the spare tire.

4. The cat was spotted by my great-grandmother up in the large tree.

5. Into a delicious bowl of cereal, my sister poured the milk.

6. The guppies were talked about by my dad and mom in the fishbowl.

7. Three small frogs were seen by Uncle Ted in the window well.

8. On the top of the tall flagpole, the infant pointed to the bird.

9. Within the patient's stomach, the doctor could feel the lump.

10. Inside the chest cavity, the doctor examined some internal organs.

11. Bernie recalled his story of cleaning elephants in the school auditorium.

12. Beneath a pile of dirty clothes, the maid found the missing pair of pants.

13. In the desk drawer, my teacher found his missing pen.

14. My sister in the apple found a worm.

15. By himself, the couple saw the man lift the very heavy carton.

(2.13) Participles and Participle Phrases

A **participle** is a verbal, which looks like a verb and acts like an adjective. Present participles end in *-ing* (as in *swimming*). Past participles end in *-ed* (as in *remembered*), *-en* (as in *eaten*), *-d* (as in *paid*), *-t* (as in *burnt*), or *-n* (as in *seen*). The participle in each sentence is italicized:

> The *hustling* runner beat the outfielder's throw.
>
> My *frenzied* approach was not successful.
>
> The *tired* joggers walked over the *fallen* leaves.
>
> The *angered* competitor questioned the *puzzled* official.
>
> The *smiling* teacher eased the youngster's concern.

A **participle phrase** consists of the participle, its modifiers, and other words that complete the idea begun by the participle. In the following sentences, the simple participle is italicized, and the participle phrase is underlined:

> That tall woman *exiting* the lab teaches chemistry.
>
> The concert *scheduled* for June was canceled.
>
> Those reporters *standing* near the hospital entrance will be leaving soon.
>
> *Standing* over seven-feet tall, the basketball player is an imposing figure.
>
> *Trusting* in her sense of direction, the guide led the group to the clearing.

✎ **WRITING TIP** *Use the participle phrase in front of and right after the noun it describes. "The man waiting for the taxi was cold" and "Waiting for the taxi, the man was cold" are two effective ways to use that particular participle phrase.*

(2.13A) Find the Six (Participles)

Only six of the following sentences do not contain participles. Write the three-letter codes for those six sentences (consecutively) in the appropriate space below the final numbered item. If your answers are correct, you will spell out an eighteen-letter word.

1. **(tre)** Repaired by the mechanic, the machine ran well again.

2. **(bri)** The machine repaired by the mechanic ran well again.

3. **(une)** The machine that was repaired by the mechanic ran well again.

4. **(ght)** The Smiths' stately home, featured in the national magazine, is quite beautiful.

5. **(nth)** The Smiths' beautiful and stately home was featured in the national magazine.

6. **(men)** Featured in the national magazine, the Smiths' stately home is quite beautiful.

7. **(nes)** Burned beyond recognition, the toast had to be thrown out.

8. **(usi)** The toast, burned beyond recognition, had to be thrown out.

9. **(dou)** The toast, burned beyond recognition, had to be thrown out.

10. **(ast)** The students heard the bell and left the classroom.

11. **(sly)** Hearing the bell, the students left the classroom.

12. **(fra)** The students, hearing the bell, left the classroom.

13. **(ica)** The crowd was clapping and cheering for the championship players and welcomed them home.

14. **(cti)** The crowd, clapping and cheering for their championship players, welcomed them home.

15. **(gue)** Clapping and cheering for their championship players, the crowd welcomed them home.

16. **(ons)** Misplaced in Washington's Union Station, the cell phone was returned.

17. **(sts)** The cell phone, misplaced in Washington's Union Station, was returned.

18. **(lly)** The cell phone was misplaced in Washington's Union Station and was returned.

The word spelled out by the three-letter codes of the sentences that do not contain participles is

_____.

 **Gerunds**

A **gerund** is a verbal that ends in *-ing* and acts as a noun. It can act as a subject, direct object, subject complement (predicate nominative), or object of the preposition. The following sentences feature a gerund in italics and the gerund's function in the parentheses after the sentence.

> *Listening* is a great asset. **(subject)**
>
> Do you think that the young soldier enjoys *jogging*? **(direct object)**
>
> His most recent exercise program is *weightlifting*. **(subject complement or predicate nominative)**
>
> Justine was given an award for *volunteering*. **(object of the preposition)**

A **gerund phrase** includes the gerund, its modifiers, and the words that complete the idea begun by the gerund. In the following sentences, the simple gerund is italicized, and the gerund phrase is underlined:

> *Skiing* during the vacation was a lot of fun for this family. **(subject)**
>
> *Reporting* the news was Brooke's dream job. **(subject)**
>
> Jimmy stopped *kicking* the ball. **(direct object)**
>
> My friend's bad habit has been *biting* his nails. **(subject complement)**
>
> We could not stop them from *yelling* at the interviewer. **(object of the preposition)**

Fill in each blank with a gerund or a gerund phrase. Remember that a gerund ends in *-ing*:

_____ is her grandmother's favorite activity.

The players enjoyed _____.

She always remembered _____.

My friends loved _____.

_____ was not impossible for this determined woman.

WRITING TIP *Although a gerund ends in* -ing *and looks like a verb, it functions as a noun. Make the distinction in your writings.* Writing *is used as a gerund in the sentence, "*Writing *is Marian's pastime." In the sentence, "Marian is* writing *her autobiography,"* writing *is a verb.*

(2.14A) Five Apiece (Gerunds)

Identify whether the gerund underlined in each of the following sentences functions as a subject (S), predicate nominative (PN), direct object (DO), or object of the preposition (OP). Write the appropriate code letter(s) on the line next to the sentence. Each of the four gerund functions—subject, predicate nominative, direct object, and object of the preposition—is used five times here:

1. _____ Our friends enjoy jogging.

2. _____ My neighbor was given a ticket for speeding.

3. _____ Lifting weights is Juan's favorite activity.

4. _____ Sylvia's pastime is collecting antiques.

5. _____ The giggling from the students was able to be heard in the next room.

6. _____ The stadium officials will not tolerate booing.

7. _____ We finished the complicated math problem before hearing the loud noise from that room.

8. _____ One of Mitch's most attractive traits is keeping others happy.

9. _____ Walking along the beach makes the couple happy.

10. _____ They enjoy walking along the beach.

11. _____ They ate dinner after walking along the beach.

12. _____ Their favorite activity is walking along the beach.

13. _____ Before seeing the sun, we were unhappy.

14. _____ Reviewing for the test was tiresome.

15. _____ My friends disliked reviewing for the challenging test.

16. _____ Witnessing the accident and its aftermath made Lucy have bad dreams.

17. _____ His most obvious flaw is making fun of others.

18. _____ She has a talent for helping those in need.

19. _____ The most difficult part of the procedure is removing these parts.

20. _____ Fred liked looking through these college yearbooks.

Infinitives

An **infinitive** is a verbal consisting of the word *to* plus a verb—for example: "to perceive," "to understand," and "to pretend." The infinitive functions as a noun, adjective, or adverb. The **simple infinitive** is the word *to* plus all the parts of the verb. The **infinitive phrase** is the infinitive, its modifiers, and all the other words that help to complete the idea begun by the infinitive.

In the following sentences, the simple infinitive is italicized, and its use is identified in the parentheses after the sentence:

> *To win* was Ted's goal. **(subject)**
>
> All of the store owners wanted *to win*. **(direct object)**
>
> Everyone wanted *to win*. **(direct object)**
>
> Ted's goal was *to win*. **(subject complement)**
>
> She possessed the desire *to win*. **(adjective)**
>
> We must strive *to win*. **(adverb)**

In the following sentences, the simple infinitive is italicized, and the infinitive phrase is underlined:

> She wanted *to be loved* by both families. (**direct object:** "To be loved by both families" answers the question, "What did she want?")
>
> The team *to beat* is the Panthers. (**adjective:** Which team is the Panthers? The Panthers are the team *to beat*.)
>
> *To win* the game was their goal. (**subject:** What was their goal? To win the game was their goal.)
>
> My aunt needed someone *to move* her cabinet. (**adjective:** Which someone did my aunt need? She needed *someone to move her cabinet*.)
>
> They needed *to feel* more comfortable. (**direct object:** "To feel more comfortable" answers the question, "What did they need?")
>
> Lindsay raced into the room *to help* the others. (**adverb:** "To help the others" answers the question, "Why did Lindsay race into the room?")

(2.15) Infinitives *(Continued)*

Fill in these blanks with infinitive phrases:

1. The president needed _____

   _____.

2. _____

   _____ you must be physically fit.

3. They are about _____

   _____.

4. My goal is _____

   _____.

5. These four politicians looked _____

   _____.

📝 **WRITING TIP** *Do not confuse an infinitive phrase with a prepositional phrase. An infinitive phrase contains a verb. A prepositional phrase does not contain a verb. Infinitive phrases include* to win, to study, to skateboard, to contribute, *and* to volunteer. *Prepositional phrases include* to the dormitory, to them, to you, to the concert, to the gas station, *and* to the mall.

(2.15A) Each of the Three Gets Five (Infinitives)

The underlined infinitive phrases in the following sentences function as nouns (N), adjectives (ADJ), and adverbs (ADVB). Write the phrase's code letters on the line next to the sentence. Each type of phrase appears five times.

1. _____ The player to draft is the running back.

2. _____ To draft that player is the team owner's goal.

3. _____ We left to get some water.

4. _____ Barring an emergency, to get up and leave during a speech is rude.

5. _____ My instructor was quite happy to receive your report.

6. _____ The card to select is this one.

7. _____ One official to talk with is Mrs. Munson.

8. _____ To be well liked was Willy Loman's goal in *Death of a Salesman*.

9. _____ In *Death of a Salesman,* Willy Loman's goal was to be well liked.

10. _____ Willy Loman's goal was to be well liked.

11. _____ He was quite fortunate to hear the news that early.

12. _____ She was happy to complete the directory by Friday.

13. _____ These are the paintings to display at the show.

14. _____ We left the building to see all the floats in the parade.

15. _____ The score to beat is 1340.

(2.15B) Infinitive Goals

Ask ten of your acquaintances (family, friends, teachers, coaches, and others) for one of their goals. This goal can be immediate or long range. Then on this sheet, write the person's name and his or her goal next to it in an infinitive phrase format. Add three of your personal goals as well. *Examples:* Bob: to win the state volleyball championship; Sevan: to be accepted into Georgetown University; Mrs. Walters: to have all my students pass the biology final exam.

Person	*Goal in Infinitive Phrase Form*
_____	_____
_____	_____
_____	_____
_____	_____
_____	_____
_____	_____
_____	_____
_____	_____
_____	_____
_____	_____

Direct Objects

A noun or pronoun that receives the *action* of a verb or shows the *result* of the action is called a **direct object.** To find the direct object in a sentence, ask the question, "What?" or "Whom?" after an action verb. In the following sentences, the action verb is underlined, and the direct object is italicized:

> Our group <u>needed</u> more *evidence.*
>
> We <u>received</u> several *envelopes* in the mail.
>
> The artist <u>finished</u> the *painting* last night.
>
> The interviewer <u>questioned</u> the *inventor* about her new product.
>
> Some of the officials <u>spotted</u> the escaped *convict.*
>
> We <u>reminded</u> *him* of the important date.
>
> We <u>buried</u> our *cat* in the pet cemetery.
>
> My former coach <u>recalled</u> that thrilling *game.*
>
> Playing hockey <u>makes</u> *her* more physically fit.

Write a direct object in the following blanks to complete each sentence:

The people selected _____ as their new leader.

Shane bought ten _____ for the class outing.

Select _____ you want.

Our new teacher instructed _____ to complete the project on time.

Ray photographed _____ in their living room.

✍ **WRITING TIP** *A direct object can be a noun or a pronoun. An indirect object needs a direct object, but a direct object does not need an indirect object. In the sentence, "Bob gave Marilyn a gift,"* Marilyn *is the indirect object, and* gift *is the direct object. You can delete* Marilyn *and still have a complete idea, but you cannot delete* gift *and still have a complete idea.*

Name _____ Date _____ Period _____

 2.16A **Five-Letter Words (Direct Objects)**

Underline the direct object in each of the following sentences. Then write the first letter of that word on the line next to its number. Write the fifteen letters consecutively on the appropriate lines below this list to spell three five-letter words.

1. _____ The girls were practicing their ballet.

2. _____ Who discovered electricity?

3. _____ Youngsters often enjoy reading.

4. _____ The vacationers toured Europe last summer.

5. _____ Most people in civilized countries respect tradition.

6. _____ In many of his college classes, Brian studied literature.

7. _____ The young doctor studied many different illnesses.

8. _____ The students played games during recess last week.

9. _____ Marian and her husband bought a new house.

10. _____ Reggie knows trivia!

11. _____ The slugger hit a homer in the bottom of the ninth inning.

12. _____ The ancients built the obelisk on that site.

13. _____ The detective shared a full understanding of the situation.

14. _____ Her favorite season is spring.

15. _____ Goodwill always attempts to conquer evil.

The three five-letter words are _____, _____, and

_____.

(2.17) Indirect Objects

An **indirect object** precedes the direct object and tells for whom or to whom the verb's action is done. An indirect object also tells who is receiving the direct object. Remember that you need a direct object in order to have an indirect object. Indirect objects must be nouns or pronouns. Like direct objects, indirect objects are never in prepositional phrases. The following verbs and their verb forms take indirect objects:

ask	bring	find	get	give	hand
lend	offer	pay	pour	promise	read
send	show	teach	tell	throw	write

Here are some examples of indirect objects and direct objects:

Frances told Yvonne the good news. (*Yvonne* is the indirect object, and *news* is the direct object.)

An office assistant gave us the correct information. (The indirect object is *us,* and the direct object is *information.*)

The waitress brought them their dessert. (The indirect object is *them,* and the direct object is *dessert.*)

My boss offered me a raise. (The indirect object is *me,* and the direct object is *raise.*)

I will show you the new plans. (The indirect object is *you,* and the direct object is *plans.*)

The journalist sent the celebrity a questionnaire. (The indirect object is *celebrity,* and the direct object is *questionnaire.*)

Will you lend us some money? (The indirect object is *us,* and the direct object is *money.*)

We sent Bill and Kylie a funny letter. (The indirect objects are *Bill and Kylie,* and the direct object is *letter.*)

Fill in the following blanks with an indirect object:

Ms. Jenkins wished _____ good luck in the race.

Can you hand _____ the pen now?

They lent _____ two hundred dollars.

📣 **WRITING TIP** *Be sure to include the direct object when using an indirect object. If there is no direct object, there can be no indirect object in a sentence. In the sentence, "Oliver passed Michelle the ball," Michelle is the indirect object, and ball is the direct object. You need ball (direct object) to make the sentence make full sense. Yet you do not need Michelle (indirect object) to make the sentence make sense.*

(2.17A) Find the Thirty Letters (Indirect Objects)

Underline the indirect object in each of the following sentences. Then write the first two letters of this word on the line next to the number. Next, write those thirty letters consecutively on the appropriate lines below the list to find the five words that these letters spell out.

1. _____ Mom showed Carlos the completed pages.

2. _____ Sherry asked the ventriloquist an interesting question.

3. _____ The wizard gave the dwarfs his magic potion.

4. _____ A veterinarian bought the elephants some more nutritious food.

5. _____ The zookeeper gave the leopard some food.

6. _____ The doctor gave the rookie some healthy advice.

7. _____ Our coach tells the blockers their assignments during practice.

8. _____ This technician brought the oncologist the x-rays.

9. _____ The séance participants told the ghost to exit the room.

10. _____ A new principal assigned the apprentice another room.

11. _____ We gave the python plenty of space.

12. _____ She handed the intern the instrument.

13. _____ My sister sent her teacher a beautiful bouquet of roses.

14. _____ We mailed our Realtor the final figures.

15. _____ Some members of the young crowd offered the stuntman their assistance.

These thirty letters spell the words _____, _____,

_____, _____, and _____.

(2.18) Predicate Nominatives and Predicate Adjectives

The **predicate nominative** is the noun that follows a linking verb and restates or stands for the subject. In these example sentences, the subject is underlined, the verb is in bold type, and the predicate nominative is italicized:

Donna **is** the new *president* of her sorority. (Donna = president)

Our most popular ice cream selections **are** *vanilla* and *chocolate*. (selections = vanilla and chocolate)

Kenneth **is** the *author* of this new play. (Kenneth = author)

Alaska **is** the largest *state* in the Union. (Alaska = state)

Predicate nominatives can also follow linking verbs that are not the verb "to be." In these example sentences, the subject is underlined, the verb is in bold type, and the predicate nominative is italicized:

My friend will **become** a *senior* in high school next month.

These photographs can **become** *postcards* very soon.

These heavy rains **seem** a *problem* for the farmers.

Kate's teacher **remains** a *constant* in the young girl's life.

Predicate adjectives also follow a linking verb that restates or stands for the subject. In these example sentences, the subject is underlined, the verb is in bold type, and the predicate adjective is italicized:

She **is** *agile*.

This mythological hunter **is** quite *brave*.

These math problems **are** certainly *challenging*.

The weather **remains** *hazy*, *hot*, and *humid*.

Aunt Theresa's lasagna **became** *legendary*.

 WRITING TIP *When you work with predicate nominatives and predicate adjectives, think of the verb as an equal sign. Both sides of the linking verb are equivalent. In the sentence, "Lydia is our representative," Lydia is the subject, and representative is the predicate nominative. Lydia and representative are equals; thus, the verb is is the same as an equal sign since one side of the sentence equals the other side of the sentence.*

Name _____ Date _____ Period _____

 2.18A **Two to One**
(Predicate Nominatives and Predicate Adjectives)

There are ten predicate adjectives and only five predicate nominatives found in these fifteen sentences. Underline the predicate adjective or the predicate nominative in each sentence. Then write the letters PA for predicate adjective or PN for predicate nominative on the line next to the number. Remember that the predicate adjectives outnumber the predicate nominatives two to one.

1. _____ Jovan Hsu is our class president.

2. _____ The contest winner is quite talented.

3. _____ The pond looks murky today.

4. _____ Bobby Andresen is our announcer.

5. _____ My grandfather has been tired throughout the day.

6. _____ That is absolutely wonderful!

7. _____ Will Mom feel lonely at home if the rest of us all go out tonight?

8. _____ Our supervisor was ecstatic when she heard that we had met our quotas.

9. _____ It is Lily knocking on your door.

10. _____ The producers appeared lethargic during the television program's taping.

11. _____ Lance Armstrong is a superstar.

12. _____ I am very happy to hear that bit of news.

13. _____ That dog is quite content.

14. _____ This painting had been considered priceless.

15. _____ During that memorable season, Joe Torre was the Yankee skipper.

(2.19) Adverb Clauses

An **adverb clause** (a group of words with at least a subject and a verb) is a subordinate or dependent clause that acts as an adverb. An adverb clause can answer any of these questions: *Why? Where? When? How? How much?* and *How often?* An adverb clause starts with a subordinating conjunction. Here are some subordinating conjunctions:

after	although	as	because	before
even though	if	in order	since	so that
that	though	unless	until	where
whether	while			

The adverb clause in each sentence that follows is italicized:

Whenever Jared introduces himself, he becomes quite nervous. (The adverb clause answers the question *when.*)

Bethany did not remember the directions *until we reached that corner.* (The adverb clause answers the question *when.*)

As soon as the program began, my cell phone rang. (The adverb clause answers the question *when.*)

After the graduation ceremony ended, we went to celebrate at a local restaurant. (The adverb clause answers the question *when.*)

You can attain that goal *if you strive for it.* (The adverb clause answers the question *how.*)

Sean looked *as if he had seen a ghost.* (The adverb clause answers the question *how* Sean looked.)

Complete the following sentences by inserting an adverb clause:

_____, she watched for crossing pedestrians.

My memory works best _____.

_____, he did not reveal anything about it.

Louise is older _____.

_____, we took it for a test drive.

 WRITING TIP *Adverb clauses combine several ideas. Use them to combine ideas and give your writing more interest. Instead of writing two simple sentences such as, "Bob saw the play" and "He later went to the restaurant," combine them into a single sentence using an adverb clause. Thus, the sentence, "After Bob saw the play, he went to a restaurant" uses the adverb clause, "After Bob saw the play," intelligently.*

(2.19A) Nine Is Fine (Adverb Clauses)

Nine of the following sentences contain adverb clauses. Underline these adverb clauses. Remember that an adverb clause must have a subject and a verb. The six other sentences contain prepositional phrases. Underline those prepositional phrases as well. Finally, write the letters AC for adverb clause and PP for prepositional phrase on the line next to the appropriate number.

1. _____ We all went to the restaurant.

2. _____ After the game concluded, we all went home.

3. _____ We will go upstate if the weather is good.

4. _____ She is pleased since you will be there.

5. _____ If he hollers, let him go.

6. _____ Considering the circumstances, I am not able to attend tomorrow's meeting.

7. _____ We will listen as soon as the crowd settles down.

8. _____ Pretend to act as if you do not know.

9. _____ Whenever I am confused, I try to do what my father would do.

10. _____ I have not seen you since last March.

11. _____ If we can conduct ourselves maturely, we can attend the gala event.

12. _____ We cannot sign the deed until tomorrow.

13. _____ Unless she decides to transfer, Dana will be here next year.

14. _____ We will not be able to make changes after that.

15. _____ You are the best students in the school.

2.20 Adjective Clauses

An **adjective clause** (a group of words with at least a subject and a verb) is a subordinate or dependent clause that functions as an adjective. It usually begins with a relative pronoun, such as *who, whom, which,* or *that.*

There are two basic types of adjective clauses.

The first type is the *nonrestrictive* or *nonessential* adjective clause. This clause simply gives extra information about the noun. In the sentence, "My older brother's car, which he bought two years ago, has already needed many repairs," the adjective clause, "which he bought two years ago," is nonrestrictive or nonessential. It provides extra information.

The second type is the *restrictive* or *essential* adjective clause. It offers essential informative and is needed to complete the sentence's thought. In the sentence, "The room that you reserved for the meeting is not ready," the adjective clause, "that you reserved for the meeting," is essential because it restricts which room.

Here are some examples of how adjective clauses function in a sentence:

The stadium *that was recently demolished* was built over seventy years ago. (The adjective clause is the subject and is restrictive or essential since it restricts the stadium to the one that was recently demolished and built over seventy years ago.)

Abraham Lincoln, *who was the sixteenth president of the United States,* fought hard for equality. (We know more about the sentence's subject, Abraham Lincoln, because of the adjective clause. Yet the adjective clause is not a necessary part of the sentence. It just adds more information about Lincoln. Therefore, the clause is nonrestrictive or nonessential.)

Here are some pieces of information regarding the italicized adjective clauses:

My older sister, *whom we spoke about last week,* will attend law school this fall. (subject) (nonessential or nonrestrictive adjective clause)

The plant *that blooms in early spring* is very beautiful. (subject) (restrictive or essential adjective clause)

She is the woman *whose daily presence and goodwill* are missed. (predicate nominative) (restrictive or essential adjective clause)

The sophomore class of *which I am a member* will be constructing the homecoming float this weekend. (object of the preposition) (nonessential or nonrestrictive adjective clause)

The trophy *that Lorena won* is tall. (subject) (restrictive or essential adjective clause)

Here is the map (that) I want you to examine. (*that* is understood) (restrictive or essential adjective clause)

 WRITING TIP *Use adjective clauses to offer several bits of information in a single sentence. When used correctly, clauses add information, fluency, and sophistication to writing. The adverb clause* who was a member of the Boston Pops orchestra *does just that in the sentence, "My uncle,* who was a member of the Boston Pops orchestra, *now lives in South Dakota."*

(2.20A) Underlining Issues (Adjective Clauses)

Underline the adjective clause in each of the following sentences:

1. He is the boy whose bike was stolen last week.

2. The road that winds its way through this part of the state is quite scenic.

3. A person who is happy will have a good life.

4. Joan Jones, who is our captain, won several medals.

5. The idea that we could raise enough money to buy that expensive equipment is startling.

6. This word that is originally from Latin is not difficult to spell.

7. Ms. Broderick recommended the play that I went to see last night.

8. This is the movie I want to see.

9. People who are curious ask many insightful questions.

10. A movie that features the National Spelling Bee is called *Spellbound*.

11. The contestant whom you voted for on the last episode should not have been eliminated.

12. This is the time when people question their priorities.

13. Here is the street corner where I fell from my bicycle.

14. These selections that you made appear to be winners.

15. A state that you have visited is Colorado.

(2.21) Noun Clauses

A **noun clause** is a subordinate or dependent clause (group of words with at least a subject and a verb) that functions as a noun. Quite simply, a noun clause does the work of a noun and can function as a subject, direct object, indirect object, object of the preposition, object complement, or predicate nominative. Often the words *that, what, where, when, who, whom, which, whose, how, why,* and *whether* start noun clauses.

In each of these six sets of examples, the italicized word(s) in the first example are replaced by a noun clause in the second example.

Subject

Example 1: *Isaac* hurt her feelings.

Example 2: *Whatever you said to Jill* hurt her feelings. (The italicized noun clause is the new subject.)

Direct Object

Example 1: Can you recall *that day*?

Example 2: Can you recall *when you were introduced to Michelle*? (The italicized noun clause is the new direct object.)

Indirect Object

Example 1: Tell *Tristan* where we will meet.

Example 2: Tell *whoever is going on the canoe trip* where we will meet. (The italicized noun clause is the new indirect object.)

Object of the Preposition

Example 1: Mackenzie is quite aware of *that*.

Example 2: Mackenzie is quite aware of *what we said to her*. (The italicized noun clause is the new object of the preposition *of*.)

Object Complement

Example 1: You can label him a *rebel*.

Example 2: You can label him *whatever name is appropriate*. (The italicized noun clause is the new object complement. It describes the direct object, *him*.)

Predicate Nominative

Example 1: Oscar's plan is *this one*.

Example 2: Oscar's plan is *what you suggested to him yesterday*. (The italicized noun clause is the new predicate nominative.)

WRITING TIP *A noun clause has many different uses. Study how these uses can make your sentences more interesting and informative.*

(2.21A) Functionally Speaking (Noun Clauses)

Indicate how each underlined noun clause in the following list functions by writing S (subject), PN (predicate nominative), DO (direct object), IO (indirect object), and (OP) object of the preposition on the line next to the sentence. When you add up the sentence numbers for each function, each will total 42. Thus, since the first sentence is a subject, S gets 1 point and so on. Find five of each function type, and look for the total of 42 as your goal for each function type.

1. __S__ What he said to you was a great compliment.

2. _____ The next governor will be whoever captures the voters' most important concerns.

3. _____ She understands what you mean.

4. _____ They asked whoever was in the audience that night.

5. _____ Send the package to whomever you choose.

6. _____ What he said still bothers some of us.

7. _____ The winner will be whoever finds the answers to all these clues.

8. _____ The group members forgot who gave you the appointment.

9. _____ They presented whoever wanted a gift a new watch.

10. _____ They will steer the discussion to whatever your concerns are.

11. _____ You will be introduced by whomever you select.

12. _____ The host presented whoever was online a free pass.

13. _____ Our committee members called whoever was on the list.

14. _____ The new mayor will be whoever receives the best media coverage.

15. _____ Whoever was there with Chrissy that night will fill in the necessary details.

16. _____ We listened to his stories about what life was like during the previous century.

17. _____ They gave whoever was a member of the club an autographed picture of the president.

18. _____ Carlotta decided that her mother would accompany her on her vacation to Puerto Rico.

19. _____ Our next major decision is whatever we deem best for the group.

20. _____ What I would like to order for dinner is the steak special.

Review Activities

REVIEW ACTIVITY 1   ADJECTIVE AND ADVERB PHRASES

Here is a quick review of the adjective and adverb phrases—with a few questions for you to answer! A prepositional phrase used as an adjective phrase is generally found immediately after the noun or pronoun that it modifies. A prepositional phrase used as an adverb phrase is found in different places within a sentence.

Here is a summary of each type of phrase:

Adjective phrase: Modifies a noun or a pronoun

Adverb phrase: Modifies a verb, an adjective, or another adverb

Adjective phrase: Answers the question, "Which one?"

Adverb phrase: Answers the questions, "Where?" "When?" "How?" "To what extent?"

Here are some example sentences illustrating the adjective and adverb phrases. The phrases are italicized.

The man *in the back seat* appears tired. (adjective phrase; Which man?)

In the back seat was the tired man. (adverb phrase; Where was the tired man?)

The show *during the afternoon* was entertaining. (adjective phrase; Which show?)

We arrived *during the show.* (adverb phrase; When?)

The package *by the door* was Dotty's. (adjective phrase; Which package?)

We left the package *by the door.* (adverb; Where?)

The incident *after the show* was memorable. (adjective phrase; Which incident?)

After the show we went home. (adverb phrase; When?)

The scene *outside the auditorium* was chaotic. (adjective phrase; Which scene?)

We stood *outside the auditorium.* (adverb phrase; Where?)

Fill in the following blanks with an adjective or adverb phrase:

1. Quincy strolled _____. (adverb)

2. The king _____ will be interviewed this evening. (adjective)

3. None _____ will be placed here. (adjective)

4. _____ John went for a jog. (adverb)

5. _____ I like to walk with my brother.
   (either an adverb or adjective)

© 2007 by John Wiley & Sons, Inc.

REVIEW ACTIVITY 2   ESSENTIAL AND NONESSENTIAL CLAUSES AND PARTICIPLE PHRASES

Underline the essential and nonessential clauses and participle phrases found in the following sentences. Each sentence contains only one phrase or clause. On the line next to the sentence, write NP for nonessential phrase, NC for nonessential clause, EP for essential phrase, and EC for essential clause. Each of these phrases or clauses appears five times. Add correct punctuation to each sentence.

1. _____ Having slept ten hours last night Rocco was well rested for the competition.

2. _____ We all heard the actors rehearsing their lines.

3. _____ The officer examining the crucial evidence will meet the reporters soon.

4. _____ Walking into the parked car Wilson hurt his knee.

5. _____ The bicycle that I own is in the garage.

6. _____ This particular treaty which was ratified a week ago will be discussed often over the next year or so.

7. _____ Our new principal who had formerly been an English teacher is very congenial.

8. _____ Anyone living in that environment needs great determination.

9. _____ Running to catch the bus the commuter was sorry that she had overslept.

10. _____ Waving to the crowd our mayor led the town's parade.

11. _____ Fans clapping for the hockey hero were happy to see such a talented player.

12. _____ Novels explaining people's motives and desires interest me.

13. _____ Recently released stamps which feature famous astronauts will be put on display in our city's library.

14. _____ Our neighbor whom I have not seen for several weeks will be buying another motorcycle this summer.

15. _____ The paintings that were sold at the recent art show are still in the museum.

16. _____ Travelers who do not get upset easily usually enjoy flying.

17. _____ Several photographers who have known each other for more than two decades were shooting pictures in the park today.

18. _____ My vacation plans that I told you about have to be canceled.

19. _____ A friend needing our help called me last night.

20. _____ This blue suit that I just purchased last night was on sale.

REVIEW ACTIVITY 3   FILLING IN THE CLAUSES

Fill in the type of clause(s) asked for in each sentence. Be sure to include a subject and a verb in each clause. Discuss your answers with your classmates.

1. **(adverb)** _____,

    she will feel stronger **(adverb)** _____.

2. The car **(adjective)** _____
    will arrive next week.

3. **(Noun)** _____
    is a generous person.

4. The librarian found **(noun)** _____.

5. **(Adverb)** _____,
    you cannot hang pictures on it.

6. Bright and blue skies are **(noun)** _____.

7. A writer **(adjective)** _____
    was Ernest Hemingway.

8. We certainly realize **(noun)** _____.

9. **(Adverb)** _____,
    his wife cooked dinner.

10. It seems **(noun)** _____.

Final Tests

FINAL TEST 1   VERBAL PHRASES

Each of the following sentences contains a gerund phrase (G), a participle phrase (P), or an infinitive phrase (I). Indicate its type by writing the appropriate letter on the line next to the sentence. Each answer is worth 5 points. Do well!

1. _____ Removing the old paint was not a fun job!

2. _____ To remove the old paint was not a fun job.

3. _____ Removing the old paint, the girls struggled to do their best work.

4. _____ The visitors sitting on the dock saw the boats.

5. _____ Sitting on the benches was a two-hour activity for the visitors.

6. _____ To sit on the dock for two hours was not easy.

7. _____ Ms. Spencer wanted to suspend the unruly students.

8. _____ Suspended, the unruly students were very bored at home.

9. _____ Suspending the students was not easy for Ms. Spencer.

10. _____ Passing through the tunnel, the drivers saw the problems ahead.

11. _____ The drivers passing through the tunnel saw the problems ahead.

12. _____ Passing through the tunnel did not take long.

13. _____ Hiring and firing workers is not an easy job.

14. _____ Hired by the former boss, Luke was let go by the new chief.

15. _____ We visited the old home built by my uncles.

16. _____ We enjoyed visiting my uncles' home.

17. _____ Settled in 1683, my home town is one of my favorite places.

18. _____ Passing the tip of the island, the ship was traveling at a slow speed.

19. _____ The ship traveling at a slow speed passed the island's tip.

20. _____ The ship needed to travel at a slow speed around the tip of the island.

Number correct _____ × 5 = _____%

FINAL TEST 2   PHRASES

Tell whether the underlined phrase in each of the following sentences is an adjective phrase (ADJ), adverb phrase (ADVB), participle phrase (P), infinitive phrase (I), gerund phrase (G), or appositive phrase (APP) by writing the phrase's abbreviation on the line before the sentence. Each correct answer is worth 5 points.

1. _____ The treacherous wind <u>during the game</u> made pitching well virtually impossible.

2. _____ The leader <u>to emulate</u> is my father.

3. _____ <u>Walking home after dinner</u>, the club's manager reflected on her trying day.

4. _____ <u>Until 2004</u>, my family vacationed at that Pennsylvania resort.

5. _____ Her summary <u>of the book</u> was quite thorough.

6. _____ Our grandmother, <u>a resilient, caring woman</u>, passed away several years ago.

7. _____ The attorney explained the case's difficult aspect <u>to her assistant.</u>

8. _____ Our skilled mechanic, <u>exhausted from the day's work</u>, asked for a ride home.

9. _____ Visitors <u>from Brazil</u> enjoyed seeing this state's attractions.

10. _____ <u>Running the campaign for her brother</u> was a challenge for Elsie.

11. _____ The capital city of North Carolina, <u>the Tar Heel State</u>, is Raleigh.

12. _____ Elvis Presley, <u>the King of Rock and Roll</u>, was born in Tupelo, Mississippi.

13. _____ <u>To read the entire book</u> was his goal.

14. _____ He is the governor <u>making the decision.</u>

15. _____ <u>By trying harder</u>, you can win this contest.

16. _____ <u>My playing the piano at that early hour</u> was not appreciated by my neighbors.

17. _____ She played the entire game <u>with gusto.</u>

18. _____ <u>Agreeing with the jury's decision</u>, the plaintiff was happy with the trial's outcome.

19. _____ The club members wanted <u>to raise the dues.</u>

20. _____ <u>Without much effort</u>, the comedian made the audience laugh.

Number correct _____ × 5 = _____%

FINAL TEST 3   COMPLEMENTS

Indicate whether the underlined word in each of the following sentences is a direct object (DO), indirect object (IO), predicate adjective (PA), or predicate nominative (PN), by writing the two-letter abbreviation on the line next to the number. Each correct answer scores 5 points.

1. _____ These hikers followed the <u>trail</u> into the deep woods.

2. _____ Our professor gave <u>her</u> the correct grade this time.

3. _____ You are the <u>champion</u>.

4. _____ Bethany informed <u>us</u> about the recent changes.

5. _____ Those tales appear <u>invented</u> to me.

6. _____ The students usually follow the <u>directions</u> quite closely.

7. _____ Our new procedure was a complicated <u>one</u>.

8. _____ We wished <u>him</u> a happy birthday.

9. _____ The bus company officials changed the <u>policy</u> last week.

10. _____ These pretzels taste very <u>salty</u>.

11. _____ Wilbur promised <u>them</u> a fresh start.

12. _____ We congratulated <u>her</u> on the surprising victory.

13. _____ Lucinda is my best <u>friend</u>.

14. _____ Mozart composed beautiful <u>music</u>.

15. _____ Raymond is the undisputed best <u>debater</u>.

16. _____ This new author is a real <u>talent</u>.

17. _____ Barbara handed the <u>ticket</u> to the customer.

18. _____ She is quite <u>intelligent</u>.

19. _____ Mark Twain is a humorous <u>writer</u>.

20. _____ This group of animals is quite <u>friendly</u>.

Number correct _____ × 5 = _____%

FINAL TEST 4   CLAUSES AND VERBAL PHRASES

Identify the underlined group of words in each of the following sentences by writing the letter assigned to the different clauses and phrases next to the appropriate sentence. Thus, use A for the adjective clause and so on. Each correct answer is worth 5 points. Do well!

A. Adjective clause
B. Adverb clause
C. Noun clause
D. Participle phrase
E. Gerund phrase
F. Infinitive phrase

1. _____ She swam well <u>after she gained back her confidence.</u>

2. _____ <u>To swim well again</u>, she had to gain back her confidence.

3. _____ <u>Gaining back her confidence</u> was crucial.

4. _____ <u>Gaining back her confidence</u>, she swam well again.

5. _____ The swimmer <u>who gained back her confidence</u> swam well again.

6. _____ Darlene sends a congratulatory note to <u>whoever wins our town's annual poetry contest.</u>

7. _____ Darlene, <u>who sends a congratulatory note to the poetry contest winner</u>, is an avid reader.

8. _____ The writer wanted <u>to win the poetry contest.</u>

9. _____ <u>After she won the poetry contest</u>, the writer received Darlene's congratulatory notes.

10. _____ <u>Winning the poetry contest</u>, the woman received a congratulatory note from Darlene, an avid reader.

FINAL TEST 4   CLAUSES AND VERBAL PHRASES (*Continued*)

11. _____ <u>Winning the poetry contest</u> was exciting for the woman.

12. _____ The poetry contest <u>that was won by the young writer</u> was exciting.

13. _____ The poetry contest award goes to <u>whoever submits the finest collection of poems.</u>

14. _____ <u>Researching her family's history</u> was Mary's final social studies project.

15. _____ Mary wanted <u>to research her family's history.</u>

16. _____ <u>Researching her family's history,</u> Mary found many new facts about her ancestors.

17. _____ Mary learned much new information about her relatives <u>while she researched her family's history.</u>

18. _____ <u>What Mary learned about her family during her research</u> is fantastic.

19. _____ The research <u>that Mary completed</u> taught her much about her family.

20. _____ <u>To learn more about her family through her research</u> was Mary's goal.

Number correct _____ **× 5 =** _____%

FINAL TEST 5   SUBORDINATE CLAUSES

Indicate the type of underlined clause by writing ADJ for adjective clause, ADVB for adverb clause, and N for noun clause on the line next to the appropriate sentence. Each correct answer is worth 5 points. Do well!

1. _____ After he washed his mud-stained football uniform, the quarterback made himself a sandwich.

2. _____ The uniform that he washed was also his older brother's uniform two years prior.

3. _____ This high school student knew exactly what he was doing.

4. _____ She set the club record that had been held by her aunt.

5. _____ Here is the university that my older brother attended.

6. _____ Give a pass to whoever needs one.

7. _____ The presenter will be whoever wins the radio contest.

8. _____ I waited in the lobby while my dad underwent an operation yesterday.

9. _____ The doctor who operated on my father had graduated from the University of Pennsylvania.

10. _____ Tell them whom you have nominated.

11. _____ The house that you have moved into was once my grandfather's home.

12. _____ He will help you whenever you ask him.

13. _____ Unless you do not need the money, you do not have to work this summer.

14. _____ My neighbor left for the subway earlier than I did this morning.

15. _____ Call us as soon as you reach that location.

16. _____ The fact that he is in great physical condition should help.

17. _____ What the reporter claimed shocked all of us.

18. _____ What he ate for dinner was talked about for days.

19. _____ She leads a life that is the dream of many.

20. _____ The teacher knew that her students would perform well on that challenging examination.

Number correct _____ × 5 = _____%

Section Three
Sentences

Diagnostic Tests

DIAGNOSTIC TEST 1   COMPLETE AND INCOMPLETE SENTENCES

Seven of these groups of words are sentences (S). Seven of these groups of words are fragments (F). Six of these groups of words are run-ons (R). Write the corresponding letter (F, S, or R) on the line next to the sentence. Each correct answer is worth 5 points.

1. _____ We are a happy family.

2. _____ Turn off the light, it's too bright in here now.

3. _____ Can you figure out these directions?

4. _____ Mary and John were married in 1948.

5. _____ All of the king's men.

6. _____ Some of that bread that you had brought over to the house.

7. _____ Detroit is a good city for sports, so is Chicago.

8. _____ My brother who lives about three hours away from here.

9. _____ Even though you can do it, do not attempt it, you could get hurt.

10. _____ In the meantime, watch out for those cars.

11. _____ There is nothing that he would not try.

12. _____ Under the bench is the hammer, bring it here please.

13. _____ I can readily see your point I do not agree with it at all.

14. _____ Most of the time during the academic year.

15. _____ Some of the cab drivers in New York City.

16. _____ Send it to me I will take care of the rest.

17. _____ Kendra is the best artist in our sophomore class.

18. _____ May I help you with that cart, Laura?

19. _____ In the very best of times with the best performers under his mentorship.

20. _____ None of these items on the top shelf.

Number correct _____ × 5 = _____%

DIAGNOSTIC TEST 2   SENTENCES BY PURPOSE

The types of sentences classified by purpose are the declarative (DEC), the interrogative (INT), the imperative (IMP), and the exclamatory (EXC) sentences. Write the abbreviation for the correct type of sentence on the line next to the number. Each type appears at least once. Each correct answer is awarded 5 points.

1. _____ He walked to the train station with his best friend.

2. _____ Do that now.

3. _____ Yippee, this is terrific!

4. _____ Would you be the one to ask here, sir?

5. _____ I am so excited!

6. _____ Hand me that hammer, Nicky.

7. _____ It said so in the newspaper.

8. _____ Are you going to the camp this summer, Betty?

9. _____ The two radio personalities will be appearing at the mall tonight.

10. _____ Can you believe that this has happened to such a good family?

11. _____ Break the record for the swim team, Lance.

12. _____ Was that you standing on the corner?

13. _____ We saw seven monkeys in the woods.

14. _____ Henry and Henrietta saved the day when they came out to take registration forms for us.

15. _____ May I assist you with that?

16. _____ This exam might be as difficult as the last test we took.

17. _____ Is this the best way to treat an ailing dog?

18. _____ Pour me some milk.

19. _____ She dropped the glasses as she came out of the drugstore.

20. _____ Will you be sending the letters out tonight?

Number correct _____ × 5 = _____%

DIAGNOSTIC TEST 3   SENTENCES BY STRUCTURE

Sentences can be classified according to their structure. The four types of sentences in this classification are simple (S), compound (CPD), complex (CPLX), and compound-complex (CC). Write the correct abbreviation on the line next to each number. Each type of sentence is used at least one time. Each correct answer is worth 5 points.

1. _____ I want an ice cream cone.

2. _____ He is the author who spoke to us, and we have never forgotten that experience.

3. _____ I know him, and he knows me well.

4. _____ The author, who has talent in others areas as well, will appear at the local bookstore tonight.

5. _____ Perry lives in the town that was featured on the news last night.

6. _____ This is the best movie out right now.

7. _____ After he left for the game, John called us, and we responded quickly.

8. _____ He did not have to go after her, but he did.

9. _____ The route that we took was long, and the bus passengers were annoyed.

10. _____ Are you going to the concert tomorrow night, Charlotte?

11. _____ I wanted to go to the game, and the other wanted to see the movie that was playing in the city.

12. _____ If you are trying to start something, do not!

13. _____ This is it, Jimmy!

14. _____ Your actions set a bad example for others, and you need to change your ways.

15. _____ Helene handled it well, but the others did not.

16. _____ I cannot defend his behavior.

17. _____ They spoke to him about it, and he did not respond.

18. _____ Because the president said that, we listened well.

19. _____ That was an innocent statement by the player.

20. _____ Come here and talk to me.

Number correct _____ × 5 = _____%

Lessons and Activities

(3.1) The Fragment

A **sentence fragment** is a group of words that lacks a complete thought and is therefore an incomplete sentence.

Here are some common types of sentence fragments. The fragment is underlined:

Prepositional phrase fragment: Vinny was very fatigued. <u>After his sixteen-mile race.</u>

Participle phrase fragment: The children were very happy. <u>Walking to school on the first day of class this year.</u>

Infinitive phrase fragment: <u>To win the first prize in the motor-building contest.</u> That was my brother's goal.

Appositive phrase fragment: Our team visited Yankee Stadium. <u>The baseball field located in New York City.</u>

Clause fragment: You would be very surprised. <u>If you saw how much your little cousin has grown this year.</u>

Three of the following groups of words are fragments or portions of a complete sentence. Circle the fragments.

1. After the meal was finished.

2. Because he was so tall, Izzy always sat in the last seat in the row.

3. Once the couple had inspected at least sixty homes in that town.

4. Mr. Thompson, a great English teacher, passed away several years ago.

5. Have you ever visited Connecticut? The Nutmeg State.

6. Roy and Estella will be married at the end of the month.

📖 **WRITING TIP** *Reading your group of words aloud should help to eliminate any fragment problem. Check that your group of words has a subject and a verb. Let your ear be your gear! "In the middle of the movie," a fragment, does not sound as if it is a complete idea. Yet, "In the middle of the movie, I fell asleep," does! This second group of words is a complete sentence, not a fragment.*

3.1A # Half a Score for Each (The Fragment)

Ten of the following groups of words are sentences, and ten are fragments. Write S for sentence and F for fragment on the line next to each group of words.

1. _____ Walking down by the mall.

2. _____ The group members were walking down by the mall.

3. _____ Over the river and through the woods.

4. _____ Returning the money to someone who used the ATM.

5. _____ It could not have come at a better time.

6. _____ The fire was started.

7. _____ The fire was started by lightning.

8. _____ Drive the ball far, Karen.

9. _____ With money left to spend at the other stores.

10. _____ Chosen by the coaches to start the season at running back.

11. _____ And nearly drowned.

12. _____ Some cities are focusing on solving crimes that were committed over a year ago.

13. _____ Catching two hours of the state's best dance entertainment.

14. _____ Grabbing life by the horns, Jeff.

15. _____ She was stretching before the start of the race.

16. _____ If you want to be a great musician, you must practice often.

17. _____ Could be the easiest way to find a solution.

18. _____ So many books, so little time.

19. _____ He can eat several large sandwiches at one sitting.

20. _____ Do you think that this group of words is truly a sentence?

(3.2) Run-Ons

A **run-on sentence** is two or more sentences incorrectly written as a single sentence. Sometimes the run-on is punctuated with a comma, as in, "Ursula walked down the street, she carried her purse." This is called a **comma splice** since the two complete sentences are spliced or joined by a comma. At other times there is no punctuation, as in, "Ursula walked down the street she carried her purse." This is a run-on sentence since one complete sentence runs on into another complete sentence.

Here are some run-on sentence examples. On the line below the comma splice or run-on problem, write a correct version of the same idea. There may be more than one correct version.

My parents bought new furniture, all the pieces fit well together.

_____

_____

She loved to have her fingernails done the cost of doing so never bothered her.

_____

_____

This watch is waterproof my father even wears it when he goes for a swim.

_____

_____

Your company had the workers sign an agreement it would bind all parties to a code of silence.

_____

_____

Four lifeguards sprinted across the beach all of them were trying to get to the helpless swimmer.

_____

_____

✍ **WRITING TIP** *Run-ons and comma splices can be eliminated by reading your writing aloud from the last sentence to the first sentence. Also, pay close attention to punctuation. If you do these two easy steps, you can reduce, or even eliminate, the number of run-ons and comma splices in your writing.*

(3.2A) Let's Get It Right! (Run-Ons)

Correct each of these run-ons by rewriting the words in a correct format on another sheet of paper or editing the run-ons here.

1. She dribbled the ball then she took a jump shot.

2. We have been practicing our music every day we really enjoy doing this.

3. When Percy swam across the lake, we congratulated him he was a bit embarrassed by our reaction.

4. My younger sister married Ernesto several years later their first child, a girl, was born.

5. I do not want to tell you again you will need to start eating a healthier diet.

6. For the past ten years my family has vacationed at the same lake it is located in Michigan.

7. We were thinking that our customers would again take advantage of this offer last year this same offer was well received.

8. Ann tried to turn off her cell phone's ringer before the lecture began unfortunately, she did not remember how to do it.

9. This sale will be in effect until the last day of August take advantage of this opportunity as soon as possible.

10. He gave us a ride home after school later we went back for the plays rehearsal in the auditorium.

(3.3) Types of Sentences by Purpose

Sentences are categorized according to their purpose. There are four types of sentences: *declarative, interrogative, imperative,* and *exclamatory*.

A **declarative sentence** makes a statement or expresses an opinion. Place a period after the sentence.

> Ida would like to attend technical school next year.

> My father will turn fifty years old next month.

An **interrogative sentence** asks a question. Place a question mark after the sentence.

> Are you interested in investing in this stock with us?

> Can you help us out at the football concession stand next Friday night?

An **imperative sentence** makes a request or gives a command. Place a period or an exclamation point after the sentence.

> Please take that book to the other room.

> Do not touch that expensive piece of artwork!

An **exclamatory sentence** expresses strong feeling. Place an exclamation point after the sentence.

> I could not believe my eyes and ears!

> This is too much for me!

There are two examples of each of the four types of sentences below. Write the sentence type on the line after the sentence.

1. This is an easy crossword puzzle. _____

2. This is fantastic! _____

3. Bring that here. _____

4. Are you available to work next Saturday morning? _____

5. You are the absolute best, best friend in the whole world! _____

6. Can they be the best band for our dance? _____

7. Open the window. _____

8. I will assist the minister in this project. _____

🖎 **WRITING TIP** *If you practice these four types of sentences, your writing will be interesting and lively. Including all of these types in your writing displays your skill and creates good variety for your readers!*

Name _____ Date _____ Period _____

(3.3A) Spelling It All Out (Types of Sentences by Purpose)

Indicate whether each sentence is a declarative (DEC), interrogative (INT), imperative (IMP), or exclamatory (EXC) sentence by writing the sentence's two-letter abbreviation on the line next to the number. Each type of sentence appears five times within these twenty sentences. Then on the line entitled "declarative" beneath the list, consecutively write the two-letter codes that follow each of the five declarative sentences. Do the same for the interrogative, imperative, and exclamatory sentences. If all of your answers are correct, you will spell out four ten-letter words. Do well, and have fun!

1. _____ I could hardly believe me eyes and ears! **(re)**
2. _____ The flight attendant talked to some of the passengers. **(ge)**
3. _____ How long have you been waiting here, Ted? **(st)**
4. _____ Take this package to the post office. **(sp)**
5. _____ She sat against the wall reading the news magazine. **(ne)**
6. _____ Do you know his address? **(re)**
7. _____ Do it now. **(ec)**
8. _____ Have you already finished your dinner? **(ng)**
9. _____ The stars were shining brightly when we landed in Miami. **(ro)**
10. _____ What a beautiful engagement ring this is! **(se)**
11. _____ These mountains are so gorgeous! **(nt)**
12. _____ Send the passengers back to the terminal lobby. **(ia)**
13. _____ Are they going to complete the crossword puzzle soon? **(th)**
14. _____ May I hitch a ride with you and your friends? **(en)**
15. _____ These are my favorite photographs. **(us)**
16. _____ Whew! That car just missed hitting me! **(me)**
17. _____ We will be moving to Europe because of Mom's new job. **(ly)**
18. _____ Store the equipment in the shed after you finish swimming. **(li)**
19. _____ Take it to the limit. **(ze)**
20. _____ That test was so easy! **(nt)**

Declarative _____

Interrogative _____

Imperative _____

Exclamatory _____

(3.3B) Sentences by Purpose

What type of sentence is each group of words? Using the three-letter abbreviations, write the sentence's type on the line next to the number. Use the following abbreviations: declarative (DEC), imperative (IMP), interrogative (INT), and exclamatory (EXC). Enjoy!

1. _____ Do this problem with a partner.

2. _____ This is the best book on the shelf.

3. _____ Teddy and Molly enjoy golfing together.

4. _____ This is too unbelievable!

5. _____ This is too good to be true!

6. _____ Will the rain hold out long enough for our picnic?

7. _____ Stop talking.

8. _____ It's too much to comprehend!

9. _____ Can you find the missing puzzle part, Tina?

10. _____ That is a fantastic slam dunk!

11. _____ Did you remember to clean your room, Kyle?

12. _____ Stand and cheer.

13. _____ Is your house the third one on the left?

14. _____ Are these the correct dresses?

15. _____ Hermie and Oscar were friends.

16. _____ Bring that here, please.

© 2007 by John Wiley & Sons, Inc.

(3.4) The Simple Sentence

Quite simply, the **simple sentence** consists of one independent clause. Yet, there may be a compound subject or a compound verb (or both) within a simple sentence.

Here are some examples of simple sentences. The subject is underlined, and the verb is italicized.

> <u>Ricardo</u> *is* a tall boy.
>
> <u>Mary</u> *spelled* the word correctly.
>
> <u>He</u> and <u>I</u> *will be going* to the movies.
>
> The <u>professor</u> *lectured* and *asked* many questions during class.
>
> <u>I</u> *wanted* to laugh and talk with the man and his friend for a long time.

Compose five simple sentences as directed. Write the sentences on the lines provided.

Use *Francine* as the subject.

_____

_____

Use *met* as the verb.

_____

_____

Use *He* and *she* as the compound subject.

_____

_____

Use *ate* and *played* as the compound verbs.

_____

_____

Use *read, studied,* and *understood* as the compound verbs.

_____

_____

📖 **WRITING TIP** *Mix simple sentences in with longer ones when you write. If most of your sentences are simple sentences, your writing will be humdrum, and your reader will become bored quite easily. Writing that sounds babyish is generally full of simple sentences without a healthy sprinkling of longer sentences within the writing piece.*

3.4A Quite Simply (The Simple Sentence)

Ten of the following twenty sentences are simple sentences. Place an X on the line next to each simple sentence.

1. _____ When he arrived, the others were relieved.

2. _____ Our sisters and brothers will be reading and reviewing the will quite soon.

3. _____ Since the cookout was such a success, let us have another!

4. _____ This artist, who also has many other hobbies, is quite talented.

5. _____ Work out and keep fit, my friends.

6. _____ Were you at the dance that night?

7. _____ This car and that scooter were involved in the accident on Fifth Avenue and Main Street yesterday, Mitch.

8. _____ I remember when we saw you that time.

9. _____ Can you recall who told you that story?

10. _____ Will you be leaving this Thursday or this Friday, Xavier?

11. _____ This is the right one for you and your friends, Nicky.

12. _____ These paintings will be replicated and sold in the next few years.

13. _____ The repairman and his helper fixed the faucet and replaced the washer machine.

14. _____ Whoever completes the puzzle first will be given a prize, and you will also meet the mayor.

15. _____ Let us try to remember when all of this fun began.

16. _____ Located on the top shelf, the doll that my sister won was brought down for her.

17. _____ These maps that have always helped us out are getting a little frayed.

18. _____ My sister helped us, and my brother did the same for you that year.

19. _____ Are you going to the fair, Perry?

20. _____ The man ate his food and chatted with his friends.

(3.5) Compound Sentences

A **compound sentence** has two or more main (or independent) clauses that should be closely related in meaning. An effective compound sentence is, "Paul likes vanilla ice cream, and his wife likes chocolate." Why is it an effective compound sentence? The two ideas are closely related in meaning. An ineffective compound sentence is, "Paul likes vanilla ice cream, and his wife is a pediatrician." Why is it an ineffective compound sentence? The two ideas are not closely related in meaning.

Here are some examples of effective compound sentences:

Henry laughed at the joke, and then the comedian told another one.

I wanted to go on vacation, and I made plans to go to Spain.

The most recent news was confusing, but we were able to make sense of it eventually.

My sister has three children, and my brother has six.

To punctuate a compound sentence:

▸ Insert a comma before the conjunction that joins the main (or independent) clauses: "Paul is an accountant, and his daughter is an artist."

▸ Insert a semicolon between the two main (or independent) closely related clauses: "Peter is an accountant; his daughter is a lawyer." This could also be written, "Peter is an accountant; his daughter, a lawyer." In this last example, the verb (*is*) is understood.

Reminder: There must be two main (or independent) clauses in a compound sentence. "Reggie loves to shoot baskets and practice his dribbling" is not a compound sentence since there is only one main (or independent) clause.

Add a main (or independent) clause to each group of words to make a complete sentence:

The raccoon spied the food, and _____.

The juice was left on the table, but _____.

Take this to the cleaners, and _____.

We would like to attend the meeting, but _____.

_____, and she was glad that she did so.

 WRITING TIP *Be sure that the two parts of your compound sentence are closely related in meaning. If the two parts do not seem to be related, it is probably not a good idea to include them in a compound sentence. Thus, "Asia is a large continent" and "my father likes to golf," would not be a good mixture for a compound sentence. Yet, "My sister likes to jog," and "My father likes to bowl," can be combined well (they are similar ideas) to form a good compound sentence. Practice these concepts in all of your assigned and free writings.*

Don't Be Confounded (Compound Sentences)

Underline the two independent or main clauses in each compound sentence below. Circle the conjunction that joins these clauses, and then write the conjunction on the line next to the number.

1. _____ She wanted to help her daughter, but society prevented that wish.

2. _____ My brother and father went fishing today, and I repainted the garage.

3. _____ Yesterday I made a hole-in-one, but today is a completely different story.

4. _____ The public address announcer recognized those in attendance, and then she gave a special welcome to the military personnel.

5. _____ I wanted to bicycle to Tucson, but the downpour prevented that from happening.

6. _____ Stay awake and drive slowly.

7. _____ Make your peace with your dad, and then come back to my house.

8. _____ The intelligent man watched the passing ships, and then he wrote an essay about the experience.

9. _____ We saw a great deal from the ranger's booth, and you would probably like to go there too.

10. _____ We flew throughout the night, and the flight attendant related her experiences about transcontinental flight to us.

11. _____ See the man about the dog, and then call me here.

12. _____ My sister lives in New Mexico, and my brother lives in Texas.

13. _____ She was accepted by three colleges, but she was rejected by her favorite college.

14. _____ Pick a card, and then we will take it to that man in the booth.

15. _____ The youngster sat still for the first two hours, but then she became restless.

3.6 Complex Sentences

A **complex sentence** has one main (independent) clause and one or more subordinate (dependent) clauses. Remember that the main (or independent) clause can stand alone. The subordinate (or dependent) clause needs the main (or independent) clause to complete the thought.

In the following sentences, the main (independent) clauses are underlined, and the subordinate (dependent) clauses are italicized.

When I found the missing book, I brought it to the library.

Since we listened to the funny radio program last night, we have retold some of the jokes.

If you attend the conference, take good notes *that will benefit our discussion group.* (This sentence contains two subordinate clauses.)

The scouts journeyed up the mountain *that we saw in the travel magazine.*

Whether you believe the story or not, it is a lesson *that we should all study.* (This sentence contains two subordinate clauses.)

Complete the following sentences by adding either a main or subordinate clause:

_____,
others will enjoy your speech.

The book _____
is an exciting tale of adventure.

Can I borrow the skirt _____

_____?

He was not allowed to play in the game

_____.

_____
if the group wants them to.

On a separate sheet of paper, compose five complex sentences. Underline the main clause, and circle the subordinate clause in each sentence.

🖎 **WRITING TIP** *To please your readers, use a variety of sentences. The complex sentence gives you the opportunity to include much information in a sophisticated way. Simple sentences alone can be deadly dull to readers. Mixing types of sentences usually increases your reader's interest in your writing.*

(3.6A) What's Left Should Be Enough (Complex Sentences)

Underline the dependent or subordinate clause(s) in each of the following sentences. To ensure that you have underlined the correct words, the words that you have left in the sentence after you have underlined (and then mentally eliminated) the subordinate or dependent clause(s) should still be a complete sentence—though not as detailed as the original.

1. He recalled that he had left his glasses in the car.

2. Because the cheetah is so fast, this animal provides much interest to us.

3. Since the motorist was lost, he decided that he would ask for directions.

4. The manual that was on your desk stated that the trip should take three hours.

5. When you think about your future, have confidence in your abilities.

6. As soon as the plane landed, Dad phoned us.

7. Two years ago, the club president stated that she wanted to make donations to the city's needy.

8. Investigating the disturbance, the police officer signaled to her partner, who was across the street.

9. Please sort these old files that are in my office.

10. While the zookeeper helped the older panda, we viewed the other pandas that were in the large exhibit.

11. The package that was delivered to your apartment was sent by my cousin whom you met in April.

12. A ferocious tiger scared the wildlife photographer, who was trying to remain calm.

13. In order to obtain concert tickets, we have to call the number that is on the screen.

14. We were allowed to leave the room after the bell rang.

15. The astonished guest could not believe what she had just witnessed.

(3.7) Compound-Complex Sentences

A **compound-complex sentence** has two or more main (or independent) clauses and one or more subordinate (or dependent) clauses.

In the following sentences, the main (or independent) clauses are underlined, and the subordinate (or dependent) clauses are italicized:

Because the singer's popularity had grown immensely over the years, she was seen on many television programs, and she sold many recordings.

Since the music coming from the next yard was so loud that night, the neighbor spoke to the police, and the noisy people were given a warning.

The waves crashed on the shore, and the surfers were enjoying the day *that was so pleasant in many ways.*

Help to create some more compound-complex sentences by adding the necessary clauses:

Add a subordinate clause to this sentence: The movie _____

_____

was very interesting, and the box office receipts proved this.

Add a main clause to this sentence: California experienced heavy rains, and

_____

because there were so many flooded areas.

Add two main clauses to this sentence: Because the prisoner was ill, _____

_____,

and _____.

Add two subordinate clauses to this sentence: _____,

Congress took immediate action, and the president made a special trip to the town

_____.

📖 **WRITING TIP** *Good writers use a number of different types of sentences to add interest and fluency to their writings. The compound-complex sentence does exactly that since it allows the writer to say much in a single sentence. Practice using the compound-complex sentence, paying close attention to its punctuation.*

(3.7A) It's Not That Complex! (Compound-Complex Sentences)

In each sentence, place brackets around the independent or main clauses and underline the dependent or subordinate clause(s).

1. A rule that needs to be changed is this one, and we plan to make the desired changes quite soon.

2. If we see that movie tonight, we will need to leave immediately, and I will be able to use my parents' car.

3. As soon as the building was occupied, the newspaper reporters interviewed the tenants and the television crews filmed the workers throughout the day.

4. This cartographer, who has made detailed maps of many neighborhoods, will sign his latest book tonight at the bookstore, and I plan to be there.

5. When the stadium was demolished, the debris was trucked off, and the workers started to prepare for the next phase of the job.

6. The wrestler who pinned all of his opponents won the county championship, and then he moved on to the state competition.

7. It was sad to see the stadium that provided so many great moments torn down, but we looked forward to a larger, more exciting stadium in its place.

8. Some of the pages that must be reprinted will be available soon, and you can pick them up in my office.

9. Stop the nonsense, and listen to me if you want to make this squad.

10. These parrots that you just bought are funny, and I intend to record their actions during the next few days.

(3.8) Starting a Sentence

Here are seven effective ways to start a sentence. Review these, and incorporate them into your writing.

Adjective

Grateful, the class sent a note to the donor.

Adverb

Quickly, the robber took the money and fled from the scene.

Prepositional phrase

In the meantime, I will research these names for you.

Infinitive phrase

To locate the correct route, check the Internet.

Gerund phrase

Renting an apartment in any major city can be a hassle.

Participle phrase

Shuffling the cards, the dealer looked closely at the players.

Adverb clause

Because Lorraine wanted to do well in that course, she studied hard each night.

Reinforcement: On a separate sheet of paper, use the seven example sentences above to write an example of each type of sentence starter. Label each type of sentence starter.

WRITING TIP *To add flavor to your writing, use as many of these sentence starters as possible in your next assigned writing. Your reader will appreciate how you vary each sentence's beginning. Your writing becomes more exciting, enjoyable, and fluid.*

(3.8A) Seven Starters (Starting a Sentence)

Here are seven ways to begin a sentence effectively and interest your reader at the same time. Write the starter's corresponding letter on the line next to the number. Each of these ways is used three times.

> A. Adjective
>
> B. Adverb
>
> C. Participle
>
> D. Prepositional phrase
>
> E. Participle phrase
>
> F. Infinitive phrase
>
> G. Subordinate clause

1. _____ Disgusted, Marty walked away.

2. _____ Clean and bright, the room that we were assigned was fine.

3. _____ Behind the screen in the front of the room, the guest speaker had hidden his props.

4. _____ To find the correct answer, Nadine browsed through the research books.

5. _____ Whenever Sam felt weak, he took a rest.

6. _____ Quietly, the magician calmed the excited children in the audience.

7. _____ Walking behind his parents, the youngster was happy.

8. _____ To be in top physical condition, you should eat properly and exercise regularly.

9. _____ Soon the pilot would announce our location.

10. _____ Tall and talented, the opposing team's center outscored the rest of his team.

11. _____ Relaxed in front of the studio audience, the contestant answered the host's first eight questions correctly.

(3.8A) Seven Starters (Starting a Sentence) *(Continued)*

12. _____ <u>Since our judo instructor had taught us that maneuver</u>, we were able to move on to more challenging moves.

13. _____ <u>Wheezing</u>, the young child tried to bring his breathing under control.

14. _____ <u>To climb El Capitan</u>, Roberta's son had to train a great deal.

15. _____ <u>Cruising down the runway</u>, the large airliner looked magnificent.

16. _____ <u>Puzzled</u>, the test taker could not remember how to solve the chemistry problem.

17. _____ <u>Because the weather conditions were so hot in Phoenix last week</u>, we spent most of the days indoors.

18. _____ <u>Confident</u>, the orchestra's conductor greeted the critics after the concert.

19. _____ <u>In the interim</u>, you can help me fold the laundry.

20. _____ <u>Slowly</u> we began to board the plane bound for Los Angeles.

21. _____ <u>Before the season's start</u>, we will have to decide who is our captain.

(3.9) Diagramming Subjects, Predicates, Modifiers, and Complements (Review)

Diagramming a sentence allows you to "draw a picture" of the sentence to see how the various parts of the sentence work. This visual representation will help you understand how the different parts of the sentence fit together.

There are two basic parts to a sentence diagram. The *subject* is on the left side of the horizontal line, and the *predicate (verb)* is on the right side of this same line, next to the subject. A perpendicular line that extends below and above the horizontal line separates these two sides.

All of the *subject's modifiers* are placed under the subject on the slanted line. The same holds true for the *predicate's modifiers*. Thus, the sentence, "The actress laughed," would be diagrammed in this way:

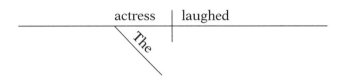

The sentence, "The famous actress laughed loudly," would be diagrammed like this:

Here is how you would diagram the sentence, "The famous, talented actress was laughing loudly":

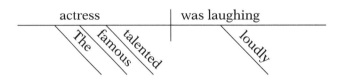

Notice how the words "The," "famous," "talented," and "loudly" are all modifiers and are placed on the slanted line below the word that they modify. The word "was" in the last sentence above is a helping verb and is placed in front of the main verb on that portion of the horizontal line.

If a *modifier is modifying another modifier,* such as the word "quite" does to "loudly" in this sentence, "The famous, talented actress laughed quite loudly," place the word "quite" on another slanted line parallel to the other modifier's line and connected to it with a shorter line attaching it to the word it modifies. This is how the diagram should appear:

© 2007 by John Wiley & Sons, Inc.

(3.9) Diagramming Subjects, Predicates, Modifiers, and Complements (Review) *(Continued)*

If the sentence is a *question,* make sure that you capitalize the helping verb (or main verb if there is no helping verb) and place it on the right side of the horizontal line. Diagram the sentence, "Is the young, talented actress laughing quite loudly?" in this format:

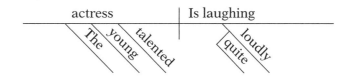

Now, let us examine how to diagram a sentence that includes a complement such as a *direct object* or an *indirect object.*

In the sentence, "The experienced salesman sold very expensive cars," the word "cars" is the *direct object,* and "expensive" modifies the direct object. To place these words into the diagram, we will draw a perpendicular line (that does not extend below the horizontal line) after the predicate, extend the horizontal line to the right, and place the direct object, "cars," on the horizontal line next to the predicate, "sold." Again, all modifiers will be placed below the word they modify. The diagram should look like this:

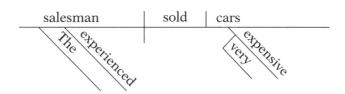

To include an *indirect object* in the sentence, we draw a slanted line beneath the predicate and attach the bottom of this line to a horizontal line that parallels the other horizontal line. Here is how to diagram the sentence, "The experienced salesman sold us very expensive cars":

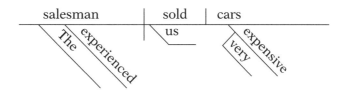

Finally, to diagram a *predicate nominative* or a *predicate adjective,* extend the horizontal line containing the subject and the predicate to the right of the predicate. From this horizontal line, draw a line that starts on the horizontal line and slants upward and toward the predicate. Thus, the predicate nominative or predicate adjective will be on the horizontal line to the right of the predicate.

139

(3.9) Diagramming Subjects, Predicates, Modifiers, and Complements (Review) (Continued)

In the sentence, "Benny is our leader," the predicate nominative is "leader," and "our" modifies the predicate nominative. Diagram this sentence in this manner:

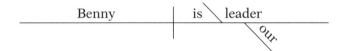

In the sentence, "Benny is very bright," the predicate adjective is "bright," and "very" modifies the predicate adjective. Diagram the sentence this way:

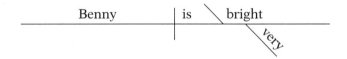

To summarize, here are the basic diagramming formats:

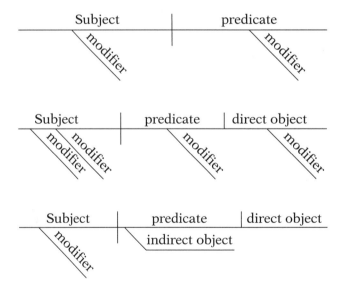

3.9A Diagramming Subjects, Predicates, Modifiers, and Complements

On a separate sheet of paper, diagram these ten sentences:

1. Laurie whispered.

2. The older dog slept.

3. My funny neighbor walks quickly.

4. These tired soldiers are marching slowly.

5. Are the musicians rehearsing?

6. Our best teachers were working quite diligently.

7. Some singers learned new songs.

8. A few players gave us their autographs.

9. Mollie's husband is an engineer.

10. My cousin is quite interesting.

(3.10) Diagramming Compound Elements and Prepositional Phrases

Diagramming compound elements such as compound subjects, compound predicates, and compound objects is not hard. Just follow these few simple rules.

The **compound elements,** whether they are compound subjects, predicates, direct objects, or indirect objects, are placed atop one another on horizontal lines, and the conjunction that joins them is placed on a vertical line of dashes. The sentence, "Hank and Rita talked and danced," would look like this:

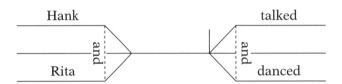

Let us now take the sentence, "The sons and daughters gave their mom and dad candies and cards." "Sons" and "daughters" are the compound subjects with the modifier "the." The conjunction "and" is on the vertical line of dashes. The simple predicate "gave" is in its usual place. "Mom" and "dad" are the compound indirect objects. They are modified by "their." Notice that the conjunctions "and" are on the vertical line of dashes. Finally, the compound direct objects, "candies" and "cards," are on lines by the conjunction "and" on the vertical line of dashes. Here is how that sentence should be diagrammed:

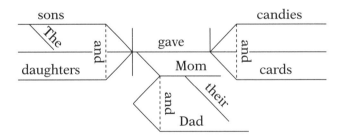

3.10 Diagramming Compound Elements and Prepositional Phrases (Continued)

Diagramming **prepositional phrases** is also quite logical. First, determine what word the prepositional phrase modifies. Does it act as an adjective or an adverb? Does it modify the sentence's subject or predicate? Prepositional phrases are placed on a lazy L beneath the word that they modify. Let us look at the sentence, "The girl in the first row was brought to the office." The prepositional phrase "in the first row" modifies "girl." Place that phrase beneath that word. The other prepositional phrase, "to the office," modifies the predicate "brought" and should be placed beneath that predicate. Here is how that sentence should be diagrammed:

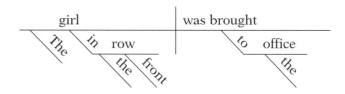

"In the morning she walks her dog around the small lake" is another sentence that contains two prepositional phrases. Both phrases modify the predicate, "walks." Diagram this sentence as such:

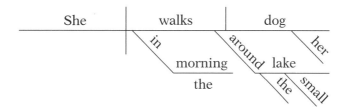

Diagramming Compound Elements and Prepositional Phrases

Diagram the following sentences on a separate sheet of paper:

1. Stan and Ollie joked.

2. David and Goliath argued and fought.

3. Beth and Georgia entertained their parents and grandparents.

4. They wrote and examined the papers and cards carefully.

5. His best friends are Tomas and Juan.

6. The three young students walked, worked, and laughed yesterday.

7. Chantelle drove around the block.

8. Delilah was swimming in the cold lake.

9. The magician in the funny suit played tricks in the park.

10. In the afternoon Grandpa went for a walk.

(3.11) Diagramming Verbals and Clauses

Remember that the three types of verbals are the gerund, the participle, and the infinitive. Here is how you can diagram each of these.

⊠ Gerunds

These -*ing* ending forms of words act as nouns. Often gerunds have modifiers. Gerunds are diagrammed with a stair-stepped line above the normal base horizontal line. The gerund line is joined to the base horizontal line by a forked line indicating where the gerund belongs in the sentence. In the sentence, "Walking was difficult for the old man," the gerund that is the sentence's subject is "Walking." "Was" is the predicate, "difficult" is the predicate adjective, and "for the old man" is the prepositional phrase that modifies the predicate, "was." Here is how that sentence should be diagrammed:

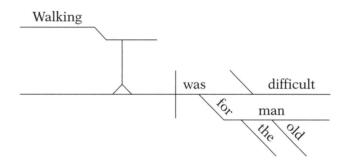

In "Walking to the store was difficult for the old man," the gerund phrase that is the sentence's subject is "Walking to the store." The predicate is "was"; the predicate adjective is "difficult"; the prepositional phrase modifying the predicate is "for the old man." Diagram the sentence in this way:

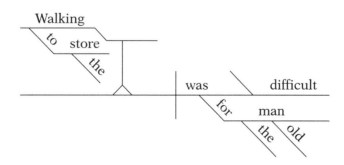

(3.11) Diagramming Verbals and Clauses *(Continued)*

⊠ Participles

These words, which often end in *-ing* or *-ed,* act as adjectives. They should be placed under the words that they modify using the "lazy L" form. Any words that modify participles should be placed beneath the participles. In the sentence, "Seeing the red light, Penny applied her brakes," "Seeing the red light" is the participle phrase that modifies "Penny," the sentence's subject. The predicate is "applied," and "brakes" is the direct object. "Her" modifies brakes. Diagram the sentence in this manner:

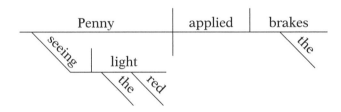

In the sentence, "Monica signaled to the children playing in the yard," "Monica" is the subject; "signaled" is the predicate; "to the children" is the prepositional phrase that modifies the predicate; and "playing in the yard" is the participle phrase that modifies "children." Here is how that sentence should be diagrammed:

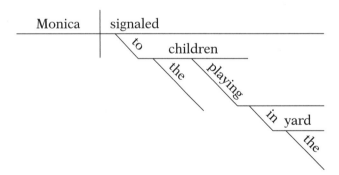

(3.11) Diagramming Verbals and Clauses *(Continued)*

⊠ Infinitives

An infinitive is the word "to" plus the verb. Examples are "to dream," "to participate," and "to yawn." Infinitives can be used as sentence subjects, direct objects, sentence complements, adjectives, and adverbs, and should be placed in one of those positions in the diagram. In the sentence, "To win the game was important," "To win the game" is the infinitive phrase and is the sentence's subject; "To win" is the infinitive; "game" is the direct object modified by "the"; "was" is the predicate; "and "important" is the predicate adjective. Diagram the sentence in this way:

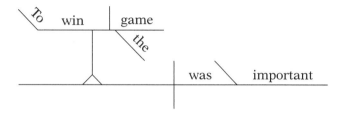

In the sentence, "Martina wanted to listen carefully," the infinitive phrase is "to listen carefully." The sentence can be diagrammed as follows:

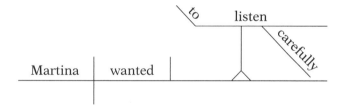

⊠ Clauses

Subordinate or dependent clauses, those groups of words that cannot stand alone, can act as adjectives, adverbs, or nouns. When diagramming a sentence that contains a subordinate or dependent clause, first diagram the main or independent clause (that portion of the sentence that can stand alone). Then diagram the subordinate or dependent clause as if it were a sentence, placing the clause below the word it modifies—whether it is a noun, verb, or, if it is a noun clause, above the main clause's line in its functional position with the sentence. Finally, connect the dependent clause portion to the main clause with a dashed line.

⊠ Adjective Clauses

In the sentence, "Paul is the student who won the contest," "who won the contest" is the adjective clause that modifies the noun "student." The sentence would be diagrammed in this manner:

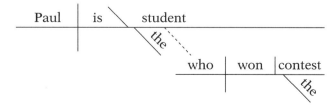

147

(3.11) Diagramming Verbals and Clauses *(Continued)*

⊠ Adverb Clauses

In the sentence, "After the storm ended, we assessed the damage," the adverb clause is "After the storm ended." It modifies the predicate "assessed." The sentence should be diagrammed in this way:

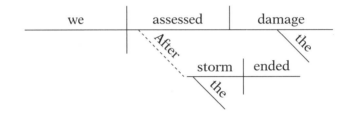

⊠ Noun Clauses

In the sentence, "We heard that you will be the champion driver," "that you will be the champion driver" is the noun clause that acts as a direct object. The main clause is, "We heard." Diagram the sentence as such:

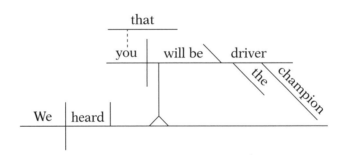

In the sentence, "That the players are drained is the reason," the noun clause is, "That the players are drained." It functions as the sentence's subject. The predicate nominative is "the reason." Here is how to diagram this sentence:

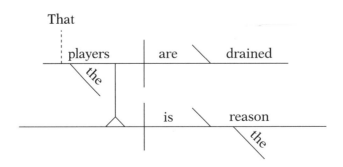

(3.11A) Diagramming Verbals and Clauses

Diagram these seven sentences on a separate sheet of paper:

1. Hearing the bad news was disturbing.

2. Reading the newspaper, Herman saw the frightening headlines.

3. Eduardo waved to his friends standing by the subway.

4. To challenge authority was not smart.

5. She is the woman who won Lotto yesterday.

6. While we were watching television on Friday, the alarm rang.

7. This is what I have been expecting.

Review Activities

REVIEW ACTIVITY 1   SENTENCES BY STRUCTURE

What type of sentence is each group of words below? Using the abbreviations simple (S), compound (CPD), complex (CPLX), and compound-complex (CC), write the correct abbreviation on the line next to the number. Each is used at least one time.

1. _____ Can you figure out this algebra problem in less than a minute?

2. _____ If you can remember these phone numbers without writing them down, you have a great memory.

3. _____ This is probably our final meeting this month, Larry.

4. _____ Eddie knew which tools we needed, but he made no effort to obtain them.

5. _____ My neighbor was working on his lawn, and my son was playing catch with his friend.

6. _____ Solve this challenging puzzle that you have in front of you, and you will win a great prize.

7. _____ Will you be there to assist with the decorating?

8. _____ My boss, who lives three miles away from here, is a very intelligent woman.

9. _____ I wanted to help you with your homework.

10. _____ We would truly love to come to your party, but we have another engagement that night.

11. _____ Kendra asked me to remind Sean about the CD that he borrowed, but I forgot to do so.

12. _____ These sea creatures that we viewed are awesome, and I look forward to seeing more of them soon.

REVIEW ACTIVITY 2   A PART HERE, A PART THERE, AND ANOTHER PART THERE ... (SENTENCE CONSTRUCTION)

Seven sentences have been broken up into three parts. To reconstruct each original sentence, select a part from each of the three groups below, and then write the seven original sentences on a separate sheet of paper.

Group One

A. A woman will be questioned

B. All of the residents were directed

C. He is a former

D. Is this your watch

E. Most of the sandwiches

F. They are looking

G. We were heading home

Group Two

H. about the incident

I. along the lonely road

J. criminal defense attorney

K. had been distributed to the homeless men

L. out of the apartment building

M. that is here

N. through the videotapes

Group Three

O. at this intersection.

P. by the police searching for the robber.

Q. in the dark.

R. on the kitchen counter, Lyle?

S. to see if they can find the evidence.

T. who has been called incompetent.

U. who stay in this city neighborhood.

© 2007 by John Wiley & Sons, Inc.

REVIEW ACTIVITY 3   COMBINING SENTENCES

Using the specified method, combine the two sentences in each item. Insert the necessary punctuation as well.

1. **Use *who:*** My sister is twenty years old. My sister will be getting married next June.

    _____

    _____

    _____

    _____

2. **Use *if:*** You want concert tickets. I can buy concert tickets for you.

    _____

    _____

    _____

    _____

3. **Use *and:*** Babe Ruth pitched and played outfield for the Boston Red Sox. Babe Ruth hit 60 home runs for the New York Yankees in 1927.

    _____

    _____

    _____

    _____

4. **Use *which:*** My uncle just bought a new car. My uncle purchased his new car last Saturday morning.

    _____

    _____

    _____

    _____

REVIEW ACTIVITY 3   COMBINING SENTENCES *(Continued)*

5. **Use an appositive phrase:** Connecticut is called the Nutmeg State. Connecticut is one of the six New England States.

   _____

   _____

   _____

   _____

6. **Use a relative pronoun:** Eduardo was selected for the Scholar-Athlete Award. Eduardo has an A average and is an All-State pitcher.

   _____

   _____

   _____

   _____

7. **Use a participle phrase:** Denise was stung by a bee. Denise immediately had to go to the hospital.

   _____

   _____

   _____

   _____

REVIEW ACTIVITY 4   LET'S COMBINE SOME MORE SENTENCES

Two sets of sentences have been combined in a number of ways in this activity. On the line next to each number in the list, write the corresponding letter of one of the seven methods of combining these sentences. Each combining device is used at least once. Two combining devices can be used for the same sentence.

> **Combining Devices**
> A. Relative pronoun
> B. Appositive
> C. Correlative conjunction
> D. Semicolon
> E. Subordinating conjunction
> F. Verbal phrase
> G. Series

For numbers 1–7: Maureen drove to school. On the way to school, Maureen saw an accident. Maureen then telephoned the police.

1. _____ Driving to school, Maureen saw an accident and then telephoned the police.

2. _____ Maureen drove to school, saw an accident, and then telephoned the police.

3. _____ While she was driving to school, Maureen saw an accident and then telephoned the police.

4. _____ Maureen, who was driving to school, saw an accident and then telephoned the police.

5. _____ Maureen not only drove to school but also saw an accident and then telephoned the police.

6. _____ Maureen was driving to school and saw an accident; then she telephoned the police.

7. _____ Maureen, a driver, saw an accident on her way to school and then telephoned the police.

For numbers 8–10: Ralph walked his garbage cans to the curb. Ralph waved to his friend. Ralph is a retired firefighter.

8. _____ Ralph, a retired firefighter, walked his garbage cans to the curb and waved to his friend.

9. _____ Ralph, who is a retired firefighter, walked his garbage cans to the curb and waved to his friend.

10. _____ Walking his garbage cans to the curb, Ralph, a retired firefighter, waved to his friend.

Final Tests

FINAL TEST 1   COMPLETE AND INCOMPLETE SENTENCES

Determine whether each group of words in the list is a sentence (S), fragment (F), or run-on (RO), by writing F, S, or RO on the line next to the number. Each correct answer scores 5 points.

1. _____ You know that this is a good plan many of us do.

2. _____ After the meal had been eaten by the hungry campers.

3. _____ Bring the cartons to the back of the store they should be stacked neatly.

4. _____ Have you decided to apply to that summer program, Paula?

5. _____ Sandy, can you contribute to the cancer fund drive?

6. _____ None of the people scheduled for the afternoon appointments.

7. _____ She quietly came down the stairs she did not want to wake up her parents.

8. _____ Hearing the motorcycles passing by on the busy highway.

9. _____ That is one bill that will never be passed in Congress.

10. _____ Now I can place some of the cups and saucers back that should help me save time tomorrow morning.

11. _____ Last week we watched the Notre Dame football game this weekend we intend to watch Northwestern's game.

12. _____ He quickly shut his book then he walked out of the main library.

13. _____ By the time he arrives in Phoenix.

14. _____ The next-to-last stop on the tourists' itinerary.

15. _____ Whether you decide to submit your application for this new position.

16. _____ The dentist will surely give you a proper cleaning this afternoon.

17. _____ She is interested in exploring new fields of science.

18. _____ These new ideas are exciting do you agree?

19. _____ Some of the new kayaks displayed in this showroom.

20. _____ What are you thinking?

Number correct _____ × 5 = _____%

FINAL TEST 2   SENTENCES BY PURPOSE

The four types of sentences classified by purpose are the declarative (DEC), the interrogative (INT), the imperative (IMP), and the exclamatory (EXC). Write the appropriate abbreviation on the line next to the sentence to indicate the type of sentence.

1. _____ Can you hear me singing?

2. _____ Do it right this time.

3. _____ What a great catch!

4. _____ This is the best way to do the problem.

5. _____ I had the most fantastic time!

6. _____ I couldn't believe my eyes!

7. _____ Is this your locker combination, Anita?

8. _____ I am glad to see that it turned out well for you and your family, Ursula.

9. _____ May we please go to lunch now?

10. _____ This article has some interesting facts.

11. _____ Listen up.

12. _____ I want to volunteer in this organization.

13. _____ Is each number correct?

14. _____ Will the kangaroo be at the zoo today?

15. _____ *Mike and the Mad Dog* is his favorite radio program.

16. _____ Have you counted all of the coins in the drawer?

17. _____ The divers were looking for the treasure.

18. _____ Take the dog out for a walk.

19. _____ Did you place the watch on this counter?

20. _____ I ate the whole thing by myself.

Number correct _____ × 5 = _____%

FINAL TEST 3   SENTENCES CLASSIFIED ACCORDING TO STRUCTURE

Determine if the sentence is simple (S), compound (CPD), complex (CPLX), or compound-complex (CC). Then write the correct abbreviation on the line next to the sentence. Each answer is worth 5 points.

1. _____ I do remember the show that you were talking about yesterday.

2. _____ There is safety in numbers.

3. _____ If you solve this puzzle, there are additional challenging ones in this book.

4. _____ Dr. Watson was the friend of Sherlock Holmes, and Professor Moriarty was Holmes's enemy.

5. _____ My friend, who has recently moved to Michigan to join his family, gave me some living room furniture that I know will be used immediately.

6. _____ I want to ask you for this book that I need, but you might not have it here with you.

7. _____ The largest of the Great Lakes is Lake Superior.

8. _____ The hostess offered us some refreshments, and we eagerly reached for them.

9. _____ While you were talking on the telephone, I rewrote this essay that Mr. Anderson assigned to us last week.

10. _____ John Glenn, who was one of America's first astronauts, returned to space in the *Discovery*, and the media enjoyed reporting on Glenn's recent space experience.

11. _____ Read this important announcement, and let me know what you think of its tone.

12. _____ Your answer is correct, and you will advance to the next round of the competition.

13. _____ I would like to go with you to the outlets today, but I have to watch my cousins instead.

14. _____ Her husband is a history professor who teaches at the local community college.

15. _____ The children spotted a stray cat on the playground.

16. _____ Mehmet could not find his watch anywhere.

17. _____ The artistic director, who is a playwright himself, works diligently on the project.

18. _____ Belinda wrote to her aunt, and then she walked to her job at the restaurant.

19. _____ Elena mentioned that she wanted to visit the home that her grandmother once owned.

20. _____ Please select this pattern that you love so much, and I will buy the couch for you.

Number correct _____ × 5 = _____%

FINAL TEST 4   WHICH IS THE BEST SENTENCE?

In each group of five sentences, select the sentence that follows the requirements of standard written English the best. In making your selection, consider grammar; usage; mechanics; sentence construction and fluency; and other elements of clear, effective, precise, and convincing writing. Circle the letter of the best sentence, and be ready to support your choice. Choice "a" in each group is the same sentence as the original one. Each answer is worth 20 points.

1. There is less fires in our town being that our residents have been educated on fire safety.

   a. There is less fires in our town being that our residents have been educated on fire safety.

   b. There is fewer fires in our town being that our residents have been educated on fire safety.

   c. There are fewer fires in our town being that our residents have been educated on fire safety.

   d. There is fewer fires in our town since our residents have been educated on fire safety.

   e. There are fewer fires in our town because our residents have been educated about fire safety.

2. Dropped from her purse, Mom lost her necklace, which had been a gift from Dad.

   a. Dropped from her purse, Mom lost her necklace, which had been a gift from Dad.

   b. Dropped from her purse, Mom lost her necklace, a gift from Dad.

   c. Mom, dropped from her purse, Dad's gift a necklace.

   d. Dropped from her purse, the necklace of Mom, that Dad had given to her.

   e. Mom lost Dad's gift, a necklace, when she dropped it from her purse.

3. Coal miners they are concerned about safety because of the fact that their job has dangers.

   a. Coal miners they are concerned about safety because of the fact that their job has dangers.

   b. Coal miners are concerned about safety because their jobs are dangerous.

   c. Concerned about safety, the dangerous jobs of the coal miners are a concern.

   d. Due to the fact that their jobs are dangerous, coal miners are concerned about their safety.

   e. Being that their jobs are dangerous, coal miners are concerned about safety.

FINAL TEST 4   WHICH IS THE BEST SENTENCE? *(Continued)*

4. One of the magazines which is on that table need to be taken with us.

   a. One of the magazines which is on that table need to be taken with us.

   b. One of the magazines that is on that table need to be taken with us.

   c. One of the magazines that are on that table needs to be taken with us.

   d. One of the magazines which are on that table need to be taken with us.

   e. On the table, one of the magazines which need to be taken with us is this one.

5. If Lucy was a little taller, she would have been able to change this ceiling light.

   a. If Lucy was a little taller, she would have been able to change this ceiling light.

   b. If Lucy were a little taller, she would be able to change this ceiling light.

   c. Had that Lucy been a little taller, she would have been able to change this ceiling light.

   d. Had Lucy, she been a little taller, she was able to change this ceiling light.

   e. Was Lucy a little taller, she would have been able to change this ceiling light.

Number correct _____ **× 20 =** _____%

Section Four
Usage

Diagnostic Tests

DIAGNOSTIC TEST 1   AGREEMENT

On the line next to each sentence, write the letter C to indicate that the sentence illustrates correct agreement regarding subject, verb, pronoun, and antecedent. Write the letter X to indicate that the sentence illustrates incorrect agreement. Each correct answer is worth 5 points.

1. _____ I was here with you.

2. _____ Some of the breads is missing.

3. _____ You were the only one who helped me then.

4. _____ One of these photos are great.

5. _____ Many of the princesses have interesting stories to tell.

6. _____ Neither of the puppies are going with us now.

7. _____ I am receiving a text message now.

8. _____ My sister and brother is here.

9. _____ The students brought their notebooks to class.

10. _____ Either of the girls are able to see the man now.

11. _____ Neither his family members nor his best friend has yet to arrive.

12. _____ Most of the paper have been read already.

13. _____ *Laverne and Shirley* was a good sitcom.

14. _____ All of the meal have been eaten.

15. _____ The comedy team is hilarious.

16. _____ Parties and others festivities is good fun.

17. _____ Many of the girls in our class seem happy about the new rule.

18. _____ One of these cells are going to be tested soon.

19. _____ Some of these newspapers need to be recycled.

20. _____ Each of these ribbons were used on the float.

Number correct _____ **× 5 =** _____%

DIAGNOSTIC TEST 2   VERB TENSES

Half of these sentences possess verbs that illustrate the correct tense. Write the letter C on the line for those ten sentences. Write the letter X for those other sentences in which the verb tense is incorrect. Each correct answer is worth 5 points.

1. _____ I rang the bell yesterday.

2. _____ Hymie goed to the movies last week.

3. _____ I write him a note a year or two ago.

4. _____ The young children builded a fort in our backyard.

5. _____ I eaten all of the cake.

6. _____ Have you bought a gift for your cousin?

7. _____ I had thought about it for a second or two.

8. _____ My friends and I am tired of that type of behavior.

9. _____ The boat sinked during the heavy rains.

10. _____ Has he ever setted the table for his family?

11. _____ The bell had rung twice by that time.

12. _____ The pipe burst during the cold spell last winter.

13. _____ Regina has rode almost every horse in this stable.

14. _____ He maked delicious desserts when he lived with us.

15. _____ Have you swum in that lake?

16. _____ I heard from my uncle last night.

17. _____ I have always drank several glasses of water each day.

18. _____ Have you recalled her last name?

19. _____ The snow fell throughout the night.

20. _____ He tore a hole in his best coat.

Number correct _____ **× 5 =** _____%

DIAGNOSTIC TEST 3   CASES

The twenty underlined pronouns in these sentences are in the nominative case (N), possessive case (P), or objective case (O). Write the appropriate letter on the line next to each sentence. Each correct answer is worth 5 points.

1. _____ This is their house.

2. _____ I would like my locker to be in this area.

3. _____ We selected you for our group, Mitch.

4. _____ You gave the gift to whom?

5. _____ They are the victors.

6. _____ Who is the new counselor?

7. _____ Has the game lost its interest?

8. _____ We students like this new policy.

9. _____ Your speech was fantastic, Nero.

10. _____ Students like her do very well in high school.

11. _____ Give them the correct directions this time.

12. _____ "My looking at you should not make you nervous," the coach told her players.

13. _____ The present was given to him.

14. _____ That was he on the telephone this morning.

15. _____ If I can make it, I certainly will be there.

16. _____ Take this to the office.

17. _____ These are my best illustrations.

18. _____ May I help you with your homework?

19. _____ Wilma handed them the required paperwork.

20. _____ Will she arrive on time?

Number correct _____ × 5 = _____%

DIAGNOSTIC TEST 4   WORDS OFTEN CONFUSED

Underline the correct word in each set of parentheses. Each correct answer is worth 5 points.

1. I (heard, herd) what you said.

2. He was a great guidance (councilor, counselor).

3. You always seem to give me good (advice, advise).

4. My family was (all together, altogether) shocked by the news.

5. The group needed more (capital, capitol) to start the new business.

6. This is a (brake, break) in the action.

7. (Where, Wear) are you going to college next year?

8. What is the (weather, whether) supposed to be tomorrow?

9. The team's (moral, morale) was very high.

10. That man had (formally, formerly) been a cab driver.

11. The teacher asked her students to be (quiet, quite).

12. This is (your, you're) best work thus far, Tina.

13. The world was not at (peace, piece) during that decade.

14. What math (coarse, course) have you signed up for this term?

15. Have you requested a meeting with the (principal, principle)?

16. The flight attendant walked into the (plain, plane) before the passengers.

17. May I go (to, too, two)?

18. Have you (all ready, already) been to my cousin's house?

19. We were very (board, bored) by that movie.

20. The group walked (threw, through) the coliseum.

Number correct _____ **× 5 =** _____%

Lessons and Activities

4.1 Agreement of Subjects and Verbs

A subject must always agree with its verb. A singular subject, one that represents a single person, place, or thing, agrees with a singular verb. A plural subject, one that represents more than a single person, place, or thing, agrees with a plural verb. Thus, a subject and verb must agree in number.

Singular nouns include *boy, girl, mother, father, sister, brother, sink, boat, tent,* and *friend.* Plural nouns include *boys, girls, mothers, fathers, sisters, brothers, sinks, boats, tents,* and *friends.*

Singular pronouns that can be the subject of a sentence include *he, she, it, I,* and *you.* Plural pronouns include *they, we,* and *you.*

The following sentences illustrate a singular subject that agrees with a singular verb. The subject is underlined, and the verb is in italics.

He *was* on time for the appointment.

The picture *costs* forty dollars.

That television program *interests* me.

The following sentences illustrate a plural subject that agrees with a plural verb. The subject is underlined, and the verb is in italics.

They *represent* our group.

The lilacs *are* in bloom.

These stories *were* disturbing.

Fill in the blank with a verb to complete the sentence. Write the letter S for singular agreement or P for plural agreement after the sentence.

Billy _____ our captain. _____

Some motorcycles _____ missing from the barn. _____

Teachers _____ to help their students. _____

WRITING TIP *Reread each of your sentences carefully to ensure that the subjects and verbs agree in number. Reading the sentences aloud can help you detect agreement problems.*

(4.1A) What's Her Name?
(Agreement of Subjects and Verbs)

Most of the following sentences contain examples of how not to use agreement. Circle the letters before each sentence that illustrate correct agreement, and then write the corresponding letter of each sentence on the line below the list. If your answers are correct, you can unscramble those letters to spell a person's first name. Write that name on the appropriate line underneath the sentences.

A. Everyone try to do well on this part of the course.

D. The table with four chairs are discounted today.

E. Morty, along with his friends, have promised to come to the party.

F. One of the kittens have gone into the next room.

G. The physicians is ready to operate.

H. Several contestants has been selected to move on to the next round.

I. All of the blanket is wet.

K. The brain cells of this animal is interesting to study.

L. Many of these boxes are empty.

N. It certainly give a good impression.

O. Neither of the cars is ready.

R. My sister's friends is coming home from summer camp today.

S. All of the assignments have been collected.

U. Some of the breads is tasty.

Y. Each of the programs are entertaining.

The letters that illustrate correct agreement are _____.

The first name that these letters spell when unscrambled is _____.

(4.2) Agreement Involving Prepositional Phrases

Prepositional phrases can affect agreement in number between the sentence's subject and verb. Here are some sentences and rules regarding the singular and plural subject-verb agreement and prepositional phrases.

Several *videos* in this pile *are* yours. (The plural word *videos* is the subject, and *are* is the plural verb. Thus, the plural subject, *videos,* agrees with the plural verb, *are.* The prepositional phrase, *in this pile,* does not affect the subject-verb agreement.)

A *plan* for the upcoming years *is* essential. (*Plan* is the singular subject, and *is* is the singular verb. Thus, the singular subject and the singular verb agree in number. The prepositional phrase, *for the upcoming years,* does not affect the subject-verb agreement.)

The *children* in this bus *recall* the incident. (*Children* is the plural subject, and *recall* is the plural verb. Thus, *children* and *recall* agree in number. The prepositional phrase, *in this bus,* does not affect the subject-verb agreement.)

The *pictures* in this hallway *remind* me of the 1950s. (*Pictures,* the plural subject, and *remind,* the plural verb, agree in number. The prepositional phrase, *in this hallway,* does not affect the subject-verb agreement.)

When working with the indefinite pronouns that can be either singular or plural, such as *all, any, most, none,* and *some,* pay attention to the prepositional phrase that follows immediately after the indefinite pronoun. Here are some examples:

***All* of this cake *has* been eaten.** (*All,* an indefinite pronoun that can be either singular or plural, takes its cue from the object of the preposition, *cake,* a singular noun. Thus, in this instance, *all* must be the same number as *cake.* Therefore, *has,* a singular verb, agrees with *all.*)

***All* of the cakes *have* been eaten.** (The subject, *all,* takes its cue from the object of the preposition, *cakes,* which is plural. Thus, *all* must be plural to agree with the object of the preposition, *cakes,* and the plural verb, *have.*)

Circle the correct verb in each sentence:

Some of this page (need, needs) to be edited.

Most of these pies (was, were) left out by mistake.

The members of this exclusive club (is, are) in session right now.

The doctors working in this hospital (deserve, deserves) much credit.

None of these pamphlets (is, are) ready to be distributed.

 WRITING TIP *Remember that the verb agrees in number with the sentence's subject, not with the object of the preposition in the prepositional phrase. In the sentence, "The number of students is fifty," the singular verb, is, agrees with the singular subject,* number. *The plural object of the preposition,* students, *does not affect the subject-verb agreement.*

(4.2A) Let's Concur!
(Agreement Involving Prepositional Phrases)

Do not let the prepositional phrases in the following sentences mar your good agreement judgment. Mentally connect each subject with its appropriate verb, disregarding the prepositional phrase in between the subject and the verb. Then read each sentence without the prepositional phrase in it. Underline the subject. After that, circle the correct verb, and write it in the space next to the number.

1. An outstanding man among hundreds of other men (is, are) a find.

2. Several veteran girls in this choir (was, were) inspirational to the younger choir members.

3. For Mets fans, a game like no other games (was, were) the sixth game of the 1986 World Series.

4. This last photograph with its many details (win, wins) this year's award.

5. Los Angeles, as well as many other major American cities, (is, are) filled with people from various cultures.

6. The aromas from this kitchen (was, were) enticing.

7. Every one of the submitted essays (is, are) given the same consideration.

8. The noises in this workout facility (was, were) quite loud.

9. A new employee in any of these many companies hardly (travel, travels).

10. Both of the signs on this narrow city street (was, were) replaced last week.

11. Misspellings in this article's text already (has, have) been detected.

12. This package, in addition to some other cartons in these rooms, (seem, seems) to be mislabeled.

13. An anticipation of possible problems (help, helps) to make the day flow more smoothly.

14. Two types of medicines (was, were) discussed at the annual convention.

15. Possible changes in the rules of this competition (had, have) been mentioned.

Name _____ Date _____ Period _____

(4.3) Indefinite Pronoun Agreement

The word to which a pronoun refers to or replaces is its *antecedent*. In the sentence, "Kenny did his homework," the antecedent is *Kenny*, and the pronoun that the antecedent must agree with is *his*, since both *Kenny* and *his* are singular. The antecedent usually comes before the pronoun.

The following pronouns are singular pronouns. They require a singular antecedent and a singular verb. Remember the mnemonic **OSANE**, the first letters of these singular pronouns:

> **o**ne
>
> **s**omeone, somebody
>
> **a**nyone, anybody, anything
>
> **n**o one, nobody, neither
>
> **e**veryone, everybody, each, either, everything

Here are some sentences that use these singular pronouns:

Somebody in our class has lost *his* (or *her*) ring. (*Somebody*, a singular pronoun, the sentence's subject and the pronoun's antecedent, must agree with *his* [or *her*], the antecedent's pronoun. *Their*, a plural pronoun, would be incorrect since the antecedent, *somebody*, is singular.)

Everyone should take *his* (or *her*) information to the front office. (The singular pronoun, *Everyone*, the sentence's subject and the pronoun's antecedent, agrees with *his* [or *her*], because the pronoun—*his* or *her*—is singular.)

Use *he*, *his*, and *him* when the antecedent is clearly masculine, as in, "*Irving* remembered *his* old phone number." Do the same with *she*, *her*, and *hers* when the antecedent is clearly feminine. "*Caroline* placed *her* sweater on the desk." Use *it* or *its* when the antecedent is neither *masculine* nor *feminine*. The *sweater* has lost *its* color over these years.

 WRITING TIP *If a word clearly means "more than one," such as, "Everyone clapped when they heard the news," use the plural pronoun,* they, *since the sentence indicates that more than a single person clapped.*

175

Who Wins? (Indefinite Pronoun Agreement)

Which of these three groups of sentences will be the winner? First, circle the correct verb in each sentence. Then count the number of letters in that word, and write the number in the space next to the sentence. Finally add up the five numbers in each group, and write that number in the "Points" space below the group's last sentence. So, which group is the big winner? Let's find out!

Group One

1. _____ Each of the reasons (was, were,) intelligently presented by the committee members.

2. _____ Neither of the fax messages (has, have) come through yet.

3. _____ (Was, Were) both of the beds moved into the larger bedroom?

4. _____ Many of the cards in the show (has, have) been sold already.

5. _____ (Do, Does) each of the officers see the problem the same way.

Points _____

Group Two

6. _____ One of the cans (was, were) picked up by the sanitation crew.

7. _____ At certain times a glitch in the programs (need, needs) to be repaired immediately.

8. _____ Each of these documentaries (is, are) interesting for most middle school students.

9. _____ Most of these transporters (travel, travels) many miles each spring.

10. _____ Some of this loaf of bread (has, have) been eaten.

Points _____

Group Three

11. _____ All of the neighbors on my block (was, were) at the Fourth of July event.

12. _____ Most of the work on this assignment (need, needs) to be completed by early October.

13. _____ None of the materials (was, were) ready to be sent out.

14. _____ Either of these women (was, were) able to attend the meeting.

15. _____ Several of the men in this grueling contest (look, looks) fatigued.

Points _____

(4.4) Compound Subjects

When compound (two or more) subjects are joined by the conjunctions *either* and *or* OR *neither* and *nor,* the verb agrees with the noun or pronoun closer to it:

Either the boy or his mother *represents* the family at gatherings. (Since *mother* is singular and closer to the verb than the other subject, *boy,* the correct verb is the singular verb, *represents.*)

Either the boy or his sisters *represent* the family at gatherings. (Since *sisters* is plural and closer to the verb than the other subject, *boy,* the correct verb is the plural verb, *represent.*)

Neither the sisters nor Ken *represents* the family at gatherings. (Since *Ken* is singular and closer to the verb than the other subject, *sisters,* the correct verb is the singular verb, *represents.*)

Neither Ken nor his parents *represent* the family at gatherings. (Since *parents* is plural and closer to the verb than the other subject *Ken,* the correct verb is the plural verb, *represent.*)

If the parts of a compound subject are joined by the conjunctions *both* and *and,* the verb must be plural:

Billy and Frankie were reading the same article. (Since *Billy* and *Frankie* are the compound subjects, the verb, *were,* must be plural.)

Reminder: Two nouns joined by the conjunction *and* are not always a compound subject. Often these nouns make up a unit. Here are some examples:

Laverne and Shirley was his favorite comedy. (*Laverne and Shirley* = comedy)

Peanut butter and jelly is her favorite sandwich. (Peanut butter and jelly = sandwich)

Yet in the sentence, "Peanut butter and jelly are the ingredients," both *peanut butter* and *jelly* are considered separate units. Thus, the plural verb should be *are.*
Here are some additional example sentences featuring compound subjects:

Jim, Karen, and *Maureen* were cutting their lawns.

Both the *girls* and the *boys* were watching the entertaining magician.

Sir Arthur Conan Doyle and *Jane Austen* are my teacher's favorite authors.

Either *Noah* or *Ellie* will cook Thanksgiving dinner this year.

Neither the *notebook* nor the *map* was located in the debris.

Where are the *hammers* and the *nails,* Richie?

Her *fingers* and *wrists* were injured in the crash.

There will be no *hamburgers* or *hot dogs* served tonight.

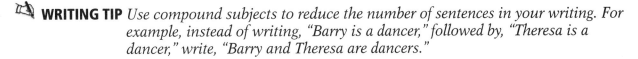 **WRITING TIP** *Use compound subjects to reduce the number of sentences in your writing. For example, instead of writing, "Barry is a dancer," followed by, "Theresa is a dancer," write, "Barry and Theresa are dancers."*

(4.4A) Two or More (Subjects) at a Time (Compound Subjects)

Underline the correct verb in each sentence:

1. _____ Neither Christina nor her friends (is, are) going to tomorrow night's concert.

2. _____ Dahlia and her friends (was, were) in attendance.

3. _____ A motorcycle driver or an automobile driver (has, have) to follow basic safety rules.

4. _____ Each month a girl and a boy (are, is) chosen to appear on the local television program.

5. _____ Ham and eggs (are, is) the ingredients.

6. _____ Laurel and Hardy (are, is) my dad's favorite comedy team.

7. _____ Jerry and Marty (travel, travels) to Europe every three years.

8. _____ Jerry or Marty (travel, travels) to Europe every three years.

9. _____ Either the president or the vice president (was, were) at that important world-wide session.

10. _____ Both the president and the vice president (was, were) at that important session.

11. _____ My brothers, my sister, and my dad (need, needs) to be there with me.

12. _____ Can the men and the women (stay, stays) on the same committee?

13. _____ Neither the man nor his sisters (forget, forgets) to send the birthday card to Kate each year.

14. _____ (Has, Have) either Yvonne, her sister, or her parents driven to the airport recently?

15. _____ California and Washington (are, is) in the West.

(4.5) Irregular Verbs

Most verbs form their past tense by adding *-ed* to the present-tense form of the verb. Examples include *reel* (reeled), *deliver* (delivered), *rush* (rushed), and *walk* (walked).

An irregular verb does not form its past and present by adding *-ed* or *-d* to the present.

An effective way to learn the irregular verbs is to memorize their tenses and use the verbs in both writing and conversation.

These seven verbs are the same in their present, past, and past participle tenses: *burst, cost, hit, hurt, let, put,* and *set.*

The helping verb for the verb in its past participle form can be *has, had,* or *have.*

Here are some other common irregular verbs and their tenses:

Present	Present Participle	Past	Past Participle
begin	beginning	began	(have) begun
blow	blowing	blew	(have) blown
break	breaking	broke	(have) broken
bring	bringing	brought	(have) brought
buy	buying	bought	(have) bought
catch	catching	caught	(have) caught
choose	choosing	chose	(have) chosen
come	coming	came	(have) come
do	doing	did	(have) done
draw	drawing	drew	(have) drawn
drink	drinking	drank	(have) drunk
drive	driving	drove	(have) driven
eat	eating	ate	(have) eaten
fall	falling	fell	(have) fallen
feel	feeling	felt	(have) felt
find	finding	found	(have) found
freeze	freezing	froze	(have) frozen
get	getting	got	(have) got or gotten
give	giving	gave	(have) given
go	going	went	(have) gone
grow	growing	grew	(have) grown

(4.5) Irregular Verbs *(Continued)*

Present	Present Participle	Past	Past Participle
hold	holding	held	(have) held
keep	keeping	kept	(have) kept
know	knowing	knew	(have) known
lay (to place)	laying	laid	(have) laid
lead	leading	led	(have) led
leave	leaving	left	(have) left
lie (to rest, to recline)	lying	lay	(have) lain
lose	losing	lost	(have) lost
make	making	made	(have) made
ride	riding	rode	(have) ridden
ring	ringing	rang	(have) rung
rise	rising	rose	(have) risen
run	running	ran	(have) run
say	saying	said	(have) said
see	seeing	saw	(have) seen
sell	selling	sold	(have) sold
send	sending	sent	(have) sent
shrink	shrinking	shrank	(have) shrunk
sing	singing	sang	(have) sung
sink	sinking	sank	(have) sunk
sit	sitting	sat	(have) sat
speak	speaking	spoke	(have) spoken
steal	stealing	stole	(have) stolen
swim	swimming	swam	(have) swum
take	taking	took	(have) taken
teach	teaching	taught	(have) taught
tear (to rip)	tearing	tore	(have) torn

Irregular Verbs *(Continued)*

Present	Present Participle	Past	Past Participle
tell	telling	told	(have) told
throw	throwing	threw	(have) thrown
wear	wearing	wore	(have) worn
win	winning	won	(have) won
write	writing	wrote	(have) written

Here are some examples of irregular verbs and their tenses:

I *keep* my coins in this jar. (present)

I am *keeping* my coins in this jar. (present participle)

I *kept* my coins in this jar. (past)

I *have kept* my coins in this jar. (past participle)

Henrietta *grew* two inches since I *saw* her. (past)

Reggie has been *catching* many fish. (present participle)

Have they *won* the last three matches? (past participle)

They *have put* much work into that project. (past participle)

The children were *swimming* in the pool. (present participle)

Most of the choral members *left* the stage. (past)

Here is the conjugation of the verb *be*:

Present: I am, you are, he/she/it is (singular); we are, you are, they are (plural)

Past: I was, you were, he/she/it was (singular); we were, you were, they were (plural)

Future: I shall (or will) be, you will be, he/she/it will be (singular); we shall (or will) be, you will be, they will be (plural)

Present perfect: I have been, you have been, he/she/it has been (singular); we have been, you have been, they have been (plural) (Remember to add *has* or *have* to the past participle.)

Past perfect: I had been, you had been, he/she/it had been (singular); we had been, you had been, they had been (plural) (Remember to add *had* to the past participle.)

Future perfect: I shall (or will) have been, you will have been, he/she/it will have been (singular); we shall (or will) have been, you will have been, they will have been (plural) (Remember to add *shall have* or *will have* to the past participle.)

(4.5) Irregular Verbs *(Continued)*

Here is the conjugation of the verb *begin*:

Present: I begin, you begin, he/she/it begins (singular); we begin, you begin, they begin (plural)

Past: I began, you began, he/she/it began (singular); we began, you began, he/she/it began (plural)

Future: I will (or shall) begin, you will begin, he/she/it will begin (singular); we shall (or will) begin, you will begin, they will begin (plural)

Present perfect: I have begun, you have begun, he/she/it has begun (singular); we have begun, you have begun, they have begun (plural) (Remember to add *has* or *have* to the past participle.)

Past perfect: I had begun, you had begun, he/she/it had begun (singular); we had begun, you had begun, they had begun (plural) (Remember to add *had* to the past participle.)

Future perfect: I shall (or will) have begun, you will have begun, he/she/it had begun (singular); we shall (or will) have begun, you will have begun, they will have begun (Remember to add *shall have* or *will have* to the past participle.)

✎ WRITING TIP *Study all the parts of these irregular verbs. You will be tested on them on future standardized tests, and you will use them often in your speech and writing. Thus, they are important to know.*

Name _____ Date _____ Period _____

(4.5A) Big and Small (Irregular Verbs)

Circle the correct verb in each sentence. Then write the three letters above the verb on the line next to the sentence. Finally, write those consecutive three-letter combinations on the lines below the last sentence. If your answers are correct, these consecutive letters will spell six words that deal with size.

ced amp lar

1. _____ They had (rode, rided, ridden) all the way home.

geh art ben

2. _____ This material will probably (shrink, shrank, shrunk) if you dry it.

sin too uge

3. _____ Several runners had (stole, stealed, stolen) home on this catcher.

mas ure

4. _____ What he (did, done) came as no surprise to us.

ree alt siv

5. _____ How many letters of acceptance were (write, wrote, written) by the admissions director?

ase tri egi

6. _____ Lesley (go, goed, went) to the concert hall with her relatives last night.

ion wes gan

7. _____ When had Stanley (began, begin, begun) the science project?

sir beg tic

8. _____ What should you have done if the bell had (ringed, rang, rung)?

dee cio col

9. _____ Have you (swimmed, swam, swum) in the Atlantic before today?

hio pio oss

10. _____ All the best concert seats have been (taked, took, taken).

© 2007 by John Wiley & Sons, Inc.

183

(4.5A) **Big and Small (Irregular Verbs)** *(Continued)*

all   alp   fes

11. _____ When you (write, wrote, written) that beautiful letter to your dad, did you anticipate his emotional reaction?

sar uny ked

12. _____ Shirley (fall, fell, fallen) as she exited the restaurant on that snowy night.

any   hes   min

13. _____ This job has (drive, drove, driven) my cousin crazy!

led   iat

14. _____ Has this type of problem (came, come) to your attention before this exam?

ore ent ure

15. _____ Some of the police personnel have (see, saw, seen) this person around the town.

The letters spell these six "size" words: _____, _____,

_____, _____, _____, and

_____.

(4.6) Regular Verbs and Tense

Verbs that are called **regular verbs** form their tenses in a common or regular way. For their past tense, these verbs end in *-ed*. For example, the past tense of the verbs *dance* and *laugh* end in *-ed*. They are consistent in that pattern, unlike irregular verbs, which form their tenses in a number of different ways. Examples of **regular verbs** are *walk, talk, wave, jump,* and *look*. Examples of **irregular verbs** are *swim, think, forget,* and *see*. Consider how a verb forms its tenses, and you can tell whether each is a regular or irregular verb.

Here are some examples of regular verbs and their tenses:

Present: *walks*—action that is going on now.

Past: *walked*—action that already occurred.

Future: *will walk*—action that will take place.

Present perfect: *have walked*—action that was completed at some other time or action that started in the past and continues now. Remember to add *has* or *have* to the past participle.

Past perfect: *had walked*—action that occurred before another past action. Remember to add *had* to the past participle.

Future perfect: *will have walked*—action that will be completed by some given time in the future. Remember to add *shall have* or *will have* to the past participle.

Here are some more examples of regular verbs and their tenses:

Believe: We *believe* your story. **(present)**

Roam: She *roamed* the neighborhood looking for her lost dog. **(past)**

Talk: I *will talk* to them for you. **(future)**

Jog: My parents *have jogged* for many years. **(present perfect)**

Listen: They *had listened* to your story. **(past perfect)**

Paint: We *will have painted* the room by then. **(future perfect)**

 WRITING TIP *If you are not sure whether a verb is a regular verb and forms its tenses in a regular (that is, common) way, consult a dictionary. There you will see how the tenses should be formed. Often a computer's spell check will do the same. Check both of these resources to ensure that you are using the correct word for the correct tense.*

4.6A # It's All in the Numbers (Regular Verbs and Tense)

Circle the correct verb in each sentence in the three groups. Then count the number of letters in that verb, and write that number on the line next to the sentence. Add up the total number of letters for each group's correct verbs, and write the total in the appropriate space. Which group's correct verbs total the highest number? See for yourself. Good luck!

Group One

1. _____ Miranda (use, used) to go to our school.

2. _____ The trainee (ask, asked) some interesting questions.

3. _____ Georgia was (walking, walk) around the lake with her brother.

4. _____ Three police officers (risk, risked) their lives saving that man last night.

5. _____ Lucinda (complete, completed, completing) her assignments for her graduate school class.

Group One's total number of letters is _____.

Group Two

6. _____ What am I (suppose, supposed) to do now?

7. _____ The crime scene investigators were (reviewed, reviewing) the evidence.

8. _____ Have the auditions (finish, finished, finishing)?

9. _____ All of the gulls (land, landed) on the railing an hour ago.

10. _____ Each of the cast members has (experience, experienced) a good time here at the camp.

Group Two's total number of letters is _____.

Group Three

11. _____ The swimmers (wonder, wondered, wondering) what had happened to the former lifeguard.

12. _____ Did you (recall, recalled) her former Charlottesville address?

13. _____ Have all of the pamphlets been (collect, collected, collecting) by the staff members?

14. _____ Unfortunately, several men (drown, drowned) when the ship sank.

15. _____ Melissa (carve, carved, carving) her name into the tree.

Group Three's total number of letters is _____.

Name _____ Date _____ Period _____

(4.7) Active and Passive Voices

The **active voice** denotes that the subject of the sentence performs the action. In the sentence, "Patsy hit the ball," *Patsy,* the subject, performs the action. Thus, this sentence is written in the active voice.

The **passive voice** denotes that the action is performed on the subject. In the sentence, "The ball was hit by Patsy," the subject, *ball,* does not perform the action. Instead, the action is performed on the subject. Thus, this sentence is written in the passive voice.

Try to use the active voice as often as possible in both written and oral communication. Use the passive voice when you want to emphasize the person or thing receiving the action. As an example, in the sentence, "A large truck was stolen at the train station last night," the writer wants to emphasize that the truck was stolen. It is not that important who stole the truck. Thus, the passive voice construction is acceptable in this instance.

Here are some examples:

Active: Herman translated the essay.

Passive: The essay was translated by Herman.

Active: The Swedish woman won the debate.

Passive: The debate was won by the Swedish woman.

Active: The director presented the award-winning film.

Passive: The award-winning film was presented by the director.

In each of the active-voice sentences, the subject performs the action. In each of the passive-voice sentences, the action is performed on the subject.

 WRITING TIP *Whenever possible, write in the active voice. Thus, instead of writing a sentence in the passive voice such as, "The test was completed by Diana," write the sentence in the active voice such as, "Diana completed the test."*

It's Better in the Active Voice (Active and Passive Voices)

Rewrite each of these sentences, and change them from the passive to the active voice. Write the new, active-voice sentence on the lines provided.

1. The dog was walked by my neighbor last night. _____

   _____

2. A good time was had by all at the picnic. _____

   _____

3. The hose in our backyard was moved by Ray. _____

   _____

4. The players were cautioned by the manager. _____

   _____

5. The hard-working assistants were congratulated by the boss. _____

   _____

6. These books were read by the top students in our class. _____

   _____

7. The challenging role was cleverly performed by Emma. _____

   _____

8. The new president was briefed by the staff. _____

   _____

9. The teammate was thrown the ball by Pedro. _____

   _____

10. The math test was completed on time by all the students. _____

    _____

4.8 Transitive and Intransitive Verbs

An action verb that has an object is a **transitive verb.** A transitive verb takes a direct object. In the sentence, "The elderly man dropped his cane," the verb is *dropped,* and the direct object is *cane.* Thus, the verb is transitive since it has an object. Remember that a direct object (always a noun or a pronoun) answers the question, *What?* or *Whom?* after the verb.

An action verb that does not have an object or complement is an **intransitive verb.** Thus, in the sentence, "Misery hurts," the verb *hurts* has no object. If you ask, *What?* or *Whom?* after the verb, you have no answer. So *hurts* in this sentence is an intransitive verb.

Here are some examples of transitive and intransitive verbs:

Jerome walked his aunt to the train station. (transitive—Jerome walked *whom?* his aunt = direct object)

Edgar walked slowly. (intransitive—No word after the verb *walked* answers the question, *What?* or *Whom?*)

Can you sing this song now? (transitive—sing *what?* song = direct object)

This house has seventeen rooms. (transitive—The house has *what?* Seventeen rooms)

He veered into the woods. (intransitive—No word after the verb *veered* answers the question, *What?* or *Whom?*)

The shortstop played well yesterday. (intransitive—No word after the verb *played* answers the question, *What?* or *Whom?*)

Two of the following sentences have transitive verbs, and two have intransitive verbs. Place a check next to the two that have transitive verbs:

I fell down.

She and I followed my cousin closely.

Some of the newspapers have good comics.

Will they help now?

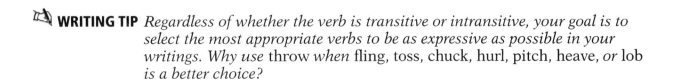

WRITING TIP *Regardless of whether the verb is transitive or intransitive, your goal is to select the most appropriate verbs to be as expressive as possible in your writings. Why use* throw *when* fling, toss, chuck, hurl, pitch, heave, *or* lob *is a better choice?*

4.8A College's Orange (Transitive and Intransitive Verbs)

Nine of the fifteen sentences in this activity have transitive verbs. The other six sentences have intransitive verbs. For each sentence that contains a transitive verb, write the letter that appears before the sentence on the line next to the sentence. Then write those nine letters consecutively on the line below the list. Those letters will spell out the college that is associated with this activity's title.

1. _____ **A**—The couple chatted for an hour.

2. _____ **S**—We heard the great news.

3. _____ **T**—Hester had been nurtured by her parents.

4. _____ **Y**—The team took the field.

5. _____ **L**—Rolando spends freely.

6. _____ **R**—The forecaster read the teleprompter.

7. _____ **A**—We ate the delicious dinner.

8. _____ **M**—Can you please slow down?

9. _____ **P**—The workers were impressed by the new boss.

10. _____ **C**—The rich man purchased the expensive piece of art.

11. _____ **O**—Our acting troupe performed at the local theater.

12. _____ **U**—I ushered my cousin to her seat.

13. _____ **S**—Take the coupons to the store.

14. _____ **T**—The parents of the deceased girl wept during the funeral.

15. _____ **E**—Prices hurt the consumer.

The letters spell out this college:

_____

(4.9) Nominative Case

The **nominative case** is used for subjects, predicate nominatives, and appositives that act as nouns—hence, the word *nominative*. In the sentence, "The best dancers are he and she," the two pronouns, *he* and *she,* are predicate nominatives in the nominative case.

The *singular nominative* pronouns are *I, you, he, she,* and *it.* The *plural nominative* pronouns are *we, you,* and *they.*

Here are several examples of pronouns used as subjects. They are all in the nominative case:

I will be there.

She will accept the trophy for the team.

They have lived there for many years.

You and *I* will be there on time. (compound subject)

Here are several examples of pronouns used as predicate nominatives. They are all in the nominative case:

The champions are *he* and *she.* (compound predicate nominatives)

That was *she* who waved to you last evening.

Our best bets are *they.*

Here are several examples of pronouns used as appositives. They are all in the nominative case:

We workers must stick together in these negotiations. (*We* is the noun appositive, and *workers* is the subject.)

The judges are *we* associates. (The noun appositive is *we,* and the predicate nominative is *associates.*)

 WRITING TIP *Remember that nominative case words always perform the action. This may become confusing when using compound subjects. You would use "She and I," not "Her and me," in the sentence, "[Compound subjects] are going to go shopping for holiday gifts this afternoon."*

Looking for 29 (Nominative Case)

In each sentence below, circle only the word that functions as a noun. Then write the number of letters in your answer on the line next to the sentence. Then add up those fifteen numbers. The total number of letters should be 29!

1. _____ (He, Him) is the winner of the radio contest.

2. _____ The contest winner is (he, him).

3. _____ (Them, These) are our best representatives for the state convention.

4. _____ (We, Us) viewers voted for the funniest television commercial.

5. _____ Melanie and (he, him) sing beautifully together.

6. _____ Melanie and (I, me) sing beautifully.

7. _____ It should have been (us, we).

8. _____ Her wish is that she and (I, me) will be in the chorus this term.

9. _____ Will it be (he, him)?

10. _____ Can you explain why he and (I, me) were eliminated from the competition?

11. _____ Neither Steve nor (I, me) can drive you to the airport tonight.

12. _____ Why do he and (I, me) work so hard to please you?

13. _____ You players and (we, us) coaches need to work out a fair practice schedule.

14. _____ Both you and (he, him) need to order your tickets before the concert sells out.

15. _____ I believe that our next state senator will be (she, her).

Objects of the Preposition

The **object of the preposition** is the noun or pronoun that ends the phrase begun by the preposition. In each of these phrases, "in the *lounge*," "near the *shoes*," "under the *pillow*," "by *herself*," and "into the *future*," the italicized or last word in the phrase is the object of the preposition.

It is always advisable to study and review the common prepositions:

aboard	about	above	across	after
against	along	among	around	as
at	before	behind	below	beneath
beside	besides	between	beyond	but(except)
by	despite	down	during	except
for	from	in	inside	into
like	near	of	off	on
onto	opposite	out	outside	over
past	since	through	throughout	till
to	toward	under	underneath	until
up	upon	with	within	without

Common compound prepositions include:

according to	aside from	because of
by means of	in addition to	in back of
in front of	in place of	in spite of
instead of	next to	prior to

(4.10) Objects of the Preposition *(Continued)*

In each of the following sentences, the first italicized word is the preposition, and the second italicized word is the object of the preposition (either a noun or a pronoun):

The group walked *between* the *buildings.*

Herm walked *with them.*

Mark groomed himself *prior to* the *dance.*

We looked *inside* the *house.*

After three *minutes,* we could not recall what had occurred.

We talked to *Ricardo* and *her.* (compound objects of the preposition)

The presents were donated by *Tom, Jill, Nancy,* and *Jack.* (compound objects of the preposition)

 WRITING TIP *Many prepositions can be placed in the blank in the sentence, "The plane flew _____ the clouds." Any word that can be placed logically in that space is a preposition. If you remember that sentence, and memorize the few prepositions that do not fit into that sentence, you will become a preposition expert.*

(4.10A) All Objects Should Be Located! (Object of the Preposition)

Underline the prepositional phrase in each sentence. Then, on the line next to the sentence, write the word that the prepositional phrase modifies.

1. _____ He sat between Robert and Rania.

2. _____ Jillian fell during the race.

3. _____ They were aboard the ocean liner.

4. _____ The stray dog was headed for the playground.

5. _____ The vendor sold the drinks to my parents.

6. _____ Take this book with you.

7. _____ He jogged by himself yesterday.

8. _____ He moved the books into the closet.

9. _____ We found the crab net beneath the dock.

10. _____ Under the eave were those escaping the rain.

11. _____ Your sorrow will decrease over time.

12. _____ Were you near the shore that night?

13. _____ The singer's new CD is selling off the charts.

14. _____ They were laughing throughout the movie.

15. _____ We have not had any dessert since last Tuesday.

(4.11) Objective Case

Direct objects, indirect objects, and objects of the preposition are all in the **objective case** since they are used as objects:

I saw *Frank* in the coffee shop yesterday. (*Frank* is the direct object since *Frank* answers the question, "*Who* was seen in the coffee shop yesterday morning?")

We gave *Frank* a ride to the museum yesterday. (*Frank* is the indirect object since the ride was given to Frank.)

The ride was given to *Frank*. (*Frank* is the object of the preposition *to*.)

Note: *Frank* could be replaced by *him* in all three example sentences. In all instances, the objective case word is used. The singular personal pronouns used in the objective case are *me, you, him, her,* and *it*. The plural personal pronouns used in the objective case are *us, you,* and *them*.

Mike took *her* to the dance last night. **(direct object)**

Will Olivia accompany *us* tomorrow night? **(direct object)**

The driver led *him* and *her* to the amusement park. **(compound direct objects)**

Louie gave *him* a quick tour of the facilities. **(indirect object)**

My choral director taught *me* a valuable lesson yesterday. **(indirect object)**

Mrs. Schuler gave *them* and *him* some advice. **(compound indirect objects)**

The police officers entered after *them*. **(object of the preposition)**

Those children formed a circle around *us*. **(object of the preposition)**

The programs were dedicated to *him* and *her*. **(compound objects of the preposition)**

📖 **WRITING TIP** *In the case of compound direct objects, compound indirect objects, and compound objects of the preposition, make sure that both of the objects are in the objective case. Write, "The teacher congratulated her and me [not her and I as the compound direct objects]." Write, "The ball was thrown to her and me [not her and I as the compound objects of the preposition]." Write, "Lola presented her and him [not her and he as compound indirect objects] with a gift."*

© 2007 by John Wiley & Sons, Inc.

Name _____ Date _____ Period _____

(4.11A) The Letter A (Objective Case Review)

Tell whether the underlined word is a direct object (DO), an indirect object (IO), or the object of the preposition (OP) by writing the corresponding letters (DO, IO, or OP) on the line next to the sentence. Then write the two letters found after each sentence on their appropriate line (direct object, indirect object, object of the preposition) below the list. If your answers are correct, you will spell out six words whose only vowel is the letter A.

1. _____ The artist signed her painting at last night's ceremony. **(ll)**

2. _____ We objected to our town's new curfew. **(ca)**

3. _____ In the meantime, you can sit here. **(na)**

4. _____ Connie helped me. **(am)**

5. _____ The club officers presented Laura with a new car. **(al)**

6. _____ The CEO offered her a new employment position. **(as)**

7. _____ My father gave my mother a surprise birthday party. **(ka)**

8. _____ Henry found the rackets in the car trunk. **(ap)**

9. _____ We could hardly wait for the new season. **(da)**

10. _____ Isabella bought her sister a new necklace. **(ga)**

11. _____ The pitcher threw the ball very quickly. **(an)**

12. _____ This new system perplexes me. **(da)**

13. _____ Yesterday we ran eight laps around the track. **(bl)**

14. _____ Coach showed our players the other team's defensive strategies. **(la)**

15. _____ They had not expected questions about that issue. **(ah)**

Direct object letters: _____

Indirect object letters: _____

Object of the preposition letters: _____

(4.12) Possessive Case

A **possessive case** word shows ownership. If the possessive case word is a noun, it is used with an apostrophe. In the sentence, "The *dog's* paw was sore," the word *dog's* is possessive since it shows ownership.

A possessive case word can also be a pronoun. In the sentence, "We noticed that *her* paw was hurt," the word *her* is possessive since it shows ownership of the paw. Possessive case pronouns do not need apostrophes.

These are singular personal possessive pronouns: *my, mine, your, yours, his, her, hers,* and *its.*

These are plural personal possessive pronouns: *our, ours, your, yours, their,* and *theirs.*

The italicized words in the following sentences are possessive since they show ownership:

> *Michelle's* car is brand new.
>
> Have you found *her* purse?
>
> Is this bracelet *yours*?
>
> The flag in *our* yard has lost *its* color.
>
> Is that piece of cake *mine*?
>
> *My* idea is not as complex as *theirs*.
>
> *His* motorcycle is parked in my *neighbor's* garage.

Fill in each blank with a possessive word. The possessive word can be a noun or a pronoun.

_____ friend met _____ sister at _____ party.

_____ spending that much money disturbed _____ father and mother.

_____ cat will be staying at _____ house for the week.

_____ essay is better than _____.

🖎 **WRITING TIP** *Remember that possessive pronouns do not use apostrophes. Words such as* his, hers, theirs, its, yours, *and* ours *do not require apostrophes.*

Name _____ Date _____ Period _____

(4.12A) Three in a Row (Possessive Case)

Can you find the three groups of three possessive words in a row? Circle each of these groups. Then, on the lines provided, write nine sentences using each of the circled possessive words in its own sentence. (Use the back of this sheet if you need more space.)

his _____

them _____

your _____

mine _____

ours _____

test _____

quarter's _____

friendly _____

one's _____

boxes' _____

boxes _____

my _____

his _____

hers _____

duties _____

ours _____

theirs _____

who's _____

whose _____

anyone's _____

girls' _____

forever _____

sheep _____

donkey's _____

donkeys _____

(4.13) Who Versus Whom

- **Who** and **whoever** are nominative (noun) case pronouns that are used as subjects and predicate nominatives.

- **Whom** and **whomever** are objective (object) case words that are used as direct objects, indirect objects, and objects of the preposition.

When a sentence has only one clause, knowing when to use *who* or *whoever* OR *whom* or *whomever* is not as complex as when a sentence has a subordinate clause. In the latter instance, first identify the main clause. Then reword the subordinate clause to see whether *who* or *whom* is the appropriate word.

Here is a rather simple sentence: "_____ is the lead singer in that group?" Answer the question. Lyle [or He] is the lead singer in the group. *He* is a nominative word. Therefore replace *He* with *Who*.

Here is a more complex sentence: "The man, _____ is the lead singer in the group, is humble." The main clause is "The man is humble." The subordinate clause is "_____ is the lead singer in the group." Fill in the blank. "*Lyle* is the lead singer in the group." *Lyle*, a nominative case word, must be replaced by a nominative case word such as *He*. So the original sentence can now read, "The man, *who* is the lead singer in the group, is humble."

Here are some more examples:

"*Who* signed your hall pass [subject]?" Answer the question: *He* (or *she*) signed your hall pass.

"The officer, *who* is also a district manager, is her neighbor [subject]." Think: He (or She) is also a district manager.

"Your first choice is *who* [predicate nominative]"? First, answer the question. Then think: He (or She) is my first choice.

"LeeAnne is the student *whom* I introduced to you at lunch yesterday." "LeeAnne is the student" is the main clause. *Whom* is the direct object of the subordinate clause that can be reworded to read, "I introduced *her* to you at lunch yesterday. Thus, *her* is the direct object of the verb *introduced*, and the word *whom* is the appropriate choice.

Name _____ Date _____ Period _____

(4.13) Who Versus Whom *(Continued)*

"The manager gave *whomever* he selected a new pass to the museum [indirect object]." "Whomever he selected" is a subordinate clause that answers the question "to whom" and can be replaced by *him* (or *her*). Thus, the revised sentence can be thought of as, "The manager gave him [or her] a new pass to the museum."

"Sherry is the director from *whom* I learned the most about acting [object of the preposition]." The word *from* is a preposition. The word that is the object of the preposition must be an objective case word. The main clause is "Sherry is the director." The subordinate clause can be thought of as "I learned the most about acting from her." *Whom* replaces *her*. Both are objective case words.

Reminder: *Who* and *whoever* are used to replace *he* and *she*. *Whom* and *whomever* are used to replace *him* and *her*. If the sentence is a question, answer it by inserting either *he* (or *she*) or *him* (or *her*). Here are two examples of this suggestion:

Who is your best friend? (*She* or *He* can replace *Who.*)

Whom will you invite to the anniversary party? (*Him* or *Her* can replace *Whom.*)

Fill in each blank with *who* or *whom:*

_____ will be your date to the prom?

The captain is the man _____ scored the most points.

That driver _____ you passed just now was going very slowly.

_____ will they select for the new position?

 WRITING TIP *The who-versus-whom dilemma troubles many writers. If you remember that* who *replaces* he *or* she *and* whom *replaces* him *or* her, *you should have no problem.*

(4.13A) Ten Times (Who Versus Whom)

Circle the correct word in each sentence. Then write that word on the line next to the sentence's number. Here is a hint: One of the words, *who* or *whom*, is the correct answer for ten of these fifteen sentences.

1. I think I remember (who, whom) she is now.

2. The pilot (who, whom) I spoke to this morning will retire next September.

3. Most of us welcomed back Teddy, (who, whom) returned from Europe last night.

4. One passenger (who, whom) I enjoyed talking with is the man in the blue suit.

5. They did not realize (who, whom) could be walking behind us.

6. These clever cartoonists, (who, whom) have won several awards, will be answering questions at tonight's session.

7. Voters (who, whom) stood in line for hours to vote should be thanked by the politicians.

8. The flight attendant is a woman (who, whom) lives in my village.

9. Unfortunately, very few people understand (who, whom) he really is underneath his facade.

10. Please address the issue with Greg, (who, whom) you know well.

11. She is truly a professor (who, whom) the students admire.

12. Can you figure out (who, whom) arranged your surprise party?

13. She is the type of point guard (who, whom) can change the course of a basketball game with little difficulty.

14. Her older cousins, to (who, whom) you have written e-mails before, will consult with you on this important topic.

15. Very few of the candidates (who, whom) are running for the state legislature are experienced in government.

Name _____ Date _____ Period _____

(4.14) Comparisons of Modifiers

Modifiers have three degrees: *positive, comparative,* and *superlative.* These degrees indicate the comparison differences in modifiers. The *positive* degree makes no comparison. It is simply a statement of fact. The *comparative* degree compares two people, places, or things. The *superlative* degree compares more than two people, places, or things. A student can be *tall* (positive degree). A student can be *taller* (comparative degree). A student can be *tallest* (superlative degree).

Here are a few basic rules for forming modifiers:

1. One-syllable modifiers form the *comparative* degree by adding *-er* and the *superlative* degree by adding *-est.* Examples: *kind* (positive degree), *kinder* (comparative degree), *kindest* (superlative degree).

2. Two-syllable modifiers form the *comparative* degree by adding *-er* or *more* or *less* and *-est* or *most* or *least* to form the *superlative* degree. Examples: *simple* (positive degree); *simpler* (comparative degree), *simplest* (superlative degree); *bashful* (positive degree), *more* (or *less*) *bashful* (comparative degree), *most* (or *least*) *bashful* (superlative degree).

3. Use *more* and *most* or *less* and *least* with adverbs that end with *-ly.* Examples: *slowly* (positive degree), *more slowly* or *less slowly* (comparative degree), *most slowly* or *least slowly* (superlative degree).

4. Use *more* and *most* or *less* and *least* with adjectives that have more than two syllables. Examples: *fantastic* (positive degree), *more* (or *less*) *fantastic* (comparative degree), *most* (or *least*) *fantastic* (superlative degree); *exciting* (positive degree), *more* (or *less*) *exciting* (comparative degree), *most* (or *least*) *exciting* (superlative degree).

5. If you are not sure if a word should use *-er* or *more* (or *less*) to form the comparative degree or *-est* or *most* (or *least*) to form the superlative degree, consult a dictionary. Also, use your ear to hear if the sound of your proposed comparison sounds correct. Thus, you would not say *peacefuler* or *peacefulest.* Instead, you would use *more peaceful* and *most peaceful.* The dictionary and your ear will tell you so!

The following are some irregular comparisons. They do not fit any of the above rules!

Positive Degree	Comparative Degree	Superlative Degree
little	less	least
many, much	more	most
bad, badly, ill	worse	worst
good, well	better	best

🖎 **WRITING TIP** *Know these few rules to clarify what is a very confusing topic for many. When in doubt, consult a dictionary.*

Half and Half (Comparisons of Modifiers)

Half of the following sentences use modifiers correctly, and half contain modifiers that are used incorrectly. Circle the number of each sentence that uses modifiers correctly, and write the three-letter code on the line next to the number. Then cross out the number of each sentence that uses modifiers incorrectly and write the three-letter code on the line next to the (crossed-out) number. Write the three-letter codes for the sentences that use the modifiers correctly on line A at the end of this activity. Then write the four words that these letters spell out on line B. Next, write the three-letter codes for the sentences that use the modifiers incorrectly on line C. Write the four words that these letters spell out on line D. Finally, on a separate sheet of paper, correct the incorrect modifier sentence in each sentence.

1. _____ The package is <u>heavier</u> than the others. **(eer)**

2. _____ These drawings are <u>worser</u> than the ones I drew last term. **(bub)**

3. _____ This new model is <u>prettier</u> than last year's contestants. **(iea)**

4. _____ She is the <u>most pleasantest</u> speaker on the debate team. **(ble)**

5. _____ We feel that you handled the situation <u>most intelligently.</u> **(ard)**

6. _____ Your drawing is the <u>neatest</u>, Jacqueline. **(var)**

7. _____ When you think of our town's two high schools, you must admit that this one is the <u>better</u> of the two. **(klo)**

8. _____ Yesterday was the <u>mostest</u> fun that I have ever had. **(gig)**

9. _____ Unfortunately, I am the <u>slower</u> of the three runners. **(gle)**

10. _____ The strong lifeguard held the struggling swimmer's arm <u>more tighter.</u> **(dli)**

11. _____ Kayaking is the <u>best</u> way to exercise and enjoy the beauty of nature. **(oph)**

12. _____ Louise is <u>more wiser</u> than her older sister. **(lli)**

13. _____ This road is the <u>bumpiest</u> of the two in this valley. **(esr)**

14. _____ Sid wrote <u>more quickly</u> than his sister did during the test. **(ole)**

15. _____ Our campgrounds were <u>more secluded</u> than yours. **(inv)**

16. _____ Of all the youngsters, Maura approached the contest <u>most eagerliest.</u> **(ear)**

17. _____ Let us find the answer <u>more quicklier.</u> **(ran)**

18. _____ Is Alaska the <u>largest</u> of the fifty states? **(isi)**

19. _____ She visited her grandmother <u>more oftener</u> than her brother had. **(ged)**

20. _____ My friend held the rope <u>more firmly</u> than her brother. **(ble)**

Half and Half (Comparisons of Modifiers) (Continued)

A. The letters from the sentences that use modifiers correctly:

   _____

B. These letters spell out these four words: _____, _____,

   _____, and _____.

C. The letters from the sentences that use modifiers incorrectly:

   _____

D. These letters spell out these four words: _____, _____,

   _____, and _____.

4.15 Dangling and Misplaced Modifiers

Modifiers help describe a word. Prepositional phrases, adjective clauses, participle phrases, and infinitive phrases are all modifiers. They should be placed as close as possible to the words that they describe within a sentence. Phrases or clauses that are incorrectly placed within a sentence are called *misplaced* phrases. Phrases that are not describing anything are called *dangling* modifiers. You can eliminate these problems by placing the phrases in the correct position.

Wrong: Jumping into the net, the crowd saw the trapeze artist. (This is a misplaced participle phrase since the crowd did not jump into the net; the trapeze artist did.)

Correct: The crowd saw the trapeze artist jumping into the net.

Wrong: Whirring in the basement, the man heard the fan. (This is a misplaced participle phrase because the man was not whirring in the basement; the fan was whirring in the basement.)

Correct: The man heard the fan whirring in the basement.

Wrong: Robert Clemens concocts interesting plots who is a mystery writer. (This is a misplaced adjective clause because Robert Clemens, and not the plots, is the mystery writer.)

Correct: Robert Clemens, who is a mystery writer, concocts interesting plots.

Wrong: To win the state lottery, a ticket must be purchased. (dangling infinitive phrase)

Correct: To win the state lottery, the contestant must purchase a ticket.

Wrong: Lifting the stack of books from her desk, her nose itched. (This is a dangling participle phrase problem since her nose cannot possibly lift the stack of books from her desk. Thus, the participial phrase modifies nothing.)

Correct: Her nose itched while Dana lifted the stack of books from her desk.

(4.15) Dangling and Misplaced Modifiers *(Continued)*

How would you correct each of these four sentences? Add any words that you think complete your thought. Write your answers on the lines provided.

Running from the scary scene, Mary's foot hurt.

_____

_____

_____

To run in that marathon, an application must be filled out.

_____

_____

_____

Shopping in the hardware store, the hammer was purchased by the older man.

_____

_____

_____

The fish was fried by the man on the grill.

_____

_____

_____

WRITING TIP *Make sure that your modifiers make sense. Read the sentence aloud. Visualize the sentence. Check to see that the modifier appears close to the noun or pronoun that it is modifying. The examples in this lesson well illustrate this dilemma of dangling and misplaced modifiers.*

(4.15A) Only Five (Dangling and Misplaced Modifiers)

Only five of the following sentences contain modifiers that are used correctly. Place a C on the line next to those five sentences. For the remaining ten sentences that use modifiers incorrectly, correct those sentences on a separate sheet of paper. Visualize each sentence, and say it aloud to help you.

1. _____ Walking to the pitcher's mound, the grass was kicked by the coach.

2. _____ Attached to the flagpole, Patty saw the beautiful new state flag.

3. _____ Seeing the boats pass, the fisherman waved to those on the decks.

4. _____ Found mangy, panting, and hungry on the curb, the police officer handed the dog to its proper owner.

5. _____ Henrietta used the cell phone given to her by her parents.

6. _____ Licking his hind leg, the owner washed his cat.

7. _____ After washing the dishes, the doorbell rang three times.

8. _____ Watching television in the den, Dad fell asleep within an hour.

9. _____ Peeking into the closet, my birthday presents were seen by me.

10. _____ Having comfortable seats and plenty of legroom, I enjoyed the treat of sitting in the first-class section.

11. _____ Rejuvenated by the workout, the gymnast felt satisfied with herself.

12. _____ After dirt-biking all day over this challenging course, my muscles were sore.

13. _____ Looking down between the clouds, the Grand Canyon was seen by the pilot.

14. _____ Before going to sleep, I sorted out all my camping gear into three piles.

15. _____ After lifting the heavy package, it was placed down on the platform by Richie.

Usage Words

You can avoid some writing difficulties by knowing how and when to use the following italicized words. Study their usage, and use them as they should be used in your future writings.

1. *beside:* next to

   We walked *beside* one another to the beach.

2. *besides:* in addition to

   Besides Maine, is there another state whose name is monosyllabic?

3. *anywhere:* in, at, or to any place

   Can I find peace *anywhere* in this house?

4. *anywheres:* There is no such word as *anywheres.*

5. *as:* a word that starts a subordinate clause; (adverb) equally; (conjunction) in the same manner; (preposition) in the role, or function

   Justin sang *as* the band accompanied him.

   The magician is just *as* good on this smaller stage.

   This woman poses *as* one who knows more than she does.

   Jill runs as fast *as* lightning.

6. *like:* a word that starts a prepositional phrase

   Geraldine walks *like* her aunt.

7. *farther:* used to designate a physical distance

   Today I walked *farther* than I had last week.

8. *further:* "additional"

   Listen for *further* instructions.

9. *can:* able to

   Ollie *can* lift those heavy weights.

10. *may:* allowed to

    May I please be excused from the table?

11. *adverse:* opposed; moving or working in an opposite direction

    We encountered *adverse* weather conditions on our ocean cruise.

4.16 Usage Words *(Continued)*

12. *averse:* "reluctant" or "not willing"

    We are *averse* to going way out on the ocean again.

13. *cent:* 1/100th of a dollar

    Gerry found one *cent* on the floor.

14. *sent:* past tense of the verb "to send"

    Reggie *sent* my sister some flowers.

15. *scent:* the smell of something or someone

    The dog was able to pick up the burglar's *scent* right away.

16. *continuous:* something that keeps happening without interruption

    They played *continuous* holiday music for more than a month on my dad's favorite radio station.

17. *continual:* that which happens again and again

    His *continual* misbehavior in class was enough to have his teacher send him to the principal's office.

18. *emigrate from:* "to leave one country to live in another country"

    My relative *emigrated* from Bohemia.

19. *immigrate to:* "to come to a new country or area"

    Did your family *immigrate* to America at the turn of the twentieth century?

20. *famous:* "well known"

    Celine Dion is a *famous* singer.

21. *notorious:* "famous but in a bad way"

    The bank robbers had become *notorious* because of their many heists.

22. *vary:* a verb that means "to change"

    To prevent boredom, I *vary* my exercise program.

23. *very:* an adjective that means "complete"

    This is the *very* thing that I was telling you!

    As an adverb, *very* means "extremely."

    The triathlete was *very* tired after his excruciating workout.

(4.16) **Usage Words** *(Continued)*

24. *right:* the opposite of wrong; the opposite of left; a power; correct or proper

    You have made the *right* decision.

    Please make a *right* turn at the next corner.

    I have a *right* to my own opinion.

    You know that this is the *right* thing to do, Celeste.

25. *write:* "to record in print"

    May I *write* down all of these fantastic quotations, Mark?

26. *rite:* a ceremony

    Obtaining one's driving license is a *rite* of passage in our country.

27. *wright:* a worker

    My uncle earns his living as a *playwright* in New York City.

28. *sight:* the "act of seeing" or "something that is seen"

    The Grand Canyon is a memorable and awesome *sight*.

29. *cite:* to quote

    The lawyer chose to *cite* a former court decision to the jury members.

30. *site:* the position or location of a building or town

    This is the former *site* of the baseball stadium.

31. *vane:* the instrument that indicates wind direction

    Have you installed the latest *vane* on the barn roof?

32. *vain:* not amounting to anything; full of oneself

    Though Robin tried her hardest, her efforts were in *vain,* for the water still flooded the basement.

    The guy was so *vain* that he thought he was even more handsome than the best looking Greek god.

33. *vein:* blood vessel

    Edward was so angry that it looked as if his *vein* was going to pop.

34. *its:* the possessive form of the pronoun *it*

    Going out to parties has lost *its* appeal for my friends and me.

(4.16) Usage Words *(Continued)*

35. *it's:* a contraction for *it* plus *is*

    It's starting to rain.

36. *lend:* to allow someone else to use what is yours

    Harry wanted to *lend* his best ice skates to his cousin, Gary.

37. *borrow:* to receive for temporary use

    Gary wanted to *borrow* ice skates from his cousin Harry.

38. *personal:* private

    This is my *personal* business that nobody else needs to know.

39. *personnel:* workers at a job

    The *personnel* at our local department store are congenial employees.

40. *pour:* to cause a flow

    Can you please *pour* the baby some milk?

41. *poor:* needy

    The *poor* soil did not allow plants to grow.

    The *poor* people of Paris revolted in 1789.

42. *pore:* a tiny opening in the skin

    Sweat seeped out of the athlete's *pores* during the marathon event.

43. *quote:* to repeat or cite

    May I *quote* your direct words as evidence, Charles?

44. *quotation:* something that is quoted

    Here are some of Ben Franklin's most practical *quotations*.

45. *set:* to put in place

    Are the arrangements for Helen's going-away party all *set*?

46. *sit:* to rest in a seated position

    Please *sit* down here, Maura.

47. *than:* to compare two or more people, places, or things

    Is your coach taller *than* you?

48. *then:* referring to time

    Then we read the next three chapters of *A Tale of Two Cities*.

(4.16) Usage Words *(Continued)*

49. *imply:* to suggest indirectly

    Did you *imply* that Diana is the one who lost your briefcase?

50. *infer:* to draw a conclusion from facts

    I did not *infer* that Diana lost your briefcase.

51. *unless:* in any other case than (subordinating conjunction that begins a subordinate clause)

    Unless you achieve the minimum score, you cannot advance in the tournament.

52. *without:* free from; not with (preposition that begins a prepositional phrase)

    They practiced *without* pain.

    Tiwana was wearing an outfit *without* jewelry.

53. *which:* pronoun that refers to things only

    The house, *which* my uncle bought recently, is in the next town.

54. *who:* relative pronoun that refers to people only

    The president *who* was reelected is ecstatic tonight.

55. *that:* pronoun that refers to both people and things

    Lucy is the type of leader that we need.

    This motorcycle is the one *that* I talked to you about yesterday.

56. *have:* a helping verb

    Hermie could *have* drawn that picture last week.

57. *of:* a preposition that is never used as part of a verb phrase

58. *aid:* to help (as a verb); help (as a noun)

    Other countries came to *aid* the country that had been devastated by the tsunami.

    Sy came to the *aid* of the drowning swimmer in time to bring him to safety.

59. *aide:* one who helps another

    My sister works as a nurse's *aide* in the local hospital.

60. *learn:* to acquire knowledge

    Can you *learn* that much about motors in one month?

61. *teach:* to instruct

    I would like to *teach* you how to fix this car's leak.

(4.16) Usage Words *(Continued)*

62. *doesn't:* contraction meaning "does not"

    The temperamental chef *doesn't* like to be told what to do.

63. *don't:* contraction meaning "do not"

    The chef's bosses also *don't* like being told what to do. (Avoid using contractions in formal writing.)

64. *discover:* to be the first to find

    Did Christopher Columbus *discover* America?

65. *invent:* to think out and produce

    Did Thomas Edison *invent* the light bulb?

66. *healthy:* pertaining to good health

    My trim and strong sister-in-law has always eaten a *healthy* diet.

67. *healthful:* that which brings good health

    My sister-in-law has always participated in many *healthful* activities.

68. *bust:* use "burst" instead of "busted"

    The pipe *burst* during the winter cold spell.

69. *busted:* use "broke" instead of "busted"

    Carlos *broke* his arm during the wrestling match.

70. *good:* an adjective

    Justina is a *good* card player.

71. *well:* an adverb

    Justina plays cards *well.*

72. *fewer:* used with plural words; answers the question, *"How many"*

    There are *fewer* opportunities for this kind of plan.

73. *less:* used with singular words; answers the question, *"How much"*

    This team has *less* spirit than last year's squad.

74. *affect:* a verb meaning "to influence"

    How will your absence *affect* your class participation grade?

(4.16) Usage Words *(Continued)*

75. *effect:* a noun meaning "result"; a verb meaning "to accomplish" or "to produce"

   What *effect* did your absences have on your class participation grade?

   To *effect* change, all of the political party members must work hard and have patience.

76. *respectfully:* politely

   The police officer *respectfully* asked us to move on to the curb so the runners could pass by more easily.

77. *respectively:* in precisely the order given

   I would like to refer to you three as Moe, Larry, and Curly, *respectively.*

78. *accept:* a verb that means "to receive willingly"

   Will you *accept* this apology from me?

79. *except:* a preposition that means "but" or "other than"

   All of the stock car drivers participated *except* Darrell.

80. *explicit:* fully and clearly expressed or demonstrated

   Pushkala thought that she had given the group members *explicit* directions on how to get to her house.

81. *implicit:* implied, rather than expressly stated

   Without Hank's being obvious, his *implicit* words told us what he wanted us to do at that time in the game.

82. *slow:* an adjective that means the "opposite of fast"

   You are not a *slow* learner!

83. *slowly:* an adverb meaning "the opposite of quickly"

   Unfortunately, we completed the task much more *slowly* than the other groups.

84. *among:* a preposition used to refer to more than two people, places, or things

   I divided the candy *among* the four youngsters.

85. *between:* a preposition used to refer to two people, places, or things

   Just *between* the two of us, this restaurant could use some improvement.

86. *likely:* probably or apparently destined to happen

   It is quite *likely* that you will be chosen for the debate team.

(4.16) Usage Words *(Continued)*

87. *liable:* legally responsible

    Since you broke this window, you are *liable* for the damages.

88. *disinterested:* impartial; showing no favoritism

    A judge should always be *disinterested* and look at only the facts of a case.

89. *uninterested:* not interested

    I was *uninterested* when Teddy was talking about his accomplishments.

90. *take:* to move something away from the speaker

    Please *take* that noisy toy into the other room immediately.

91. *bring:* to move something toward the speaker

    Please *bring* that pitcher of water to me, Raymond.

92. *leave:* to depart; to let stay or be

    I must *leave* in an hour or so.

    Leave that book here.

93. *let:* to allow

    Let me help you with that heavy package, Marion.

94. *in:* within a particular place

    I am studying *in* my room right now.

95. *into:* indicates the movement from one specific area to another specific area

    I am now walking from my brother's room *into* my room.

96. *red:* a color

    Jason loves to color with his *red* crayon.

97. *read:* the past and past participle of the verb *read*

    I *read* that article today.

🖎 **WRITING TIP** *Pay attention to how published writers use these words in context. Be wise, and imitate these skilled writers. In addition, your computer's spell-check program will not always detect if you use these words incorrectly. Thus, depend on yourself to know how these words are spelled and used. Be your own best resource!*

(4.16A) Be Upbeat! (Usage Words)

Circle the correct word in each sentence. Then, on the line next to the sentence, write the word's corresponding two-letter code that appears above the word. Finally, write the two-letter code answers consecutively on the lines below the last question. If your answers are correct, they will spell out a proverb.

                        as   pl

1. _____ I wanted to sit (beside, besides) my best friend at that table.

                                         mi   ac

2. _____ We could not find the missing cat (anywhere, anywheres).

                    el le

3. _____ Luke walks (as, like) his older brother.

                             is   fo

4. _____ Our school year is longer (than, then) yours.

                                                 ju   ne

5. _____ The hotel manager will not allow us to enter (unless, without) we show her our key.

                          ts   st

6. _____ Here is the woman (which, who) won the town's tennis championship.

                             af ek

7. _____ Do you think that he could (have, of) landed that airplane more skillfully?

                  or   ro

8. _____ Can you (learn, teach) us how to repair the burner?

                  wn   er

9. _____ This car (doesn't, don't) have great acceleration, so be very cautious when you drive it.

                           te   tu

10. _____ Is he the scientist who (discovered, invented) the light bulb?

(4.16A) Be Upbeat! (Usage Words) *(Continued)*

rn   io

11. _____ Last winter, two of the stadium's large pipes (burst, busted) due to the frigid weather.

ed   hi

12. _____ Lucinda, a professional athlete, is a very (good, well) basketball player.

up   et

13. _____ We have (fewer, less) assistant principals in our school this year.

si   gh

14. _____ How will this injury (affect, effect) your contract?

ed   de

15. _____ All of the swimmers (accept, except) the tall boy qualified for the state championships.

do   oo

16. _____ The director divided up the jobs (among, between) the four workers.

rd   wn

17. _____ (Leave, Let) me complete this math problem by myself please.

The thirty-four letters spell out this proverb: _____

_____

_____

More Usage Words

Match each word in Group One with its definition in Group Two by writing the correct number in its box in the magic square. If your answers are correct, each row, each column, and each diagonal will add up to the same number.

Group One

A. leave
B. invent
C. let
D. except
E. than
F. affect
G. between
H. effect
I. among
J. then
K. learn
L. accept
M. besides
N. teach
O. discover
P. beside

Group Two

1. to influence
2. a preposition used to refer to more than two people, places, or things
3. to be the first to find
4. a preposition and a conjunction meaning "with the exception of" or "yet"
5. in addition to
6. to think out and produce
7. the result; to bring about change
8. to acquire knowledge
9. to allow
10. next to
11. referring to time
12. a conjunction and preposition that introduces the second element in a comparison
13. a verb meaning the opposite of "to reject"
14. a preposition used to refer to two people, places, or things
15. to depart
16. to instruct

A =	B =	C =	D =
E =	F =	G =	H =
I =	J =	K =	L =
M =	N =	O =	P =

(4.16C) Knowing When to Use What (Usage Words)

On the lines provided, write a sentence for each word in each pair below. Your sentences should clearly display the difference between the two words, which are often confused, in each pair.

1. anywhere, anywheres

_____

_____

_____

_____

2. who, whom

_____

_____

_____

_____

3. affect, effect

_____

_____

_____

_____

4. unless, without

_____

_____

_____

_____

5. fewer, less

_____

_____

_____

_____

(4.16C) Knowing When to Use What (Usage Words) *(Continued)*

6. **beside, besides**

   _____

   _____

   _____

   _____

7. **learn, teach**

   _____

   _____

   _____

   _____

8. **among, between**

   _____

   _____

   _____

   _____

9. **accept, except**

   _____

   _____

   _____

   _____

10. **leave, let**

   _____

   _____

   _____

   _____

(4.17) Words Often Confused (Part One)

Do you know the difference between *board* and *bored*? These words are just two of the confusing words that you should know. Study the spellings, pronunciations, and definitions of these words, and you will be *all ready* to *advise* others about these words.

advice: opinion given; counsel

   What is your *advice* to solve this problem, Hillary?

advise: to give advice or counsel

   I would *advise* you to seek an attorney's guidance on this difficult issue.

all ready: everyone is ready

   Are they *all ready* to listen to the joke?

already: by or before the given time; even now or even then

   When she entered the restaurant, her friends had *already* started their meals.

   Milton is *already* taking his belongings to go home.

affect: to influence (verb)

   How will the judge's decision *affect* our school's budget?

effect: the result or consequence (noun); to bring about change (verb)

   The *effect* of this decision will not be felt for a few years.

   These new politicians plan to *effect* change immediately.

all together: everyone in the same place

   We were *all together* waiting for the important announcement.

altogether: totally; completely

   The town administrators were *altogether* unhappy that they had to raise taxes.

board: piece of wood; a group; meal served at a college or camp

   The carpenter had to cut the *board* twice.

   We had to ask permission of the town *board*.

   Many of the college dormitory students did not enjoy the tasteless *board* served each Sunday night.

bored: not enthused; made tiresome or weary (verb); made a hole in (verb)

   Jack was *bored* during the speech and almost fell asleep.

   His stories *bored* everyone in the room.

   The contractor *bored* a hole in the dining room wall.

(4.17) Words Often Confused (Part One) *(Continued)*

brake: a stopping device

Luckily, he pushed down on the car's *brake* and avoided the accident.

break: to smash, shatter, sever (verb); rest or respite (noun)

Did you break that *plate,* Toshio?

Let's take a *break* from this boring task.

capital: city (noun); money (noun); that can be punished by death; most important

Des Moines is the *capital* of Iowa.

Can you raise the *capital* to build that large office?

Are you in favor of *capital* punishment?

The *capital* reason we were called together is for this important announcement.

capitol: building; statehouse (noun)

Can you locate the *capitol* on this street?

choose: to select

Will you *choose* something from this menu now?

chose: past tense of "to choose"

You *chose* the hamburger special the last time we ate here.

coarse: not refined; harsh

His *coarse* comments embarrassed all who heard those words.

course: a path; onward movement; part of an expression

Did you follow this *course* through the woods?

We have made some fantastic progress over the *course* of history.

Of *course,* try my racket, Perry.

 WRITING TIP *Do not allow any of these words to throw you off* course! Choose *the right word for the right* effect! *Consult your dictionary when necessary.*

(4.17A) Add Up the Points (Words Often Confused—Part One)

Each of the words in the box should be inserted into either Group One, Group Two, or Group Three only once. All of the boxed words will be used. Each word has the point value of its number. Thus, *advice* is worth 1 point, *advise* is worth 2 points, and so forth. After you have inserted the words into each group, count up the point value of the five words in that group. Each group's total is 40. So if the total of each group is 40 points, you have mastered this activity!

1. advice
2. advise
3. all ready
4. already
5. affect
6. effect
7. all together
8. altogether
9. board
10. bored
11. brake
12. break
13. capital
14. capitol
15. choose

Add Up the Points (Words Often Confused—Part One) (Continued)

Group One

A. Because we had worked for several hours in a row and needed a rest, the supervisor told us to take a _____.

B. Since we had _____ completed the project with time to spare, we took a look at the new project.

C. With so many options to _____ from, I requested more time to make my final decision.

D. We seek the _____ of John Miller because of his wisdom and decision-making abilities.

E. My friends were _____ unhappy with Reggie's behavior at the dance last weekend.

Group Two

F. The most devastating _____ of these conflicts will be felt in a short time.

G. The humdrum routine of her job made her easily _____ on a daily basis.

H. The building in which the state legislature meets is called the
_____.

I. When we were _____ to leave for the hiking trip, the rain began to fall.

J. Because we were _____ when the news was announced, we were able to share our reactions immediately.

Group Three

K. The carpenter measured the _____ twice before she made the cut.

L. Phoenix is the _____ city of Arizona.

M. I would _____ against attempting that foolish jump from the garage roof.

N. Will this low math test grade really _____ your quarter's grade?

O. The driver stepped down on the _____ instead of the accelerator of the automobile.

Words Often Confused (Part Two)

Can a *consul* give a *compliment* to a *counselor* so that no one else will *hear* what he has been *led* to say? These five italicized words, among those words that are often confused, appear in this activity. Memorize the spellings, pronunciations, and meanings of these words, which are often confused. Whenever possible, use these words in your writings.

compliment: (noun) a formal act of courtesy; (verb) to offer praise

> The director gave Marcia a *compliment* on her role as Juliet.

> Please *compliment* the chef on this delicious swordfish.

complement: (verb) to complete or bring to perfection; (noun) that which completes or brings to perfection

> Do you think that this bracelet will *complement* my outfit?

> This bracelet is a fitting *complement* to your outfit.

consul: a foreign country's representative

> My grandfather introduced me to Spain's *consul* at last night's banquet.

council: a group that works toward a common goal

> Will you run for a seat on the student *council* this year, Matthew?

councilor: a member of a council

> Jenny Jenkins is a *councilor* on our town's planning committee.

counsel: (noun) advice; (verb) to give advice

> The psychologist always offers sage *counsel*.

> She will often *counsel* me on how to get along better with my peers.

counselor: a person who counsels; an adviser (or advisor)

> My guidance *counselor*, Ms. Kennedy, has helped me to select some interesting classes.

desert: (verb, dĭ-ˊzərt) to leave; (noun, ˊde-zərt) a dry region

> Did the others *desert* you at that crucial moment?

> The camels are accustomed to travel in the *desert*.

dessert: the final course of a meal

> Would you like ice cream and pie for *dessert*?

(4.18) Words Often Confused (Part Two) *(Continued)*

formally: in a dignified manner

They all dressed *formally* for the banquet.

formerly: in the past

Rasheed had *formerly* been the library's director.

hear: to perceive with the ears

Did you *hear* what she just said?

here: this place

I'm going to stay *here* and wait for them to come back.

its: personal pronoun

The game has lost *its* excitement.

it's: contraction for *it* plus *is*

It's time to go home, Pedro.

lead: graphite (´led); to go first (´lēd); a distance ahead (´lēd)

The pencil's *lead* has run out.

Will you *lead* the class in song, Yacub?

The base runner took her *lead* and watched the pitcher's motion.

led: past tense of "to lead"

The singer *led* her group in song.

 WRITING TIP Its *is a possessive pronoun.* It's *is a contraction. Know the difference! Use the dictionary when the need arises.*

4.18A # Parade of Animals (Words Often Confused—Part Two)

If you correctly match the fifteen words in Column A with their definitions in Column B, you will spell out the names of six animals. First, write the two-letter answer from Column B on the line next to the appropriate number in Column A. Write the thirty consecutive letters on the lines below the final numbered item. If you are correct, the thirty letters will spell out the names of six animals.

Column A

1. _____ complement
2. _____ compliment
3. _____ consul
4. _____ council
5. _____ counsel
6. _____ desert
7. _____ dessert
8. _____ formally
9. _____ formerly
10. _____ hear
11. _____ here
12. _____ its
13. _____ it's
14. _____ lead
15. _____ led

Column B

ac—in a dignified way

am—the part of the meal following the main course

an—a group united for a specific task

ap—the representative of a foreign country

br—a flattering remark; to say something flattering

da—advice or to give advice

er—past tense of "to lead"

ga—to pick up through the ears

ig—a heavy metal; pencil's graphite

io—possessive of "it"

ll—to leave; a dry region

nt—*it* plus *is*

ou—previously; in the past

rl—this place

ze—something that completes or makes better; to complete or make better

The names of the six animals are _____, _____,

_____, _____, _____, and

_____.

(4.19) Words Often Confused (Part Three)

Can a belt be too *loose* or too *lose*? What is the difference between *moral* and *morale*? Is *piece* or *peace* the opposite of war? These questions can be answered using the information found in this activity. Words such as these are often confused because of their pronunciation or their closeness in spelling. Study the spelling, pronunciation, and meaning of these words. Use them in your writing when it is appropriate to do so.

piece: a fragment; a part

He found a *piece* of the cloth in the closet.

peace: the opposite of war

The protestors wanted *peace,* not war, in their country.

moral: lesson of conduct; the idea of right and wrong

The protestor felt that killing another person was not *moral.*

morale: spirit or mental condition

The team's *morale* was high after they soundly defeated their rivals in football.

loose: not tight

Because the bike rack was *loose,* both bicycles fell off.

lose: opposite of "to gain"

They thought that they would win, not *lose,* this match.

quiet: not loud

We should be *quiet* in the library.

quite: completely; to a high degree

The office manager was *quite* pleased with his team's performance.

principle: a rule of conduct; main fact; law

What is the scientific *principle* behind how a heavy object like a plane can lift off the ground?

principal: the leader of a school; the most important

Both the teachers and the students respected the *principal* for her courage in making difficult decisions.

This is the *principal* export of the country.

(4.19) Words Often Confused (Part Three) *(Continued)*

plain: not complex; a tract of land

It is *plain* to see that you are handsome.

The distance runners began to cross the *plain* during their training run.

plane: an airplane; a flat surface; a level; a tool

How does a *plane* move that quickly?

Humanity should operate on a high *plane* of civilization.

The shop teacher showed his students how to smooth wood with a *plane.*

shone: past tense of "to shine"

The sun has not *shone* in three days.

shown: past tense of "to show"

Have you *shown* your mom and dad your fabulous report card yet?

past: (noun) a time word meaning "of a former time"; (adjective) just gone by; (preposition) farther on than

The elderly woman loves to reminisce about the *past.*

His *past* performances indicate that he should do well here today.

We walked *past* the mansion.

passed: past tense of "to pass"

The three runners *passed* me during the race.

 WRITING TIP *A computer's spell-check program might not pick up if these confused words are used correctly. Be your own spell checker and know how these closely related but often confused words are different from each other. It is* quite plain *that a* principal piece *of your skill as a writer is to know these words!*

(4.19A) Shady Characters (Words Often Confused—Part Three)

Circle the word that is defined by the few words in each number. Then write the corresponding three-letter codes next to the question's number. Finally, write the three-letter codes consecutively on the lines beneath the last question to spell out the names of six shady characters.

1. _____ opposite of war

   (umb) peace   **(bro)** piece   **(car)** loose

2. _____ right and wrong issues; lesson of conduct

   (the) lose   **(rel)** moral   **(too)** morale

3. _____ opposite of loud

   (law) quiet   **(rom)** quite   **(sel)** principle

4. _____ past tense of shine

   (eep) shone   **(loo)** plain   **(ent)** shown

5. _____ flat surface; a level; a tool; an airplane

   (nor) principle   **(bel)** plain   **(ing)** plane

6. _____ rule of conduct

   (ane) principal   **(wil)** principle   **(sti)** moral

7. _____ past tense of "to pass"

   (bee) morale   **(urn)** past   **(low)** passed

8. _____ mental condition; spirit

   (dow) moral   **(cra)** morale   **(win)** peace

9. _____ most important; leader of a school

   (yon) principal   **(art)** principle   **(oon)** plain

10. _____ completely; to a great extent

    (onl) quiet   **(gee)** loose   **(map)** quite

(4.19A) Shady Characters (Words Often Confused—Part Three) *(Continued)*

11. _____ unadorned; flat area of land; clear

   (pel) plane   **(lep)** plain   **(elp)** principle

12. _____ time gone by

   (onn) passed   **(enc)** past   **(wod)** shown

13. _____ to suffer loss

   (ilp) lose   **(pen)** loose   **(roo)** morale

14. _____ a portion of something

   (doi) morale   **(ara)** piece   **(ene)** peace

15. _____ displayed

   (sol) shown   **(lon)** shone   **(ert)** plain

The names of the six shady characters are _____,

_____, _____,

_____, _____, and

_____.

(4.20) Words Often Confused (Part Four)

Do you know the difference between *there, their,* and *they're*? Does sound travel *threw* or *through* a wall? Is *week* or *weak* the opposite of strong? These answers can be found in this list of words and their meanings and illustrative sentences:

stationary: not moving; set in a position

Scared, Rex thought it would be best to remain *stationary* until the noise stopped.

stationery: paper used for writing

Can you buy me some more *stationery* when you go to the office supply store tonight?

their: possessive for *they*

This is *their* best effort.

there: a place; a sentence starter

May I drive *there* with you, Nicky?

There are fifty states in the United States.

they're: contraction for *they* plus *are*

Did you think that *they're* going to paint the mural with us?

threw: past tense of "to throw"

The outfielder *threw* the ball to the shortstop.

through: a preposition meaning "in one side and out the other"

Will you walk *through* the large office complex later?

to: a preposition; an infinitive

I walked *to* the store for my mother.

The French word *fumer* means "*to* smoke."

too: in addition

Wally seemed *too* happy after receiving that bit of news.

two: one plus one

There are at least *two* people waiting outside your office.

(4.20) Words Often Confused (Part Four) *(Continued)*

waist: the middle part on one's body

After exercising over a period of time, Tomas lost two inches off his *waist.*

waste: garbage

The *waste* management company recycles bottles, papers, and cans.

weak: opposite of strong

After his operation, Jim felt too *weak* to exercise as rigorously as he previously had.

week: a seven-day period

With only three days left in the *week,* the group had to work overtime to complete the project on time.

weather: conditions outdoors

We hope that the *weather* will cooperate for our annual picnic this Saturday.

whether: if it is true or likely; in either case

Whether you select this college or the college in California, I know that you will be happy in either place.

who's: contraction for *who* plus *is*

Who's knocking at the door, Ned?

whose: possessive of *who*

We need to know *whose* jacket this is, so we can return it.

your: possessive of *you*

Have you finished *your* part of the project, George?

you're: contraction for *you* plus *are*

You're in for a big surprise if you do that.

🖎 **WRITING TIP** Their, there, *and* they're *are three of the most confused words in the English language. Study them so you will not confuse them.* They're *not going to have* their *way with you* there, *are they?*

© 2007 by John Wiley & Sons, Inc.

(4.20A) A Balancing Act (Words Often Confused—Part Four)

Match the words in Column A with their meanings in Column B by writing the two-letter code associated with each answer. The answer for question 13, ka, is already given to you. If your answers are correct, your consecutive two-letter responses will spell out a famous saying (and a synonym for a saying). Write those letters on the lines provided at the bottom.

Column A

1. _____ stationary
2. _____ stationery
3. _____ their
4. _____ there
5. _____ they're
6. _____ threw
7. _____ through
8. _____ to
9. _____ too
10. _____ two
11. _____ waist
12. _____ waste
13. __ka__ weak
14. _____ week
15. _____ weather
16. _____ whether
17. _____ who's
18. _____ whose
19. _____ your
20. _____ you're

Column B

ac—to destroy or ruin; garbage

al—not moving; fixed

ay—in the direction of; toward

bo—if it is true or likely that; in either case that

du—a period of seven days

ka—not strong

ka—at or in that place; that place or point

ke—one more than one; one less than three

ll—the general condition of the atmosphere at a particular time and place

lw—writing materials

ma—also; in addition to

nd—contraction for *they* plus *are*

no—past tense of "to throw"

or—of, belonging to, made by, or done by them

pl—in one side and out the other side of

rb—contraction for *you* plus *are*

ro—possessive form of the pronoun *who*

sj—the part of the body between the ribs and hips

ve—of, belonging to, made by, or done by you

yp—contraction for *who* plus *is*

The saying is: _____

_____

Synonym for "saying": _____

(4.21) Double Negatives

A **double negative** is using two negatives to express a negation. For example, "He did not do nothing," is a double negative since *not* and *nothing* are both negative words. In this instance, the two negative words negate or cancel each other out. The correct form of this idea is either, "He did not do anything," or "He did nothing." In short, use only a single negative word.

Negative words include *no, not, nobody, never, hardly, but* (meaning "only"), *nothing, only,* and *scarcely.*

Here are some examples of double negatives followed by suggested corrections:

> *Wrong:* I can not get no happiness.
>
> *Correct:* I can get no happiness. (or) I can not get any happiness.
>
>
> *Wrong:* Carlotta has not gone nowhere.
>
> *Correct:* Carlotta has gone nowhere. (or) Carlotta has not gone anywhere.

Correct these double negative problems. Write your answers on the lines provided:

We do not need no help.

_____

_____

I haven't no friends.

_____

_____

There aren't no empty seats in this section.

_____

_____

📖 **WRITING TIP** *Although you might hear double negatives used in conversation and nevertheless understand the speaker's intention, double negatives are not permitted in formal writing. "I don't want no more hassles," for example, is not proper English. What is the correct way to say this?*

(4.21A) This Can't Get No Harder! (Double Negatives)

What an inappropriate and incorrect title! Yet it is an example of a double negative problem because both *can't* and *no* are negatives and cancel each other out in meaning. "This can't get any harder" is the correct way to say what is intended in this instance since there is only one negative, *can't*. Each of the following sentences contains a double negative. Correct each, and write the revised sentence beneath the original one.

1. I don't have no friends.

   _____

2. He can't get no satisfaction from his job.

   _____

3. We can't hardly hear the band from our seats.

   _____

4. There wasn't no reason to stay around any longer waiting for our ride.

   _____

   _____

5. They haven't but three weeks to finalize the New York City Marathon plans.

   _____

   _____

6. How come she never did nothing about it?

   _____

7. Julio does not ever do nothing wrong.

   _____

8. These directions from Dad don't make no sense to me.

   _____

9. I hadn't scarcely enough money to afford the birthday present.

   _____

   _____

10. We don't need no motivation.

    _____

Review Activities

REVIEW ACTIVITY   WORDS OFTEN CONFUSED

Match the word from Group One with its definition in Group Two. Write the correct number in the appropriate box of the magic square. If your numbers are correct, each row, each column, and each of the two diagonals will add up to the same number.

Group One

A. break

B. lead

C. counsel

D. course

E. choose

F. advise

G. brake

H. dessert

I. led

J. advice

K. consul

L. here

M. desert

N. council

O. capital

P. all ready

Q. affect

R. hear

S. board

T. already

U. capitol

V. bored

W. effect

X. coarse

Y. chose

Group Two

1. the final course of a meal

2. to smash or shatter

3. not enthused; made tiresome or weary

4. a piece of wood; group

5. city; money; that can be punished by death; most important

6. to influence

7. a group that works toward a common goal

8. to select

9. the result or consequence

10. to counsel

11. not refined; harsh

12. opinion given; counsel

13. to leave; a dry region

14. everyone ready

15. graphite; to go first; a distance ahead

16. by or before the given time

17. advice; to give advice

18. building; statehouse

19. this place

20. past tense of "to go first"

21. a foreign country's representative

22. a stopping device

23. path; onward movement

24. past tense of "to select"

25. to perceive with the ears

REVIEW ACTIVITY   WORDS OFTEN CONFUSED *(Continued)*

A =	B =	C =	D =	E =
F =	G =	H =	I =	J =
K =	L =	M =	N =	O =
P =	Q =	R =	S =	T =
U =	V =	W =	X =	Y =

Final Tests

FINAL TEST 1   AGREEMENT

Circle the correct answer for each sentence. Each correct answer scores 5 points.

1. Each of the chorus members brought (her, their) music sheets.

2. *Thelma and Louise* (is, are) an interesting motion picture.

3. Some of these pictures in the album (was, were) taken in Chicago.

4. Either the minister or the members of the church (is, are) going to the mission this weekend.

5. Her favorite sandwich (are, is) bacon, lettuce, and tomato.

6. All of the magazine (has, have) to be read by Wednesday's class.

7. All of the benches (has, have) to be placed in storage for next season.

8. Most of the newspaper (was, were) placed in the recycling can.

9. Several of the people (has, have) been contacted about the newest plans.

10. Bobby and Eduardo (is, are) playing handball in the schoolyard.

11. (Has, Have) any of the missing packages been located?

12. None of my personal information (was, were) known to that group of people.

13. (Was, Were) all of the participants aware of the rule changes?

14. Neither Miguel nor his parents (was, were) told of the recent park renovations.

15. Christine brought (her, their) purse to the movies this past weekend.

16. (Has, Have) you spotted that necklace?

17. The older flag has lost (its, their) bright colors.

18. These television critics and their magazine editor (is, are) unfair in their criticism of that program.

19. Both the cellist and her family members (was, were) thrilled with the good news.

20. Some of the singers in this contest (seem, seems) nervous.

Number correct _____ × 5 = _____%

FINAL TEST 2   VERB TENSES

Circle the correct verb tense in each sentence. Each correct answer scores 5 points.

1. Until he (reach, reached) home plate, we did not have a sense that we could score against the talented rival team.

2. She would have (prefer, preferred) to write her memoirs without an editor's assistance.

3. My aunt (laid, lay) her belongings on the counter.

4. Had she (swam, swum) that many laps in that short span of time?

5. Michael (leads, led) a discussion about the Internet each Thursday evening at our local library.

6. If I (was, were) he, I would choose to remain in this group.

7. The Smiths were still driving the car that they (bought, had bought) many years ago.

8. This magazine would have been more interesting if it (would have been, had been) filled with more exciting articles.

9. When the weather became cooler, Ricardo (became, become) more at ease.

10. The fatigued worker (sleep, slept) for twelve hours.

11. After the explorer entered the cave, she (knew, know) that it would be a memorable journey.

12. The rain had (fallen, fell) for more than seven consecutive days.

13. If we (had, had had) the opportunity to call you, we would have done so.

14. My friend (came, come) to the door after I knocked two times.

15. This long-distance record had not been (broke, broken).

16. These street performers (amaze, amazed) the crowd yesterday.

17. (Threw, Throw) the ball to your sister, Maddy.

18. If your leg hurts, (lay, lie) down, and do some stretching.

19. Had the pipes (burst, bursted) last winter?

20. They had (began, begun) the new procedure.

Number correct _____ × 5 = _____%

FINAL TEST 3   VERB TENSES

Half of the underlined verbs are in the wrong tense. For these incorrect verbs, write the correct tense of the verb on the line next to the sentence. For the other ten verbs, write the letter C for "correct" on the line next to the sentence. Each correct answer is worth 5 points.

1. _____ The birds have already <u>flied</u> away.

2. _____ Have you <u>brought</u> your bathing suit with you?

3. _____ They should have <u>answered</u> the police officer's questions immediately.

4. _____ Did you <u>swum</u> in the lake this season?

5. _____ Last week the wind <u>blowed</u> down our fence.

6. _____ No, I had not <u>choosed</u> this brand of detergent, Jim.

7. _____ Had the boat already <u>sunk</u>?

8. _____ I had <u>rode</u> almost twenty miles before stopping for breakfast.

9. _____ Most of the mourners <u>wept</u> during the eulogy.

10. _____ I thought that we had <u>asked</u> for syrup with the pancakes.

11. _____ The Boy Scout had <u>lit</u> the candle to begin the ceremony.

12. _____ The gardeners were <u>supposed</u> to dig out these bushes.

13. _____ The custodian <u>throwed</u> out all of the empty boxes this morning.

14. _____ It <u>seems</u> to me that this problem is not that difficult to solve.

15. _____ Has this shirt already <u>shrank</u>?

16. _____ They have <u>ringed</u> the bell several times this hour.

17. _____ These pictures had <u>falling</u> from the wall during the hurricane.

18. _____ We <u>given</u> all we could to try and make it possible to be accepted here.

19. _____ It <u>took</u> all afternoon for us to prepare for this party.

20. _____ When the dogs <u>began</u> to bark, we decided to go indoors.

Number correct _____ × 5 = _____%

FINAL TEST 4   CASES

Circle the correct word in each set of parentheses. Each correct answer scores 5 points.

1. We afforded (her, she) the highest compliments.

2. These gifts are to be given to Tamika and (he, him).

3. (We, Us) women sponsor this charity event each year.

4. Please take this text to (they, those) students.

5. The representative from the local police department spoke to (us, we) students about safe driving.

6. Permit (us, we) to go along with you, Ronaldo.

7. (You and I, Me and you) are going to report on the oil crisis next week.

8. Are (them, they) happy with the new television schedule?

9. The most qualified candidate for governor is (her, she).

10. Either Manuel or (he, him) will be helping to move that very heavy sofa.

11. Is it (them, they) in the photograph?

12. Since (us, we) left early, you can use our studio.

13. Please allow (she, her) to assist you with the decorations.

14. The sportscaster sat behind (she and I, her and me) at the restaurant last night.

15. Maureen, Kate, and (her, she) will be the next ones to sing.

16. Do you recall (who, whom) said that to you?

17. William Shakespeare, (who, whom) the panel members greatly admire, was the subject of the discussion.

18. On (who, whom) did you place your bet?

19. (Who, Whom) won last year's election?

20. The announcer helped you and (they, us).

Number correct _____ **× 5 =** _____%

FINAL TEST 5   WORDS OFTEN CONFUSED

Underline the correct word in each set of parentheses. Each correct answer scores 5 points.

1. Have you (shone, shown) this picture to your sister?

2. What are we going to order for (desert, dessert)?

3. This is as heavy as (lead, led).

4. We have often (complemented, complimented) the chef for his culinary skills.

5. Have you been really (board, bored) with this television program?

6. The ship's captain had gone off the designated (coarse, course).

7. A few of the runners (passed, past) out on that steamy day.

8. Did you (hear, here) that?

9. I had (formally, formerly) lived in Seattle, but now I live in Spokane.

10. They had to decide (weather, whether) they wanted to spend their money on that item.

11. The tourists walked (threw, through) the luxurious home.

12. That television program was a gigantic (waist, waste) of her time!

13. Would you like to borrow our (stationary, stationery) bike?

14. How is the team's (moral, morale) this evening?

15. Do not (lose, loose) sleep over this.

16. Do you know (who's, whose) jacket this is, Mindy?

17. In another (weak, week) we will graduate from high school.

18. Please deposit the goods right (hear, here).

19. These critics were (quiet, quite) happy with the actor's performance.

20. John Marfen is our student (council, counsel) president.

Number correct _____ × 5 = _____%

Section Five
Mechanics

Diagnostic Tests

DIAGNOSTIC TEST 1   CAPITALIZATION

Fifty of the words in the following sentences should be capitalized. Circle the first letter of each of these fifty words. Each correctly circled letter scores 2 points. Each incorrectly circled letter reduces your score by 2 points. Do well!

1. my sister, nancy, owns a toyota camry.

2. raised in alabama, this gentleman wrote many interesting stories.

3. he does his shopping at pathways, the local supermarket.

4. andy warhol's famous paintings of campbell's soup cans were part of our dinner conversation.

5. we studied the korean war in our history class last november.

6. did you drive to jones beach last memorial day?

7. the play *hello dolly* will be performed tonight in pleasantville, new york.

8. she is a very popular brazilian dancer.

9. we discussed the serious matters involving both the united states congress and the house of representatives.

10. both of my uncles attended the university of miami.

11. this holiday inn will host a visit by superintendent alston.

12. the airport is near shea stadium in queens.

13. the woman asked her colleagues, "are you going home for lunch?"

14. my neighbor had been a colonel for seventeen years.

15. some of these tomatoes are unripe.

A: **Number of correctly circled letters** _____ **× 2 =** _____

B: **Number of incorrectly circled letters** _____ **× 2 =** _____

A _____ **− B** _____ **= Final score** _____%

DIAGNOSTIC TEST 2   COMMAS

Twenty-five commas need to be inserted within these sentences. Each sentence needs at least one comma. In a series, place a comma before the word *and*. Each comma is worth 4 points. Each incorrectly inserted comma deducts 4 points. Do well!

1. Tomasita is this the correct way to Jackson Mississippi?

2. You need to carry the crate the flag and the two packages.

3. Having read the newspaper that morning Georgia a sophisticated and well-read editor walked to her limo.

4. Since I do not have the correct change for the bus could you lend me some coins David?

5. John G. Loweret Jr. a college professor would like to visit Madrid Spain in a few months.

6. When my sister was born on June 4 1987 my aunt stayed at our house for a few days and helped with the chores.

7. Rex would like to run for Congress and many think that he a charming intelligent man would make a good leader.

8. No this is the wrong way to my cousin's cabin.

9. After the principal read the afternoon's announcements the members of our club the Brainstormers met for practice.

10. This saleswoman who is also a noted book editor will be visiting several of our town's stores next month.

A: Number correct _____ **× 4 =** _____
B: Number wrong _____ **× 4 =** _____
Final score A − B = _____%

Lessons and Activities

⑤.1 Capitalization

Use capital letters for:

- **Proper adjectives** (American customs, Spanish civilization)

- **Names of courses with numbers or letters after them** (Math 101, Geography 4)

- **Names of language courses** (Russian, French, English)

- **Geographical names** (St. Louis, Missouri; Madrid)

- **Brand names** (Hallmark cards, Ford automobiles)

- **Specific time periods and events** (the Spanish Inquisition, the Great Depression)

- **Salutations and closing of letters** (Dear Teresa, Sincerely)

- **Religions and religious references** (Protestantism, the Jewish readings)

- **Titles showing family relationships** (Uncle Dave, Grammy Smith)

- **Proper nouns** (Michael, Rosa, Coca-Cola)

- **Titles used with names of people** (Dr. Isaacs, President Richards)

- **Names of works of art and literature** (*The Last Supper, Mona Lisa, David Copperfield, The Notebook*)

- **Names of ships, trains, and aircraft** (USS *Constitution*, Long Island Railroad, *Air Force One*)

- **Names of buildings and monuments** (Empire State Building, Mount Rushmore)

- **Names of stars, planets, and constellations** (the North Star, Mars, Orion)

- **Names of nationalities, races, and languages** (Polish, Caucasian, Gaelic)

WRITING TIP *Study these few capitalization rules. Once you know them, you will become more confident and proficient with capital letters!*

(5.1A) Half and Half (Capitalization)

Half of the following words are correctly capitalized. Place a C on the line next to groups of words that are correctly capitalized.

1. _____ Sixty-Third Avenue

2. _____ Fourth of July

3. _____ spanish class

4. _____ burger king Restaurant

5. _____ a high school near me

6. _____ Forty-Fifth Street

7. _____ Louisville Slugger Bat

8. _____ science class

9. _____ Clinton, New york

10. _____ *An american Tragedy* (novel)

11. _____ the San Francisco giants (baseball team)

12. _____ Chapter 14

13. _____ James P. Murphy sr.

14. _____ German class

15. _____ Home economics Class

16. _____ mathematics

17. _____ History 101

18. _____ Spring fever

19. _____ the English countryside

20. _____ Madison Square garden (arena)

(5.1B) Sporting Around (Capitalization)

For each pair of names or phrases, identify the one that is correctly punctuated. Then write the letters that are in parentheses next to that correct group of words on the line after the number. Write the thirty letters consecutively on the lines below the list. If your answers are correct, you will spell the names of two movies about sports.

1. _____ Senator Clinton **(re)**

    senator Clinton **(to)**

2. _____ a general in an army **(me)**

    a General in an Army **(ri)**

3. _____ Aunt priscilla **(rt)**

    Aunt Priscilla **(mb)**

4. _____ President Carter **(er)**

    president Carter **(es)**

5. _____ Hello, doctor Affrot **(on)**

    Hello, Doctor Affrot **(th)**

6. _____ *Webster's New World Dictionary* **(et)**

    Webster's New World dictionary **(te)**

7. _____ my Sister, Jill **(re)**

    my sister, Jill **(it)**

8. _____ President Wilson **(an)**

    president Wilson **(am)**

9. _____ *sports Illustrated* **(es)**

    Sports Illustrated **(sf)**

10. _____ high school memories **(ie)**

    High School memories **(rr)**

11. _____ Nassau County residents **(ld)**

    Nassau County Residents **(me)**

12. _____ Science class **(il)**

    science class **(of)**

Sporting Around (Capitalization) *(Continued)*

13. _____ Mayor Arnold Smithers **(dr)**

mayor Arnold Smithers **(fe)**

14. _____ Bill of Rights **(ea)**

Bill Of Rights **(oi)**

15. _____ *good Morning America* (television show) **(st)**

Good Morning America (television show) **(ms)**

These thirty letters spell the names of these two movies:

_____

_____

Name _____ Date _____ Period _____

(5.1C) Ten Letters at a Time (Capitalization)

Select the correctly capitalized phrase in each numbered item. Then, on the line next to the number, write the letter that appears after the phrase. Finally, write those twenty letters consecutively on the lines below the list. If your answers are correct, you will spell out two ten-letter words. Do well!

1. _____ Raymond Herrick Jr. **(m)**

   Raymond Herrick jr. **(r)**

2. _____ west of the town's center **(i)**

   West of the town's center **(e)**

3. _____ Thirty-Third Street **(c)**

   Thirty-third Street **(g)**

4. _____ Michelle J. O'Brien **(r)**

   Michelle J. O'brien **(a)**

5. _____ the Spanish Civilization **(p)**

   the Spanish civilization **(o)**

6. _____ books from South America **(s)**

   books from south america **(i)**

7. _____ the Mississippi river **(t)**

   the Mississippi River **(c)**

8. _____ Grand Coulee Dam **(o)**

   Grand Coulee dam **(e)**

9. _____ the main Street **(s)**

   Main Street **(p)**

10. _____ an Italian painting **(e)**

    an Italian Painting **(r)**

11. _____ Yellowstone National park **(e)**

    Yellowstone National Park **(f)**

12. _____ Eddie Minter **(r)**

    eddie Minter **(t)**

(5.1C) Ten Letters at a Time (Capitalization) *(Continued)*

13. _____ the Detroit Tigers Baseball team **(d)**

         the Detroit Tigers baseball team **(a)**

14. _____ Lincoln boulevard **(m)**

         Lincoln Boulevard **(u)**

15. _____ Malibu beach **(e)**

         Malibu Beach **(d)**

16. _____ French cuisine **(u)**

         french Fries **(r)**

17. _____ the play, *Macbeth* **(l)**

         the Play, *Macbeth* **(b)**

18. _____ Milford high School **(a)**

         Milford High School **(e)**

19. _____ the world Series **(o)**

         the World Series **(n)**

20. _____ *The Old Man And the Sea* **(n)**

         The Old Man and the Sea **(t)**

These letters spell out two ten-letter words:

_____ and _____

(5.2) 100 Challenging Spelling Words

Here are one hundred difficult spelling words. Study all of these words, perhaps working with ten to twenty at one time. Practice spelling them orally, and practice spelling and saying these words with another person. There are four fun activities that will test your ability to spell these one hundred words. Enjoy!

absence	disease	jealousy	preferred
accommodate	eighth	knowledge	preparation
accomplish	embarrass	laboratory	proceed
accordion	encouraging	legitimate	psychology
analysis	equivalent	leisure	quantity
analyze	existence	length	quizzes
apparent	explanation	maintain	really
auxiliary	familiar	maintenance	receive
balloon	February	marriage	recommend
barbecue	foreign	medicine	repetition
beginning	forty	mosquito	safety
benefit	fulfill	naturally	scary
business	governor	necessary	strategy
calendar	grammar	neighbor	subtle
changeable	guarantee	noticeable	technique
column	happily	occasion	thorough
commission	height	occurred	toward
condescend	humorous	omitted	twelfth
convenient	hypocrite	overrun	unforgettable
courteous	imaginary	parallel	usually
defendant	implement	penetrate	village
deferred	inactivity	perceive	villain
describe	information	permitted	visible
desirable	insurance	pleasant	Wednesday
desperate	introduce	potatoes	young

✒ **WRITING TIP** *Knowing these one hundred challenging words will help you in your writing. You will save time since you will not have to look these words up in the dictionary. Plus, you will not have to rely on the computer's spell-check program. You will become your own best resource!*

(5.2A) Finding the Missing Letters

One letter from each word in the following list is missing. On the line next to the word's number, write the letter that belongs in that word. Then cross off that letter in the box below. When you are finished crossing off the last letter in the box, you should have found the missing letters!

1. _____ accordi_n

2. _____ analys_s

3. _____ anal_ze

4. _____ ben_fit

5. _____ bus_ness

6. _____ chang_able

7. _____ conven_ent

8. _____ descr_be

9. _____ equiv_lent

10. _____ govern_r

11. _____ hypocrit_

12. _____ impl_ment

13. _____ insur_nce

14. _____ lengt_

15. _____ med_cine

16. _____ nat_rally

17. _____ omit_ed

18. _____ over_un

19. _____ perc_ive

20. _____ permit_ed

21. _____ prep_ration

22. _____ ps_chology

23. _____ quant_ty

24. _____ su_tle

25. _____ thoro_gh

Here are the missing twenty-five letters. Cross each one out after you use it.

a	e	i	i	t
a	e	i	o	u
a	e	i	o	u
b	e	i	r	y
e	h	i	t	y

5.3 **Commas**

Use the **comma** (,) to:

> **Separate items in a series:** The manager spoke to Tim, Brian, Mike, and Rob.

> **Separate short, independent clauses in a series:** The pilots chatted, they looked at the map, they prepared to lift off, and they greeted the passengers.

> **Separate two or more adjectives preceding a noun:** The model is a tall, handsome man.

> **Separate independent clauses:** We wanted to stay on that road, but it was closed due to the accident.

> **After words such as *well, yes, no,* and *why* when they begin a sentence:** Yes, this is the correct answer.

> **After an introductory participle phrase:** Wanting to help the stranded motorist, Dad steered his car off the parkway.

> **After several consecutive introductory prepositional phrases:** In the middle of the night, that noise scared the youngsters.

> **After an introductory adverbial clause:** Because the rain is still falling, we will have to cancel the picnic.

> **Set off parenthetical expressions:** This type of machinery, in my opinion, is outdated.

> **Set off the salutation of a friendly letter and the closing of any type of letter:** Dear Maria, Yours truly,

> **Set off items in dates and addresses:** My friend was born on July 21, 1978.

> **Set off names in direct address:** Greg, are you going to apply for summer work this year?

> **Set off nonessential clauses and nonessential participle phrases:** These doctors, who have been in the same practice for fifteen years, are going to be at my cousin's wedding.

> **Set off appositives and appositive phrases:** New Jersey, the Garden State, is where my uncle lives.

> There is no need to insert a comma before Jr. or Sr. as in Thomas Jones Jr. or Michael Gavigan Sr.

WRITING TIP *Editors will tell you that one of the biggest problems that writers confront is how to use the comma correctly. If you study the comma rules in this lesson, pay attention to how professional writers use the comma, and consult a grammar book or an Internet source when you need to, you will fare well with commas.*

(5.3A) Why We Use Commas (Part One)

Commas are needed in the sentences in this activity for eight reasons:

A. Separate items in a series

B. Separate short independent clauses in a series

C. Separate two or more adjectives preceding a noun

D. Separate independent clauses

E. After words such as *well, yes, no,* and *why* when they begin a sentence

F. After an introductory participle phrase

G. After several consecutive introductory prepositional phrases

H. After an introductory adverbial clause

Read each sentence, and pay attention to the inserted commas. Then, on the line after the number, write the corresponding letter of the reason that the commas were inserted.

1. _____ Jenkins is a talented, articulate, versatile speaker.

2. _____ They shot baskets, they wrestled, they bowled, and finally they rested.

3. _____ The singers whom my parents enjoy are Elvis, Madonna, Stevie Wonder, Cher, and the Four Tops.

4. _____ No, my car is not parked behind the gymnasium.

5. _____ In the middle of the day in June, we decided to go to my uncle's vacation cabin on the lake.

6. _____ Since we drove so many miles yesterday, we plan to take it easy today.

7. _____ Stung by his supervisor's remarks, the electrician decided to call his union leader for advice.

8. _____ Designed by Frederick Olmstead, Central Park in New York City is an oasis in the concrete jungle.

9. _____ A vote was scheduled for December 3, and the citizens were eager to cast their ballets.

(5.3A) Why We Use Commas (Part One) *(Continued)*

10. _____ We ordered three pizzas, two hero sandwiches, and four bottles of soda.

11. _____ Whenever I feel afraid, I take a deep breath.

12. _____ The teacher lectured, some students copied notes, and some others doodled.

13. _____ The athletic, motivated high school student set the state high jump record.

14. _____ The Three Stooges were Moe, Larry, and Curly.

15. _____ Yes, we have no bananas.

16. _____ By the stores in the middle of town, we spotted the celebrity.

17. _____ When you see your sister, tell her that we will meet tomorrow afternoon.

18. _____ Mrs. Maiori is a friendly, caring vice principal.

19. _____ We did enjoy the movies, and we were pleased with its thrilling ending.

20. _____ Today we will attempt to organize all these folders, and tomorrow we will start to call more volunteers.

(5.3B) Why We Use Commas (Part Two)

Commas are needed in the sentences in this activity for six reasons:

> A. Set off parenthetical expressions
>
> B. Set off the salutation of a friendly letter and the closing of any type of letter
>
> C. Set off items in dates and addresses
>
> D. Set off names in direct address
>
> E. Set off nonessential clauses and nonessential participle phrases
>
> F. Set off appositives and appositive phrases

For each sentence below, determine why the comma is inserted within that particular sentence. Write the reason's corresponding letter on the line next to the number. Each of the letters will be used at least once, and some will be used more than once.

1. _____ George, are you implying that he is less than honest?

2. _____ Dwayne was born on July 22, 1994.

3. _____ These counselors, who like to visit different American colleges, will meet with the transfer students this morning.

4. _____ The White House is located at 1600 Pennsylvania Avenue, Washington, DC, 20500.

5. _____ Of course, we will let you know as soon as we can.

6. _____ Nevertheless, I will answer her question.

7. _____ Respectfully yours,

8. _____ Sincerely yours,

9. _____ Jeremy, are you hearing this?

10. _____ My new home, which is located near the mall, needs to be painted.

11. _____ George Costanza, a character on *Seinfeld*, is hilarious.

12. _____ The most incriminating piece of evidence, the knife, has been located by the detectives.

13. _____ Dear Serena,

14. _____ Are you looking for this book, Peter?

15. _____ Rosita, looking at her target, concentrated on hitting the bull's-eye.

5.4 Apostrophes

Use an **apostrophe** ('):

▸ **For common contractions** (I'd, he'd, can't, didn't, hadn't)

▸ **In place of omitted letters or numbers** (Class of '07)

▸ **To express time or amount** (yesterday's newspaper, a minute's times, five dollars' worth of grapes)

▸ **To form possessives with compound nouns** (my mother-in-law's advice)

▸ **To form certain plurals** (two's, C's, and 6's)

Rules for Apostrophes and Possession

▸ To form the possessive of a singular word, add an apostrophe and an *s*. (girl's dress, gentleman's courtesy)

▸ To form the possessive of a singular word (of more than one syllable) that ends with *s* or *z*, either add the apostrophe after the *s* (Kansas' population) or add the apostrophe and another *s* (Kansas's population) depending on how the resulting word sounds. You could write and say *James'* or *James's,* but you would be hard pressed to pronounce *Ulysses's*! Thus, listen to how it sounds to see if you will add the apostrophe.

▸ To form the possessive of a plural word that ends in *s,* usually add an apostrophe. (girls' dresses, boys' behavior)

▸ To form the possessive of a plural word that does not end in *s,* add an apostrophe and an *s.* (women's club, people's voting habits)

▸ To form the possessive of a shared item, add an apostrophe and an *s* to the last item in the series. (This is Uncle Henry, Grandpa Tommy, and Aunt Judith's car.)

▸ To form the possessive of individual ownership in a series, add an apostrophe and an *s* to each item. (We read Isaac's, Tina's, Monty's, and George's essays.)

▸ To form the possessive of indefinite pronouns, add an apostrophe followed by an *s.* (Is this anyone's business but hers?)

 WRITING TIP *Apostrophes can be confusing! Yet, they do not have to be. Study these few basic rules concerning apostrophes, and you will do just fine when using them.*

(5.4A) Showing Your Apostrophe Skills

There is a need for at least one apostrophe in each of the following sentences. Some require more than one. Insert the necessary apostrophes.

1. Hed rather read last weeks magazine.
2. My mother belongs to the womens club.
3. Can you estimate this boxs weight?
4. We followed the mices path.
5. A secretarys job is not an easy one!
6. Uncle Jack, Grandpa Frank, and Grandmother Anna signatures are interesting.
7. She graduated with the Class of 05 from high school.
8. Is this somebody elses coat?
9. Have you painted the mens faculty bathroom yet?
10. How many *toos* did he misspell in the essay?
11. This is his father-in-laws radio.
12. Have you read the governors new proposal?

Show the possessive of each of the following. Write each possessive form on the line.

13. the watches owned by the men _____

14. the equipment worth fifty dollars _____

15. the medals that Rich owns _____

16. the contract of *they would* _____

17. the stamp collection owned by Chris _____

18. the house owned by Aunt Shelia and Uncle Tony _____

19. the lair of the wolves _____

20. the fort of the children _____

(5.5) Quotation Marks

Use **quotation marks** (" ") to:

- Indicate a speaker's exact words. **Examples:** Izzy remarked, "I have lost my appetite." "My best friend is leaving town," said Jeff, "and I will miss him."

- Indicate a quotation or quotations within quotations. **Examples:** Mark asked, "Did you hear Helen say, 'I am tired'?" Sally remarked, "My favorite holiday song is 'White Christmas' by Bing Crosby."

- Indicate exact words from a quoted source. **Example:** In the play *Macbeth,* the witches say, "Double, double toil and trouble; Fire burn, and cauldron bubble."

- Punctuate the following titles: a song ("Cat's in the Cradle"); a poem ("The Charge of the Light Brigade"); a short story ("After Twenty Years"); a newspaper or magazine article ("My Neighborhood is Great"); a chapter in a book ("Kenny Knows What's Up"); a television episode ("George, the Marine Biologist").

- Emphasize a specific word. **Example:** I have heard him use "yowza" about a million times!

Punctuating Quotation Marks

- Place periods and commas inside quotation marks. **Examples:** Perry responded, "I want more ice cream." "I want more ice cream," said Perry.

- If a question mark or an exclamation mark punctuates the quotation, the mark belongs inside the quotation marks. **Example:** His sister asked, "May I go with you tonight?"

- If the question mark or exclamation mark punctuates the main sentence, place it outside. **Example:** Was it Romeo who said, "I am fortune's fool"?

- Semicolons and colons should be placed outside the quotation marks. **Examples:** My principal concluded his speech to the graduating class with the famous line: "To thine own self be true." The politician called it "disturbing"; the critic called it "business as usual."

🖎 **WRITING TIP** *Quotation marks can be perplexing. By learning and using the rules in this lesson, you will be able to solve any punctuation problem.*

(5.5A) Quotation Marks in Every Sentence

Each sentence in the following list needs at least one set of quotation marks. Punctuate the sentences with quotation marks as needed.

1. I have read the short story, The Story of an Hour, by Kate Chopin.

2. I am not going to go home just yet, Lily remarked.

3. We will watch the television episode, The Rascals Are Here, tonight, said Fern.

4. I really enjoyed the lecture, The Way We Live, by Thomas Devlin.

5. Hymie asked, Did Hamlet say, To be or not to be?

6. I believe, said Hank, that all people can better themselves.

7. Sandy said, I enjoyed reading the short story, Bernice Bobs Her Hair, by F. Scott Fitzgerald.

8. The director screamed, I see a tornado in the distance!

9. Are they being sarcastic toward you? I asked Vivian.

10. The poem, Boy Wandering in Simms Valley, is great, said Joey.

11. Is Love Is All You Need your mother's favorite Beatles song? Ollie asked Stanley.

12. Tommy told us, I know how much you are trying to do better.

(5.6) Semicolons, Colons, Italics, and Hyphens

Use a **semicolon** (;):

- Between the clauses of a compound sentence if they are not joined by a conjunction. These clauses must be closely related. **Examples:** My sister is a prize figure skater; she will compete in Tokyo next month [closely related clauses]. My sister is a prize figure skater. She has many friends [clauses are not closely related].

- Between clauses that are joined by certain transitional words and phrases in a compound sentence. These transitional words are *accordingly, consequently, for example, for instance, furthermore, however, instead, moreover, nevertheless, otherwise,* and *therefore.* **Example:** The movie director wanted to start filming; however, the weather prevented her from doing so.

- Between the items in a series if the items contain commas. This will avoid a confusing number of commas. **Example:** He presented his book proposal to publishers in San Francisco, California; Helena, Montana; Detroit, Michigan; and Atlanta, Georgia.

Use a **colon** (:):

- To introduce a list of items. **Example:** Our English teacher introduced us to the following American writers: Emily Dickinson, Ernest Hemingway, F. Scott Fitzgerald, Kate Chopin, and Eudora Welty.

- After the salutation of a business letter. **Example:** Dear Mr. Kennedy:

- To divide hours from minutes. **Example:** It is 5:40 in the afternoon.

- To separate chapter from verse in biblical references. **Example:** John 3:22

Use *italics* (or an underline) for:

- Book titles: *To Kill a Mockingbird*

- Full-length play titles: *Death of a Salesman*

- Long poems: *The Odyssey*

- Magazine title: *Sports Illustrated*

- Newspaper titles: *New York Times*

- Movie titles: *Rocky*

- Television programs: *The Tonight Show*

- Paintings and sculptures: *The Last Supper* (painting), *The Thinker* (sculpture)

- Ships and planes: USS *Intrepid* (ship), *Air Force One* (plane)

5.6 Semicolons, Colons, Italics, and Hyphens *(Continued)*

Use a **hyphen** (-):

▸ To separate parts of certain compound nouns. **Example:** She is the *editor-in-chief* of the magazine.

▸ Between two words that comprise a single adjective only when the adjective precedes the noun that it modifies. **Example:** The *bramble-covered* path was not a popular one for the tourists.

   You do not have to use the hyphen if the first word of the two-word adjective ends in *-ly*. **Example:** The *heavily traveled* road was full of potholes.

▸ When writing out the numbers *twenty-one* to *ninety-nine* inclusive. **Example:** There are *fifty-six* people waiting to see this movie.

▸ To syllabicate words at the end of the line of typing or writing. Divide words of two or more syllables only between syllables. Single-syllable words should not be divided.

🖎 **WRITING TIP** *These four marks of punctuation will add variety to your writing. They will also display your punctuation skills and your ability to use words and signs correctly when you write. Review them often. Once you learn them, you will become more confident and proficient when using these punctuation marks.*

(5.6A) Working with Punctuation

Insert commas, periods, question marks, underlinings (or italics), apostrophes, hyphens, quotation marks, semicolons, and colons in the following fifteen sentences.

1. We could not believe that he ate two hamburgers three helpings of macaroni salad four hard rolls twenty six pretzels six hot dogs and a dozen olives

2. Are you going to the prom with Maria Torres Miguel

3. We will have this window installed this Saturday otherwise we will have to wait until the spring

4. My favorite novel by Ernest Hemingway is A Farewell to Arms

5. May we go on a field trip to see the battleship the USS Intrepid

6. Where is Auguste Rodin's statue The Thinker

7. What do you intend to do about our drinking water problem is the question to ask the politician at today's meeting

8. I will meet you at the railroad station at 745 tomorrow morning

9. Nadia remarked I am confused about this math problem

10. Georgette reads the New York Times at least three days a week

11. The movers intended to lift the piano by themselves however the home owner insisted on helping them

12. Have you read F. Scott Fitzgerald's short story Bernice Bobs Her Hair

13. Both the Republicans and the Democrats bickered over Senator Larsens remarks more-over neither side wanted to back off the issue

14. He can bat from both the left and right side of the plate slides well and is very disciplined

15. Tad is reading the article How to Succeed in High School by Johnny Matzuka

(5.6B) Using Semicolons, Colons, Italics, and Hyphens

Insert semicolons, colons, italics (underlining), and hyphens correctly in the following sentences. Each of these is used at least one time.

1. Dear President Gavigan

2. I read The Great Gatsby and Julius Caesar this summer.

3. My father has a subscription to Games magazine.

4. You will need to have the following items for the trip tent, lantern, matches, and a compass.

5. There are between forty seven and fifty one tickets left to be sold for tonight's performance.

6. My best friend would like to attend college however he has to earn a scholarship in order to do so.

7. The newly appointed editor in chief is Millie Wilson.

8. Have you watched reruns of Friends lately?

9. Kent is a terrific company president he will be honored for his business achievements at the banquet this evening.

10. We saw a film about the USS Constitution last evening.

11. I will pick you up at 645 tomorrow morning, Harry.

12. We attended the theater and saw The Sound of Music this past winter.

13. Our class studied the works of the following painters Degas, Manet, Monet, Sisley, and Gauguin.

14. My thirty two year old sister loves to discuss the articles from the Boston Globe.

15. Her favorite painting is Grant Wood's American Gothic.

(5.7) Brackets, Parentheses, Ellipsis Marks, and Dashes

Use **brackets [ ]** to:

▸ Enclose corrections or explanations or comments within a quoted passage. **Examples:** "My father's friends told of their 1945 [actually 1946] experiences overseas." Many of James Joyce's years [1882–1941] were spent pondering Irish traditions and customs.

Use **parentheses ( )** to:

▸ Enclose material that explains. **Example:** Winston Churchill's years as British prime minister (1940–1945, 1951–1955) were memorable ones.

▸ Enclose supplementary materials. **Example:** His many jobs (newspaper deliveryman, custodian, truck driver, and machinist) have taught him much about life.

▸ Enclose numbers or letters in a series within a sentence. **Example:** There are four types of sentences by purpose: (1) declarative, (2) imperative, (3) interrogative, and (4) exclamatory.

Use **ellipsis marks (. . .)** to:

▸ Show that material has been omitted from a quotation. **Example:** The theater manager went on to say, "I have never in all my years ... witnessed such a magnificent acting performance."

▸ Show that more of a statement or series could be continued. **Example:** My niece thought that the Seven Dwarfs (Dopey, Bashful, Doc ...) were interesting.

Use the **dash [—]** to:

▸ Show a sudden break in the sentence. **Example:** We could not remember the combination—every one of us!

▸ Emphasize or explain a word or a series or group of words in a sentence. **Example:** The vowels—a, e, i, o, u, and sometimes y—appear frequently in the English language.

▸ Show an interruption in speech. **Example:** The painting is—well—it is—let's just say—interesting.

 WRITING TIP *Although these four punctuation marks are not used as often as many of the other punctuation marks, they are useful in the right construction. It is advisable to review them often even though they are used more infrequently than the others.*

Proper Punctuation, Please! (Brackets, Parentheses, Ellipsis Marks, and Dashes)

5.7A

Write two sentences exemplifying the four punctuation marks requested below. If there is need for other marks of punctuation within the sentences, use them as well.

1. Write two sentences that include brackets.

_____

_____

_____

_____

2. Write two sentences that include parentheses.

_____

_____

_____

_____

3. Write two sentences that include ellipsis marks.

_____

_____

_____

_____

4. Write two sentences that include dashes.

_____

_____

_____

_____

(5.8) End Marks

End marks are important in that they effectively close or end your thought. Here are four end punctuation marks.

- Use a **period** at the end of a declarative sentence. *Examples:* This is the best way to fix that plumbing problem. I have seen many musicians, but none were as good as she.

- Use a **period** at the end of an imperative sentence or an **exclamation mark** if the command is said with great emphasis or excitement. *Examples:* Let's fix the plumbing problem soon. Take the newspaper up to Grandma May's room. Call the police right away!

- Use a **question mark** at the end of an interrogative sentence. *Examples:* Are you sixteen years old yet? Have you remembered to walk the dogs? Will this be the year that he retires from coaching?

- Use an **exclamation mark** at the end of an exclamatory sentence. *Examples:* It's all over! What a mess you started! I cannot believe my eyes and ears!

For practice, place the correct end mark after each of these sentences. Use five periods, two exclamation marks, and two question marks.

1. How are you

2. I am feeling fine

3. This is absolutely ridiculous

4. The physician explained the procedure to my dad

5. He is a friendly dog

6. I am very astonished

7. We needed to study for the history test

8. Kenny landed the plane with little difficulty

9. May I borrow some money from you

WRITING TIP *These basic marks of punctuation are used often. They should be more recognizable and easier for you to use than some of the lesser-used punctuation marks.*

(5.8A) Putting the End Mark in Its Place

Place an end punctuation mark (period, question mark, or exclamation mark) after each of the following sentences:

1. Hand me the hammer, Hank

2. Is that your uncle sitting in the fourth row

3. This is my final lap

4. You have got to be kidding me

5. Could you please pass the pepper, Peter

6. She wished me well

7. Will both workers be able to complete this job by tomorrow night

8. He spotted his mother's car in the parking lot

9. Stop talking now

10. What a relief that was

11. What a great surprise

12. We quietly resumed our conversation

13. Please turn off that radio

14. Catch that thief

15. Congratulations

16. Have you had enough to eat

17. Where are you going to college, Jessica

18. What a gorgeous dress

19. Listen carefully to what I am going to tell you

20. There were a few of the Madison High School students at the concert

Review Activities

REVIEW ACTIVITY 1   TRAVELING ALONG
(CAPITALIZATION)

Circle the first letter of each word that should be capitalized in the following sentences. Then write each of these first letters, consecutively, on the lines after the list. If your answers are correct, you will spell out the names of six places on the map.

1. i took tommy alder and linda young to the mets game last night.

2. annual checkups with doctor richards should put your mind at ease.

3. instantly david started talking to the texans and ohioans.

4. peter studied english literature while he lived in kansas.

5. anyone who travels with charley will book a room in this fancy hotel.

6. harry loves india's landscape and the north american climate.

7. surely edward visited both oklahoma and utah last year.

8. look at sweden's culture for that inspiration.

9. alan levine was the recipient of this year's award.

10. eventually the martin family members will purchase a home in our town.

The letters spell out these places: _____, _____,

_____, _____, _____,

and _____.

REVIEW ACTIVITY 2   SHOWING YOUR COMMA SKILLS

1. Write two sentences each using a comma to separate a nonessential clause from the rest of the sentence.

   _____

   _____

   _____

   _____

   _____

2. Write two sentences each using a comma to separate a nonessential participle phrase from the rest of the sentence.

   _____

   _____

   _____

   _____

   _____

3. Write two sentences each using a comma to separate the name(s) in direct address from the rest of the sentence.

   _____

   _____

   _____

   _____

   _____

REVIEW ACTIVITY 2   SHOWING YOUR COMMA SKILLS
(Continued)

4. Write two sentences each using a comma to separate a parenthetical expression from the rest of the sentence.

_____

_____

_____

_____

_____

_____

5. Use a comma after a friendly letter's salutation.

_____

6. Use a comma after the closing of any type of letter.

_____

7. Use a comma after a name followed by Ph.D.

_____

8. Use a comma to separate items in a date.

_____

9. Use a comma to separate items in an address.

_____

REVIEW ACTIVITY 3   INSERTING COMMAS

Insert at least one comma in each of the following sentences. Reread each sentence after you have placed the punctuation mark(s) to ensure that your choice is correct.

1. Cooking Thanksgiving dinner Mom carried on several conversations with our relatives.

2. They talked they laughed and they danced during the reunion weekend.

3. In the span of two weeks in May my brother bought and sold three houses.

4. When Stuart dieted he lost more than twenty pounds.

5. Dr. Brown wanted to suspend the students but she decided against it.

6. Yes you should try to see that movie soon.

7. While she was reading the mail Aretha talked with her friend on the telephone.

8. Hillary's three favorite colors are red blue and purple.

9. These scary tall creatures are rather interesting.

10. Motivated by his coach's words the quarterback worked hard during practice today.

11. The caustic ill-tempered supervisor was immediately removed from this position.

12. No I do not need any help.

13. After Aunt Dolly finished gardening she went to see a movie.

14. Italy's capital city is Rome and Spain's capital city is Madrid.

15. If you need an experienced carpenter call Mike Barnes.

REVIEW ACTIVITY 4   WRITING AND PUNCTUATING

1. Write a sentence that contains an introductory participle phrase.

_____

_____

2. Write a sentence that contains a nonessential participle phrase.

_____

_____

3. Write a sentence that contains a nonessential clause.

_____

_____

4. Write a sentence that starts with *Well, No, Why,* or *Yes.*

_____

_____

5. Write a sentence that includes a name or names in direct address.

_____

_____

6. Write a sentence that contains a parenthetical expression.

_____

_____

7. Write an example of a friendly letter's salutation.

_____

_____

8. Write a sentence that contains the name James Donald Reins, Ph.D.

_____

_____

9. Write a sentence that contains an address, including the house number, street name, city, state, and ZIP Code.

_____

_____

10. Write a sentence that contains items in a series.

_____

_____

Final Tests

FINAL TEST 1   CAPITALIZATION

Fifty of the letters in these sentences should be capitalized. Circle those letters. Each correct answer counts 2 points. Incorrectly circled letters will cost you 2 points each. Do well!

1. we read homer's two major writings in literature 101 last fall.

2. syracuse university played against many good teams last season.

3. listening to professor finkel lecture had been a treat for the dowling college students.

4. my parents enjoy going to hear harry reynolds do his comedy routine.

5. the deliveryman drove up to the manthas' house on east linden boulevard.

6. he had formerly held an important position in the u.s. department of defense.

7. our spanish and french friends took us to an italian restaurant called mario's.

8. tom glavine pitched for several national league teams.

9. the plaza is a major hotel.

10. we enjoy looking at photographs in *national geographic* magazine.

11. you should speak to dean jones about your troubling situation.

12. will you help to promote this new album?

13. has your class studied the declaration of independence this semester?

14. congresswoman marla jensen felt that this was a complex issue.

15. the principal of our school greeted the new students from china and india.

A. **Number correct** _____ × 2 = _____

B. **Number incorrect** _____ × 2 = _____

Final score: A − B = _____%

© 2007 by John Wiley & Sons, Inc.

FINAL TEST 2   COMMAS

Fill in the twenty-five missing commas in the following sentences. Each sentence needs at least one comma. Each correct comma is worth 4 points. An incorrectly placed comma will be penalized 4 points.

1. Bobby do you still live in Spokane Washington?

2. Running after the city bus Geraldine a college student was late for school.

3. The deliveryman brought pickles olives celery and apricots.

4. The speaker who has already won several awards will be appearing at another location on July 28.

5. Yes I did hire you on August 15 2004 Steve.

6. She grabbed the pillow and then she threw it at her tall pretty sister.

7. To tell you the truth I do not remember that incident.

8. Since Kendra has not filled out the required application we cannot be admitted to the festival.

9. After the song was over all the dancers headed toward the refreshments tables.

10. Henrietta is this the way to the festival in Boston Massachusetts?

11. The man who caused the disturbance went home and the authorities started the investigation that night.

12. After he read the motion picture's reviews Larry a computer sales representative decided to take his friendly older neighbor to the movies with him.

A. Number correct _____ **× 4 =** _____

B. Number incorrect _____ **× 4 =** _____

Final score: A − B = _____%

Section Six

Meeting the Tests Head-On

The Past Participles of Irregular Verbs

Fill in the correct letters of each irregular verb's past participle. Enjoy!

Across

4. lead
6. throw
7. sing
9. come
11. steal
12. bring
14. write
15. drink

Down

1. fall
2. make
3. blow
5. tear
6. teach
7. swim
8. give
9. catch

10. grow
11. say
13. tell
14. win

6.2 Pairing the Prepositions

Use the pair of prepositions in each numbered item to construct a sentence. Include details and specific verbs to make your sentences come alive! Share your answers with your classmates.

1. behind, within

   _____

   _____

2. except, during

   _____

   _____

3. against, besides

   _____

   _____

4. around, within

   _____

   _____

5. off, with

   _____

   _____

6. after, by

   _____

   _____

7. past, at

   _____

   _____

8. of, beneath

   _____

   _____

9. between, for

   _____

   _____

10. along, over

    _____

    _____

6.3 Clauses and Verbal Phrases

Fourteen clauses and phrases are underlined in the sentences below. Write the five-letter code word for the appropriate clause or phrase when you fill in the blanks of this crossword puzzle. Here is the code:

adjective clause = hurry
adverb clause = happy
noun clause = handy
participle phrase = hasty
gerund phrase = hefty
infinitive phrase = hardy

Across

1. Diving into the shallow water is not a smart idea, Rob.

2. The table that we bought this past weekend will blend well into our apartment.

3. The residents enjoyed cleaning the stream together.

4. Moving along at a comfortable pace, the surgeons were happy with the operation thus far.

5. What we remembered from the accident was told to the authorities.

6. We cannot start until we get the director's approval.

7. These are the same garden tools that my neighbor owns.

8. He wanted to win the tennis match very badly.

Down

1. To succeed in college was Maria's goal.

2. Researching the topic on the Internet was exciting.

3. The worker polishing the brass is my uncle.

4. Freddy sent the brochure to whoever signed up for the course.

5. Whenever Quinn poses for a photograph, he is complimented on his good looks.

6. This is the road to take to Toledo.

6.3 **Clauses and Verbal Phrases** *(Continued)*

Phrasing It the Correct Way

The directions here are quite specific. Use the parts of speech and other requirements given in each number to compose sentences that include all the elements. Reread your sentences to ensure that you have fulfilled the requirements. Share your sentences with your classmates.

1. Adverb phrase/proper noun/appositive phrase/present-tense verb/pronoun-adjective/noun

_____

_____

_____

2. Infinitive phrase/present-tense verb/article/common noun

_____

_____

_____

3. Participle phrase/proper noun/past-tense verb/article/common noun

_____

_____

_____

4. Article/common noun/verb/pronoun-adjective/common noun/preposition/pronoun-adjective/
   adjective/plural noun

_____

_____

_____

5. Article/common noun/past-tense verb/article/common noun/prepositional phrase

_____

_____

_____

(6.4) Phrasing It the Correct Way *(Continued)*

6. Proper noun/appositive phrase/helping verb/main verb/prepositional phrase

_____

_____

_____

7. Singular pronoun/ad.verb/past-tense verb/infinitive phrase

_____

_____

_____

8. Prepositional phrase/article/co.mmon noun/present-tense verb/infinitive phrase

_____

_____

_____

9. Present-tense verb/article/common noun/participle phrase

_____

_____

_____

10. Participle phrase/article/common noun/past-tense verb/article/common noun

_____

_____

_____

(6.5) Placing the Words in Their Proper Places

Here is your chance to show your sentence completion skills. Use the words in Group One to complete sentences 1 to 5. Do the same with the words in Group Two for numbers 6 to 10. After inserting the words, reread the sentences to ensure that your answers are correct.

Group One

and	for	not	Take
but	have	or	very
car's	in	range	wanted
debris	it	Should	
department	mountaineers	Since	

---

1. I _____ to fix my _____ noise, _____ I could _____.

2. _____ the deer entered our backyard, we _____ fed _____ twice a day.

3. _____ the book _____ the wallet to the lost-and-found _____.

4. _____ they remove the _____ from the road _____ wait _____ the police to arrive?

5. The _____ climbed the _____ tallest mountain _____ that _____.

Group Two

attempted	into	sale	Trying
call	investments	securely	will
different	loyal	Several	you
down	mate	that	
If	May	together	

---

6. _____ to secure the boat, the _____ tied the rope _____ to the dock.

7. The financial planner had _____ to select _____ types of _____ for his _____ clients.

8. _____ we assist _____ in moving the packages _____ the basement?

9. _____ of these couches _____ be on _____ starting tomorrow.

10. _____ you believe _____ you can settle the dispute, let us _____ the two parties _____.

Placing the Phrases and Clauses as Directed

On a separate sheet of paper, write sentences that fulfill the following directions:

For A–C: Place the prepositional phrase "in the middle of the night" as:

A. An adverb phrase that starts the sentence

B. An adverb phrase that ends the sentence

C. An adjective phrase that follows the word it modifies

For D–F: Place the participle phrase "trying to lift the heavy stationary bicycle" in these ways:

D. Start the sentence with this phrase.

E. Place the phrase immediately after the noun that it describes.

F. End the sentence with this phrase.

For G–H: Place the adverb clause "while the rain continued to fall" in these ways:

G. Start the sentence with this clause.

H. End the sentence with this clause.

For I–K: Place the infinitive phrase "to win the lottery" in these ways:

I. Use the phrase as the sentence's subject.

J. Use the phrase as a predicate nominative.

K. Use the phrase as a direct object.

For L–M: Use the adjective clause "who won the Tour de France bicycle race" in these ways:

L. Place the clause within the middle of the sentence.

M. End the sentence with the clause.

For N–Q: Use the gerund phrase "accepting her party's nomination" in these ways:

N. Use the phrase as the sentence's subject.

O. Use the phrase as a direct object.

P. Use the phrase as an object of the preposition.

Q. Use the phrase as a predicate nominative.

(6.7) Picking Apart the Sentences

These twenty identifications will test your grammar knowledge. On the line next to each number, write the correct word(s) from that group's sentence.

He walked slowly down the street.

1. _____ adverb

2. _____ preposition

3. _____ past-tense verb

4. _____ object of the preposition

5. _____ article

6. _____ pronoun

Since the magician practices so much, he has improved his act.

7. _____ main clause

8. _____ consecutive adverbs

9. _____ subordinating conjunction

10. _____ direct object

11. _____ possessive pronoun/adjective

12. _____ helping verb

13. _____ dependent clause

Kim and Ricky, my brother, will be married on the last day in March.

14. _____ coordinating conjunction

15. _____ first object of the preposition

16. _____ second preposition

17. _____ adjective that is not an article or a pronoun

18. _____ verb phrase

19. _____ first helping verb

20. _____ appositive phrase

Let's Pick Apart Another Sentence

Using the words in the sentence, "Hank was a policeman and a very good friend of mine, but I never understood a single opinion that he had," fill in the twenty blanks that follow.

1. _____ main clause

2. _____ first coordinating conjunction

3. _____ relative pronoun

4. _____ second dependent clause

5. _____ first predicate noun

6. _____ main clause's subject

7. _____ first adjective

8. _____ last verb

9. _____ first verb

10. _____ first adverb

11. _____ *single*'s part of speech

12. _____ first pronoun

13. _____ first preposition

14. _____ last pronoun

15. _____ *never*'s part of speech

16. _____ proper noun

17. _____ *understood*'s verb tense

18. _____ coordinating conjunction

19. _____ number of nouns in the sentence

20. _____ number of pronouns in the sentence

Putting It All Together

Phrases and clauses help to combine the ideas within sentences. Identify how each related pair of the following sentences is combined by using the following identification code: adverb clause (ADVC), adjective clause (ADJC), noun clause (NC), participle phrase (PP), infinitive phrase (IF), or gerund phrase (GP). Each combining method is used at least once within this activity. Write the code letters on the line next to the sentence.

For sentences 1–3: "The principal congratulated the three students" has been combined with "The three students won the citywide writing contest."

1. _____ The principal congratulated the three students after they won the citywide writing contest.

2. _____ The principal congratulated the three students who won the citywide writing contest.

3. _____ Winning the citywide writing contest, the three students were congratulated by the principal.

For sentences 4–8: "Suzanne would like to attend Vanderbilt University, a competitive university" has been combined with "Suzanne is an excellent student."

4. _____ Suzanne, who is an excellent student, would like to attend Vanderbilt, a competitive university.

5. _____ Wanting to attend competitive Vanderbilt University is the dream of Suzanne, an excellent student.

6. _____ Because Suzanne is an excellent student, she would like to attend Vanderbilt University, a competitive university.

7. _____ To attend competitive Vanderbilt University is a goal for Suzanne, an excellent student.

8. _____ What Suzanne, an excellent student, desires is acceptance into Vanderbilt, a competitive university.

For sentences 9–10: "Frederick is a terrific debater" has been combined with "Frederick has had extensive speech training."

9. _____ Frederick, who has had extensive speech training, is a terrific debater.

10. _____ Because Frederick has had extensive speech training, he is a terrific debater.

Putting the Sentences Together—Bit by Bit

Use the twenty groups of words below to compose seven sentences. Use each group only once. Pay attention to the capital letters and periods to help you in composing these sentences. Write your seven answers on the lines below.

1. treated the ailing child.
2. I travel frequently
3. without exercising.
4. at Michigan State University.
5. Mariah is
6. This company decided
7. He hardly ever
8. to that radio station
9. throughout the year.
10. as a young teen.

11. to create
12. the richest, most delicious
13. An experienced doctor
14. candy possible.
15. goes a day
16. We listen
17. She experimented
18. almost four hours a day.
19. with mascara
20. a full-time graduate student

_____
_____
_____
_____
_____
_____
_____
_____
_____
_____
_____
_____

(6.11) Putting the Sentences Together Again—Bit by Bit

Use the twenty groups of words below to compose seven sentences. Use each group only once. Pay attention to the capital letters, commas, and periods to help you in composing these sentences. Write your seven answers on the lines below.

1. of the car
2. If you need tickets
3. Although Charley has tried to
4. wonderful books for her grandchildren.
5. for the play,
6. in your notebook
7. May I please
8. My mother always bought
9. change his eating habits,
10. borrow that book from you?

11. We looked out the front window
12. Reserve a special section
13. for your new vocabulary words.
14. it has been a struggle for him.
15. for the Super Bowl,
16. dearly for them.
17. After memorizing our lines
18. you will probably pay
19. and saw the deer crossing the road.
20. we performed a dress rehearsal.

_____

_____

_____

_____

_____

_____

_____

_____

_____

_____

_____

_____

_____

_____

(6.12) Is There an Error? (Part One)

Three portions of each of the following sentences are underlined, and each has a letter in front of it. Circle the letter of the underlined portion that contains an error in grammar, usage, or mechanics. Then, either above or below the sentence, correct the error. If there is no error, simply circle the letter D. Be ready to explain your answers.

1. Hester **(A)** implied that she has **(B)** begun working on the project by **(C)** herself. **(D)** No error

2. **(A)** Him losing his hat at the **(B)** site added to the confusion **(C)** of the moment. **(D)** No error

3. The spectators applauded **(A)** as they have never **(B)** did before at any **(C)** other game. **(D)** No error

4. There **(A)** are **(B)** less cartoons on television these days **(C)** than there were thirty years ago. **(D)** No error

5. The troop members walked **(A)** farther today **(B)** than they **(C)** has yesterday. **(D)** No error

6. **(A)** Although I looked **(B)** everywhere for my missing dog, I could not find him **(C)** anywheres. **(D)** No error

7. He and **(A)** her would never refuse to help **(B)** anyone who needed **(C)** their assistance. **(D)** No error

8. **(A)** Having spended so many hours on that project, they **(B)** then worked on carrying their bundles **(C)** down the stairs. **(D)** No error

6.13 Is There an Error? (Part Two)

Three portions of each of the following sentences are underlined, and each has a letter in front of it. Circle the letter of the underlined portion that contains an error in grammar, usage, or mechanics. Then, either above or below the sentence, correct the error. If there is no error, simply circle the letter D. Be ready to explain your answers.

1. A large **(A)** number of spectators **(B)** had attended the race **(C)** at the older track. **(D)** No error

2. This **(A)** here photograph has **(B)** affected many **(C)** who have seen it recently. **(D)** No error

3. They and **(A)** we could **(B)** hardly anticipate what would **(C)** happen next. **(D)** No error

4. **(A)** Being as my uncle is **(B)** quite intelligent, we asked him to try out **(C)** for the television quiz program. **(D)** No error

5. **(A)** Since the temperature has **(B)** fell, we started to **(C)** wear warmer clothes. **(D)** No error

6. Please **(A)** leave me **(B)** learn this math problem by **(C)** myself. **(D)** No error

7. All of the reporters should **(A)** of **(B)** done more investigating instead **(C)** of immediately reporting the news. **(D)** No error

8. **(A)** Even though the officer **(B)** supposedly looked in every room, he never walked from the hallway **(C)** in this room here. **(D)** No error

6.14 Can You Find the Two Errors?

Each of the following sentences contains two errors in grammar, usage, or mechanics. Circle the two errors, and then correct the error in the space either above or below the sentence.

1. The hostess and him chosen the best way to accommodate all the guests.

2. Less then twenty protestors were interviewed for the program.

3. Who should I of asked for that favor?

4. Sherrie acted like she knew which of the two candidates was the intelligenter.

5. The tax increase for these services have been met with frequently protests.

6. I didn't realize that these scientists invented those oil fields.

7. We think that the affects of that hurricane will really hurt less people than you think.

8. Several of the branch managers was transferred, and these workers are not to happy about the changes.

9. Neither the parents nor the child seem bothered by the acception to the rule.

10. These stories was read by my teacher and he during the morning classes.

What's Wrong Here?

There is a problem in grammar or usage in each sentence below. No sentence contains more than a single error. Circle the problem, and on the lines below the sentence, explain what the problem is and how it can be corrected. Your explanation does not have to be in complete sentences.

1. My neighbor said that she sleeps good.

   _____

   _____

2. There is a few items that I would like to address with you.

   _____

   _____

3. If you think that you will be successful on this examination, one should have confidence.

   _____

   _____

4. After the traffic passed, I ride my bike across the street.

   _____

   _____

5. Rhonda and Felicity plans to go to the mall after practice.

   _____

   _____

6. Lenny and Geraldine wants to be attorneys.

   _____

   _____

(6.15) What's Wrong Here? *(Continued)*

7. We went shopping, ate lunch, and gone to see a movie.

_____

_____

8. Looking into the bottom of the bottle, the lemon seeds were spotted by Dad.

_____

_____

9. The hockey team's loss diminished the players' moral.

_____

_____

10. The conversation between you and I was quite long.

_____

_____

11. John is much taller from his older brother.

_____

_____

12. After Tyrone finish building his motorbike, he took it for a ride.

_____

_____

6.16) **Which Is the Best Sentence?**

In each group of five sentences, select the sentence that follows the requirements of standard written English the best. In making your selection, consider grammar, usage, mechanics, sentence construction and fluency, and other elements of clear, effective, precise, and convincing writing. Circle the letter of the best sentence, and be ready to support your choice.

Group 1

a. Being that he is so tall, he can easily dunk the basketball.

b. Since that he is so tall, he can easily dunk the basketball.

c. Since he is so tall, he can easy dunk the basketball.

d. Since he is so tall, he can easily dunk the basketball.

e. Being he is so tall, he can easily dunk the basketball.

Group 2

a. Madeline, one of the most talented dancers in the troupe, she has danced in many American cities.

b. Madeline, one of the most talented dancers in the troupe, because she has danced in many American cities.

c. Madeline, one of the most talented dancers in the troupe, has danced in many American cities.

d. Madeline, one of the most talented dancers in the troupe, since she has danced in many American cities.

e. Madeline, one of the most talented dancers in the troupe, and has danced in many American cities.

Group 3

a. The *New York Times* and the *Boston Globe* are two newspapers that my grandfather reads each day.

b. The *New York Times* and the *Boston Globe* are two newspapers who my grandfather reads each day.

c. The *New York Times* and the *Boston Globe* are two newspapers when my grandfather reads each day.

d. The *New York Times* and the *Boston Globe*, two newspapers that my grandfather reads each day, are them.

e. The *New York Times* and the *Boston Globe* are two newspapers that my grandfather reads each day are they.

(6.16) **Which Is the Best Sentence?** *(Continued)*

Group 4

   a. A social worker's salary is usually not as high as a lawyer.

   b. A social workers' salary is usually not as high as a lawyer.

   c. A social workers' salary is usually not as high as a lawyer's salary.

   d. A social worker's salary is usually not as high as a lawyer's salary.

   e. A social worker's salary is usually not as high as a lawyers' salary.

Group 5

   a. Many workers in this county are organizing unions because they will help them to earn better pay.

   b. Many workers in this county are organizing unions, in order that they get better pay.

   c. Many workers in this county are organizing unions for the purpose of them earning better pay.

   d. Many workers in this county are organizing unions so better pay can be had by them.

   e. Many workers in this county are organizing unions to earn better pay.

Answer Key

Section One: Parts of Speech

Diagnostic Tests

⊠ Diagnostic Test 1: Parts of Speech

1. V	6. CONJ	11. ADV	16. PRO
2. PREP	7. PRO	12. ADJ	17. ADV
3. ADV	8. INT	13. N	18. PREP
4. ADJ	9. PRO	14. V	19. INT
5. PREP	10. N	15. PRO	20. N

⊠ Diagnostic Test 2: Parts of Speech

1. around	3. help	5. lock
2. she	4. eraser	6. margarine
7. older	14. over	21. yet
8. agile	15. between	22. Jeepers
9. kind	16. joke	23. Ah
10. fast	17. overcharged	24. No
11. intelligently	18. eat	25. eventually
12. really	19. for	
13. by	20. and	

The four trees are *ash, elm, oak,* and *fir*.

The four first names are *Bob, Joe, Fay,* and *Jane*.

Lessons and Activities

⊠ 1.1A: Plus a Quotation (Nouns)

1. Wendy, housekeeper

2. answers, test, electricity

3. violin, easel

4. rabbit, yard, officer

5. umbrella, Alabama

6. rain, electrician, box

7. end, afternoon

8. group

9. ostrich, orangutan

10. doctor, orthodontist, neighbors

11. evening, Archie, boating

12. rash, allergy

13. height, agility, match

14. Linda, infant, night

15. carton, oven, licorice, noodles

Quotation and author: "Whatever you are, be a good one." Abraham Lincoln

⌗ 1.1B: Nouns Abound in the Classroom

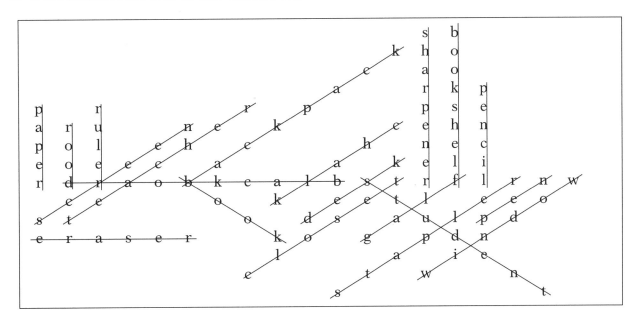

backpack	closet	paper	sharpener
blackboard	desk	pen	stapler
book	door	pencil	student
bookshelf	eraser	ruler	teacher
chalk	flag	screen	window

⌗ 1.2A: Two at a Time (Pronouns)

1. This (DEM), it (PER)

2. He (PER), himself (REF)

3. you (PER), they (PER)

4. Who (INT), her (PER)

5. I (PER), them (PER)

6. him (PER), we (PER)

7. Ours (PER), theirs (PER)

8. Neither (IND), them (PER)

9. she (PER), someone (IND)

10. Those (DEM), ones (IND)

11. yours (PER), us (PER)

12. he (PER), it (PER)

13. Everything (IND), us (PER)

14. they (PER), themselves (REF)

15. All (IND), both (IND)

⌧ 1.2B: Naming the Pronouns

Possible answers are the following:

1. you, him, she, her, our, its, who, all, any, few, one

2. they, them, themselves, this, that, these, those

3. all, another, any, anybody, anyone, anything, both, each, either, everybody, everyone, everything, few, many, more, most, much, neither, nobody, none, no one, one, other, several, some, somebody, someone, such

4. ourselves, themselves, yourselves

5. myself, yourself, himself, herself, itself

6. who, whom, which, and whose

7. The ten pronouns are *I, It, somebody, me, most, This, myself, other, All,* and *my.*

⌧ 1.3A: And a Trip to the Zoo (Adjectives)

The adjectives (and their numbers) are pretty (2), attractive (5), nice (7), dainty (9), agile (10), mean (12), odd (14), noisy (15), kind (17), easy (19), young (20), brave (22), interesting (23), smart (25), old (26), nasty (28), proud (30), infantile (31), great (33), zany (35), elegant (36), boastful (37), rigid (38), and average (40).

The animals are the *panda* (numbers 2, 5, 7, 9, and 10), the *monkey* (numbers 12, 14, 15, 17, 19, and 20), the *bison* (numbers 22, 23, 25, 26, and 28), the *pig* (numbers 30, 31, and 33), and the *zebra* (numbers 35, 36, 37, 38, and 30).

⌧ 1.3B: Listing Three Adjectives

Answers will vary.

⊠ 1.4A: Where the Boys Are (Verbs)

1. r (remember)	8. e (erased)	15. t (told)
2. u (understands)	9. w (withered)	16. e (etched)
3. s (shuffle)	10. i (inspired)	17. f (forgot)
4. s (send)	11. l (leaped)	18. r (recalled)
5. j (jokes)	12. l (loved)	19. e (ended)
6. o (omitted)	13. p (pedaled)	20. d (decided)
7. s (simulated)	14. e (envies)	

The boys are *Russ*, *José*, *Will*, *Pete*, and *Fred*.

⊠ 1.4B: Connecting Verbs and Vocabulary

Walk: meander, parade, plod, shuffle, stride, trek

Talk: chatter, confess, gossip, pronounce, soliloquize, verbalize

Laugh: chuckle, giggle, guffaw, howl, roar, snicker

Succeed: accomplish, achieve, conquer, overcome, score, triumph

Catch: apprehend, claw, collar, corral, snare, trap

⊠ 1.4C: You Will Not Need Help Here (Verbs)

Answers will vary.

⊠ 1.5A: Scrambled Up for You! (Adverbs)

1. fast	6. always	11. first
2. here	7. before	12. often
3. weekly	8. rather	13. now
4. well	9. still	14. also
5. ever	10. not	15. kindly

⊠ 1.5B: Dressing Up (Adverbs)

1. verb—b	6. verb—l	11. adjective—s
2. adjective—s	7. adjective—o	12. adverb—n
3. adjective—h	8. adverb—a	13. adverb—t
4. verb—e	9. verb—t	14. verb—s
5. adverb—p	10. adjective—e	15. adverb—s

Numbers 1, 4, 6, 9, and 14 spell *belts*.

Numbers 2, 3, 7, 10, and 11 spell *shoes*.

Numbers 5, 8, 12, 13, and 15 spell *pants*.

All three items are part of dressing up!

⊠ 1.6A: Finding the Four Words (Prepositions)

1. (b) beyond
2. (i) into
3. (b) below
4. (a) around
5. (c) concerning
6. (i) in
7. (d) during
8. (u) underneath
9. (n) near
10. (d) down
11. (o) over
12. (t) to
13. (a) across
14. (u) under
15. (t) toward

The four words are *bib* (numbers 1–3), *acid* (numbers 4–7), *undo* (numbers 8–11), and *taut* (numbers 12–15).

⊠ Activity 1.7A: Appropriately Chosen! (Conjunctions)

1. both … and
2. neither … nor
3. Either … or
4. for
5. and
6. Not only … but also
7. Whether … or
8. but
9. yet
10. or
11–15. Sentences will vary.

⊠ 1.8A: With Great Feeling!!! (Interjections)

Answers will vary.

Review Activities
⊠ Review Activity 1: O What an Activity! (Parts of Speech)

A = 15	B = 6	C = 9	D = 4
E = 12	F = 1	G = 14	H = 7
I = 2	J = 11	K = 8	L = 13
M = 5	N = 16	O = 3	P = 10

⊠ Review Activity 2: Finding the Missing Link (Parts of Speech)

1. C	6. PN	11. P	16. ADVB
2. ADVB	7. N	12. PN	17. ADVB
3. ADJ	8. V	13. C	18. N
4. I	9. V	14. N	19. N
5. P	10. ADJ	15. ADJ	20. V

⊠ Review Activity 3: Checking Out the Two Sentences (Parts of Speech)

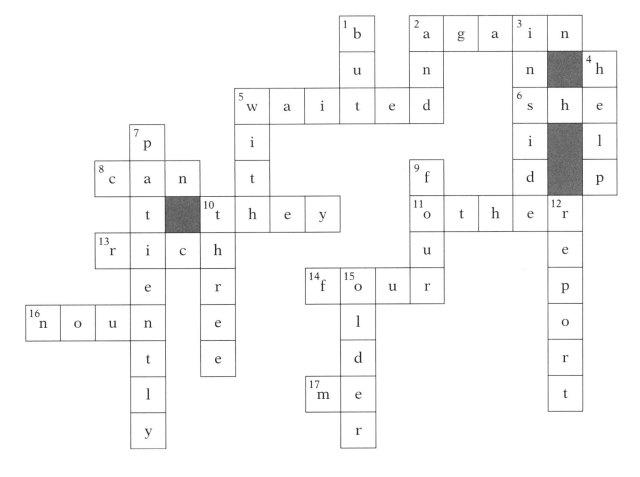

Final Tests

⊠ Final Test 1: Parts of Speech

1. V	6. I	11. N	16. ADVB
2. C	7. P	12. PN	17. V
3. ADVB	8. P	13. ADVB	18. PN
4. PN	9. ADJ	14. C	19. ADVB
5. N	10. C	15. V	20. ADJ

⊠ Final Test 2: Parts of Speech

These are possible answers.

1. You can solve the problem by yourself.

2. Some of these clams are tasty.

3. Read this article now.

4. John and Bridget were married in July.

5. These newspapers should not be sold on these corners.

6. Will you grab the other end of the heavy carton?

7. I would go, but I have homework.

8. Ricardo loves you very much.

9. The boatman finally took his boat out into the bay.

10. With their help, the youngster went up the slide.

Section Two: Parts of a Sentence

Diagnostic Tests

⊠ Diagnostic Test 1: The Parts of a Sentence

For the first five sentences, the simple subject is italicized, and the complete subject is underlined.

1. The *musicians* in the orchestra are paid well.

2. Some *books* in the library need to be restocked.

3. My *friends* in Nebraska should be coming here this summer.

4. The *colors* of the mural are exhilarating.

5. *Each* of the gymnasts will perform this evening.

For the next five sentences, the simple predicate is italicized, and the complete predicate is underlined.

6. He *helps* with the shopping.

7. The singers *performed* last night.

8. The message *tells* much.

9. Our new director *hosted* a meeting at his house.

10. Several fish *swam* toward the boat.

The verb phrase in each of these sentences is underlined.

11. The bed <u>will be shipped</u> tomorrow.

12. Our friends <u>are traveling</u> in Europe.

13. <u>Will</u> you <u>help</u> with the packages?

14. David and Fran <u>were stopping</u> at the store.

15. We <u>had heard</u> the beautiful music.

The compound subjects in these sentences are underlined.

16. The <u>boss</u> and her <u>workers</u> will meet in Boston next week.

17. <u>You</u> and <u>I</u> can handle this problem, Nera.

18. The <u>cat</u> and the <u>mouse</u> watched for each other.

19. <u>Windows</u> and <u>walls</u> need to be cleaned tomorrow.

20. There are <u>Bob</u> and <u>Hank</u>.

⊠ Diagnostic Test 2: Prepositional and Verbal Phrases

The prepositional phrase in each of these five sentences is underlined.

1. Mom cooked the meal <u>within an hour</u>.

2. He broke the record <u>by three seconds</u>.

3. <u>In a minute</u> I can help you.

4. Some <u>of the pretzels</u> are stale.

5. Will you go <u>to the game</u> tonight?

The appositive phrase in each sentence is underlined.

6. Gary Thomas, <u>our professor</u>, is extremely intelligent.

7. Chicago, <u>the Windy City</u>, is in Illinois.

8. My cousin, <u>a broadcaster</u>, is quote well spoken.

9. The heart of the book, <u>the eighth chapter</u>, is touching.

10. Manhattan College, <u>the home of the Jaspers</u>, is a great school.

The misplaced or dangling modifier in each of these five sentences is underlined.

11. <u>Following the path</u>, the flower was spotted by the hikers.

12. <u>At the age of nine</u>, my grandmother taught me how to sew.

13. <u>While drinking the water</u>, the bottle was dropped by the spectator.

14. <u>After winning the contest</u>, the ticket was turned in by the happy family.

15. We saw the flowers <u>walking to the library</u>.

The verbal phrases are underlined in these five sentences. The type of verbal is indicated by the letter preceding the sentence: P = participle; I = infinitive; G = gerund.

16. (I) <u>To win the contest</u> was her goal.

17. (G) <u>Collecting stamps</u> is a good hobby for older people as well.

18. (P) <u>Seeing the stray cat</u>, the police officer stopped the oncoming traffic.

19. (I) Ted needed <u>to finish his essay</u>.

20. (P) The worker <u>wiping his brow</u> is my neighbor.

☒ Diagnostic Test 3: Complements

1. PN	6. IO	11. DO	16. PA
2. DO	7. IO	12. PA	17. IO
3. PA	8. DO	13. IO	18. PN
4. IO	9. PA	14. PN	19. DO
5. PN	10. PN	15. DO	20. PA

☒ Diagnostic Test 4: Subordinate Clauses
The adverb clauses are sentence numbers 3, 6, 7, 9, and 11.

The adjective clauses are sentence numbers 1, 5, 10, 14, and 15.

The noun clauses are sentence numbers 2, 4, 8, 12, and 13.

Lessons and Activities
☒ 2.1A: Look for Something Easy (Simple Subjects)

1. Tennis	6. Asteroids	11. Olives
2. Halloween	7. Newfoundland	12. Eavesdropping
3. Incas	8. beginnings	13. arm
4. solitude	9. elements	14. sousaphone
5. chances	10. shoulders	15. youngster

The sentence reads, "This can be so easy."

⊠ 2.2A: Healthy Advice (Complete Subjects)

1. an	6. yk	11. oc
2. ap	7. ee	12. to
3. pl	8. ps	13. ra
4. ea	9. th	14. wa
5. da	10. ed	15. y!

The familiar proverb is, "An apple a day keeps the doctor away!"

⊠ 2.3A: You Name Them (Subjects in Unusual Positions)

1. Rudy	6. this	11. mirror
2. states	7. election	12. kerchief
3. you	8. margin	13. registrants
4. liver	9. loneliness	14. giants
5. velocity	10. larceny	15. nature

The six names are *Rusty, Olive, Thelma, Lola, Mike,* and *Regina.*

⊠ 2.4A: Matching Them Up (Simple Predicates)

1. permitted—a	6. debated—e	11. strutted—o
2. recalled—l	7. guffawed—g	12. peruse—b
3. assisted—f	8. hurled—m	13. circulated—i
4. sprinted—k	9. started—d	14. veered—n
5. vacated—h	10. selected—c	15. rehearse—j

⊠ 2.5A: A Walk in the Park (Compound Verbs)

1. chatted, exchanged	9. tackled, broke
2. are (not a compound verb)	10. raised, yelled
3. nail, tack	11. argued, negated, triumphed
4. read, ask, listen	12. recognized (not a compound verb)
5. pleases, respects	13. read, investigate, validate, explore
6. remember (not a compound verb)	14. roll, sit
7. offers, suggests	15. imparted, defied, exposed
8. prepare, execute, control	

The four New York City parks are *Central, Prospect, Bryant,* and *Riverside.*

⌧ 2.6A: Yours to Complete (Complete Predicates)

Answers will vary.

⌧ 2.7A: Phasing In Verb Phrases

1. were running	6. had enjoyed	11. will tolerate
2. had been sewing	7. will help	12. are going
3. will be moving	8. had been previewing	13. can find
4. do remember	9. has helped	14. had resurfaced
5. may appear	10. will make	15. will begin

⌧ 2.8A: Hidden Prepositional Phrases

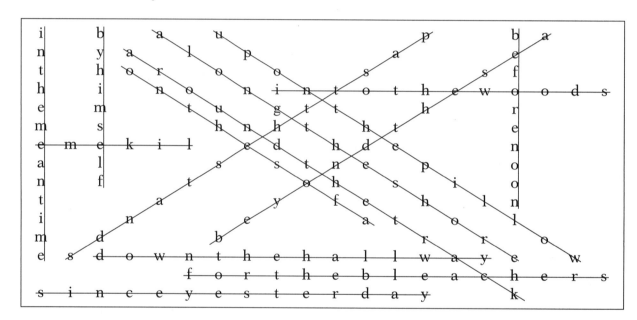

⌧ 2.8B: One to a Sentence (Prepositional Phrases)

The italicized word in each phrase is the preposition.

1. *by* the backstage noise	9. *for* a favor
2. *in* the last inning	10. *concerning* your eligibility
3. *under* the large beach umbrella	11. *for* only a few moments
4. *in* the pond	12. *near* Fenway Park
5. *beyond* the mountain	13. *in* the morning
6. *of* the police force	14. *aboard* the ship
7. *within* the castle	15. *at* the office
8. *during* the wrestling match	

⊠ 2.9A: Making Sense of the Adjective Phrase
Answers will vary.

⊠ 2.10A: Traveling the World (Adverb Phrases)
1. near the podium
2. for that orchestra
3. under the ladder
4. to the arena
5. around the neighborhood
6. Near the daffodils
7. into the election
8. near the garage
9. with their yo-yos
10. past the playground
11. in the truck
12. around that lake
13. to her accountant
14. On that occasion
15. since last semester

The three countries are *Poland, Egypt,* and *Laos.*

⊠ 2.11A: Be Positive About Appositives
1. ap
2. po
3. si
4. ti
5. ve
6. sr
7. ei
8. nf
9. or
10. ce
11. an
12. id
13. ea
14. we
15. ll

The sentence reads, "Appositives reinforce an idea well."

⊠ 2.12A: Misplaced Information (Prepositional Phrases)
These are possible ways to correct the misplaced prepositional problem in each sentence:

1. The guests beckoned to the disobedient dog under the bed.
2. My dad turned over the steak in the oven.
3. We moved the spare tire in the trunk of my car.
4. My great-grandmother spotted the cat up in the large tree.
5. My sister poured the milk into a delicious bowl of cereal.
6. My dad and mom talked about the guppies in the fishbowl.
7. Uncle Ted saw three small frogs in the window well.
8. The infant pointed to the bird on the top of the tall flagpole.
9. The doctor could feel the lump within the patient's stomach.
10. The doctor examined some internal organs inside the chest cavity.

11. In the school auditorium, Bernie recalled his story of cleaning elephants.

12. The maid found the missing pair of pants beneath a pile of dirty clothes.

13. My teacher found his missing pen in the desk drawer.

14. My sister found a worm in the apple.

15. The couple saw the man lift the very heavy carton by himself.

✠ 2.13A: Find the Six (Participles)

The six sentences that do not contain participles are numbers 3, 5, 8, 10, 13, and 18. Their three-letter codes spell *unenthusiastically*.

✠ 2.14A: Five Apiece (Gerunds)

1. DO	6. DO	11. OP	16. S
2. OP	7. OP	12. PN	17. PN
3. S	8. PN	13. OP	18. OP
4. PN	9. S	14. S	19. PN
5. S	10. DO	15. DO	20. DO

✠ 2.15A: Each of the Three Gets Five (Infinitives)

1. ADJ	6. ADJ	11. ADVB
2. N	7. ADJ	12. ADVB
3. ADVB	8. N	13. ADJ
4. N	9. N	14. ADVB
5. ADVB	10. N	15. ADJ

✠ 2.15B: Infinitive Goals

Answers will vary.

✠ 2.16A: Five-Letter Words (Direct Objects)

1. ballet	6. literature	11. homer
2. electricity	7. illnesses	12. obelisk
3. reading	8. games	13. understanding
4. Europe	9. house	14. spring
5. tradition	10. trivia	15. evil

The three five-letter words are *beret*, *light*, and *house*.

⊞ 2.17A: Find the Thirty Letters (Indirect Objects)

1. Carlos
2. ventriloquist
3. dwarfs
4. elephants
5. leopard
6. rookie
7. blockers
8. oncologist
9. ghost
10. apprentice
11. python
12. intern
13. teacher
14. Realtor
15. stuntman

The thirty letters spell the words *cave, dweller, oblong, happy,* and *interest.*

⊞ 2.18A: Two to One (Predicate Nominatives and Predicate Adjectives)

The predicate nominatives are found in sentences 1 (president), 4 (announcer), 9 (Lily), 11 (superstar), and 15 (skipper). The predicate adjectives are found in sentences 2 (talented), 3 (murky), 5 (tired), 6 (wonderful), 7 (lonely), 8 (ecstatic), 10 (lethargic), 12 (happy), 13 (content), and 14 (priceless).

⊞ 2.19A: Nine Is Fine (Adverb Clauses)

1. PP (to the restaurant)
2. AC (After the game concluded)
3. AC (if the weather is good)
4. AC (since you will be there)
5. AC (If he hollers)
6. PP (Considering the circumstances)
7. AC (as soon as the crowd settles down)
8. AC (as if you do not know)
9. AC (Whenever I am confused)
10. PP (since last March)
11. AC (If we can conduct ourselves maturely)
12. PP (until tomorrow)
13. AC (Unless she decides to transfer)
14. PP (after that)
15. PP (in the school)

⊞ 2.20A: Underlining Issues (Adjective Clauses)

1. whose bike was stolen last week
2. that winds its way through this part of the state
3. who is happy
4. who is our captain
5. that we could raise enough money to buy that expensive equipment
6. that is originally from Latin
7. that I went to see last night
8. (that) I want to see
9. who are curious
10. that features the National Spelling Bee

11. whom you voted for on the last episode

12. when people question their priorities

13. where I fell from my bicycle

14. that you made

15. that you have visited

⊠ 2.21A: Functionally Speaking (Noun Clauses)

1. S	6. S	11. OP	16. OP
2. PN	7. PN	12. IO	17. IO
3. DO	8. DO	13. DO	18. DO
4. IO	9. IO	14. PN	19. PN
5. OP	10. OP	15. S	20. S

Review Activities

⊠ Review Activity 1: Adjective and Adverb Phrases

Answers will vary.

⊠ Review Activity 2: Essential and Nonessential Clauses and Participle Phrases

The phrase or clause in each sentence is underlined.

1. NP; <u>Having slept ten hours last night</u>, Rocco was well rested for the competition.

2. EP; We all heard the actors <u>rehearsing their lines</u>.

3. EP; The officer <u>examining the crucial evidence</u> will meet the reporters soon.

4. NP; <u>Walking into the parked car</u>, Wilson hurt his knee.

5. EC; The bicycle <u>that I own</u> is in the garage.

6. NC; This particular treaty, <u>which was ratified a week ago</u>, will be discussed often over the next year or so.

7. NC; Our new principal, <u>who had formerly been an English teacher</u>, is very congenial.

8. EP; Anyone <u>living in that environment</u> needs great determination.

9. NP; <u>Running to catch the bus</u>, the commuter was sorry that she had overslept.

10. NP; <u>Waving to the crowd</u>, our mayor led the town's parade.

11. NP; Fans, <u>clapping for the hockey hero</u>, were happy to see such a talented player.

12. EP; Novels <u>explaining people's motives and desires</u> interest me.

13. NC; Recently released stamps, <u>which feature famous astronauts</u>, will be put on display in our city's library.

14. NC; Our neighbor, <u>whom I have not seen for several weeks</u>, will be buying another motor-cycle this summer.

15. EC; The paintings <u>that were sold at the recent art show</u> are still in the museum.

16. EC; Travelers <u>who do not get upset easily</u> usually enjoy flying.

17. NC; Several photographers, <u>who have known each other for more than two decades</u>, were shooting pictures in the park today.

18. EC; My vacation plans <u>that I told you about</u> have to be canceled.

19. EP; A friend <u>needing our help</u> called me last night.

20. EC; This blue suit <u>that I just purchased last night</u> was on sale.

⊠ Review Activity 3: Filling In the Clauses

These are possible answers:

1. Whenever she works out, she will feel stronger after the workout is completed.

2. The car that you ordered from the dealer will arrive next week.

3. Whoever pays for their tickets is a generous person.

4. The librarian found whatever they needed.

5. Until the wall is repaired, you cannot hang pictures on it.

6. Bright and blue skies are what we want for this weekend.

7. A writer who was a member of the expatriates was Ernest Hemingway.

8. We certainly realize that they have some problems.

9. While Terry worked on his car, his wife cooked dinner.

10. It seems that nothing ever changes.

Final Tests

⊠ Final Test 1: Verbal Phrases

1. G	6. I	11. P	16. G
2. I	7. I	12. G	17. P
3. P	8. P	13. G	18. P
4. P	9. G	14. P	19. P
5. G	10. P	15. P	20. I

✠ Final Test 2: Phrases

1. ADJ	6. APP	11. APP	16. G
2. I	7. ADVB	12. APP	17. ADVB
3. P	8. P	13. I	18. P
4. ADVB	9. ADJ	14. P	19. I
5. ADJ	10. G	15. G	20. ADVB

✠ Final Test 3: Complements

1. DO	6. DO	11. IO	16. PN
2. IO	7. PN	12. IO	17. DO
3. PN	8. IO	13. PN	18. PA
4. IO	9. DO	14. DO	19. PN
5. PA	10. PA	15. PN	20. PA

✠ Final Test 4: Clauses and Verbal Phrases

1. (B) adverb clause	11. (E) gerund phrase
2. (F) infinitive phrase	12. (A) adjective clause
3. (E) gerund phrase	13. (C) noun clause
4. (D) participle phrase	14. (E) gerund phrase
5. (A) adjective clause	15. (F) infinitive phrase
6. (C) noun clause	16. (D) participle phrase
7. (A) adjective clause	17. (B) adverb clause
8. (F) infinitive phrase	18. (C) noun clause
9. (B) adverb clause	19. (A) adjective clause
10. (D) participle phrase	20. (F) infinitive phrase

✠ Final Test 5: Subordinate Clauses

1. ADVB	6. N	11. ADJ	16. ADJ
2. ADJ	7. N	12. ADVB	17. N
3. N	8. ADVB	13. ADVB	18. N
4. ADJ	9. ADJ	14. ADVB	19. ADJ
5. ADJ	10. N	15. ADVB	20. N

Section Three: Sentences

Diagnostic Tests

☒ Diagnostic Test 1: Complete and Incomplete Sentences

The sentences are numbers 1, 3, 4, 10, 11, 17, and 18.

The fragments are numbers 5, 6, 8, 14, 15, 19, and 20.

The run-ons are numbers 2, 7, 9, 12, 13, and 16.

☒ Diagnostic Test 2: Sentences by Purpose

Sentences 1, 7, 9, 13, 14, 16, and 19 are declarative sentences.

Sentences 2, 6, 11, and 18 are imperative sentences.

Sentences 3 and 5 are exclamatory sentences.

Sentences 4, 8, 10, 12, 15, 17, and 20 are interrogative sentences.

☒ Diagnostic Test 3: Sentences by Structure

The simple sentences are numbers 1, 6, 10, 13, 16, and 19.

The compound sentences are numbers 3, 8, 14, 17, and 20.

The complex sentences are numbers 4, 5, 12, 15, and 18.

The compound-complex sentences are numbers 2, 7, 9, and 11.

Lessons and Activities

☒ 3.1A: Half a Score for Each (The Fragment)

The sentences are numbers 2, 5, 6, 7, 8, 12, 15, 16, 19, and 20.

The fragments are numbers 1, 3, 4, 9, 10, 11, 13, 14, 17, and 18.

☒ 3.2A: Let's Get It Right! (Run-Ons)

These are possible answers. There are others.

1. She dribbled the ball. Then she took a jump shot.

2. We have been practicing our music every day. We really enjoy doing this.

3. When Percy swam across the lake, we congratulated him. He was a bit embarrassed by our reaction.

4. My younger sister married Ernesto. Several years later their first child, a girl, was born.

5. I do not want to tell you again. You will need to start eating a healthier diet.

6. For the past ten years, my family has vacationed at the same lake. It is located in Michigan.

7. We were thinking that our customers would again take advantage of this offer. Last year, this same offer was well received.

8. Ann tried to turn off her cell phone's ringer before the lecture began. Unfortunately, she did not remember how to do it.

9. This sale will be in effect until the last day of August. Take advantage of this opportunity as soon as possible.

10. He gave us a ride home after school. Later we went back for the play's rehearsal in the auditorium.

⊠ 3.3A: Spelling It All Out (Types of Sentences by Purpose)

1. EXC	11. EXC
2. DEC	12. IMP
3. INT	13. INT
4. IMP	14. INT
5. DEC	15. DEC
6. INT	16. EXC
7. IMP	17. DEC
8. INT	18. IMP
9. DEC	19. IMP
10. EXC	20. EXC

The declarative sentences spell *generously*.

The exclamatory sentences spell *resentment*.

The interrogative sentences spell *strengthen*.

The imperative sentences spell *specialize*.

⊠ 3.3B: Sentences by Purpose

Declarative sentences are numbers 2, 3, and 15.

Imperative sentences 1, 7, 12, and 16.

Interrogative sentences are numbers 6, 9, 11, 13, and 14.

Exclamatory sentences are numbers 4, 5, 8, and 10

⊠ 3.4A: Quite Simply (The Simple Sentence)

The simple sentences are numbers 2, 5, 6, 7, 10, 11, 12, 13, 19, and 20.

⊠ 3.5A: Don't Be Confounded (Compound Sentences)

The conjunction found in each sentence is listed below. The independent clauses in each sentence are the words that precede and follow the conjunction.

1. but	6. and	11. and
2. and	7. and	12. and
3. but	8. and	13. but
4. and	9. and	14. and
5. but	10. and	15. but

⊠ 3.6A: What's Left Should Be Enough (Complex Sentences)

1. that he had left his glasses in the car

2. Because the cheetah is so fast

3. Since the motorist was lost; that he would ask for directions

4. that was on your desk; that the trip should take three hours

5. When you think about your future

6. As soon as the plane landed

7. that she wanted to make donations to the city's needy

8. who was across the street

9. that are in my office

10. While the zookeeper helped the older panda; that were in the large exhibit

11. that was delivered to your apartment; whom you met in April

12. who was trying to remain calm

13. that is on the screen

14. after the bell rang

15. what she had just witnessed

⊠ 3.7A: It's Not That Complex! (Compound-Complex Sentences)

1. [A rule that needs to be changed is this one], and [we plan to make the desired changes quite soon.]

2. If we see that movie tonight, [we will need to leave immediately], and [I will be able to use my parents' car.]

3. As soon as the building was occupied, [the newspaper reporters interviewed the tenants], and [the television crews filmed the workers throughout the day.]

4. [This cartographer, who has made detailed maps of many neighborhoods, will sign his latest book tonight at the mall,] and [I plan to be there.]

5. When the stadium was demolished, [the debris was trucked off,] and [the workers started to prepare for the next phase of the job.]

6. [The wrestler who pinned all of his opponents won the county championship,] and [then he moved on to the state competition.]

7. [It was sad to see the stadium that provided so many great moments torn down,] but [we looked forward to a larger, more exciting stadium in its place.]

8. [Some of the pages that must be reprinted will be available soon,] and [you can pick them up in my office.]

9. [Stop the nonsense,] and [listen to me] if you want to make this squad.

10. [These parrots that you just bought are funny,] and [I intend to record their actions during the next few days.]

⊠ 3.8A: Seven Starters (Starting a Sentence)

1. C (participle)

2. A (adjective)

3. D (prepositional phrase)

4. F (infinitive phrase)

5. G (subordinate clause)

6. B (adverb)

7. E (participle phrase)

8. F (infinitive phrase)

9. B (adverb)

10. A (adjective)

11. E (participle phrase)

12. G (subordinate clause)

13. C (participle)

14. F (infinitive phrase)

15. E (participle phrase)

16. C (participle)

17. G (subordinate clause)

18. A (adjective)

19. D (prepositional phrase)

20. B (adverb)

21. D (prepositional phrase)

⊠ 3.9A: Diagramming Subjects, Predicates, Modifiers, and Complements

1.   Laurie | whispered

2.   dog (The, older) | slept

3.   neighbor (My, funny) | walks (quickly)

4.   soldiers (These, tired) | are marching (slowly)

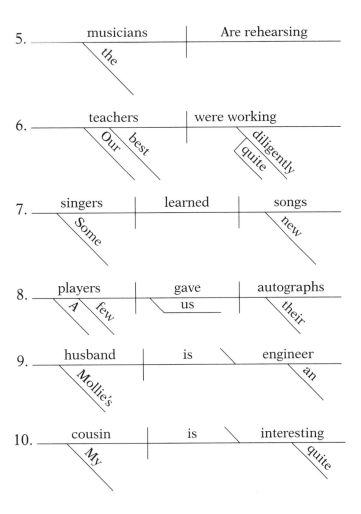

⊠ 3.10A: Diagramming Compound Elements and Prepositional Phrases

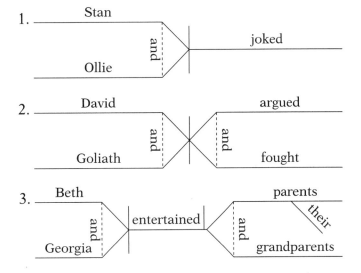

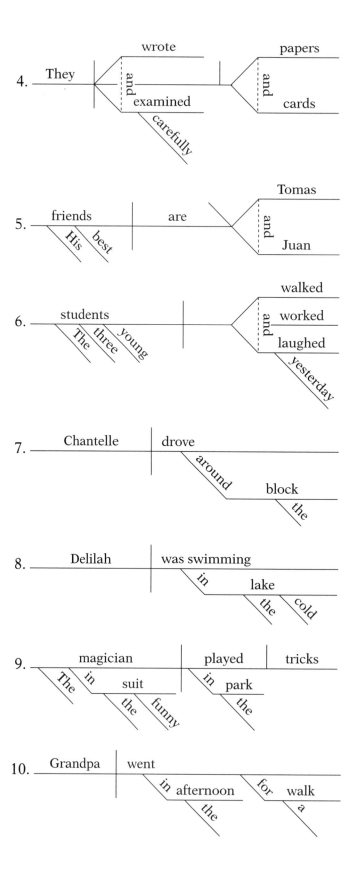

⊠ 3.11A: Diagramming Verbals and Clauses

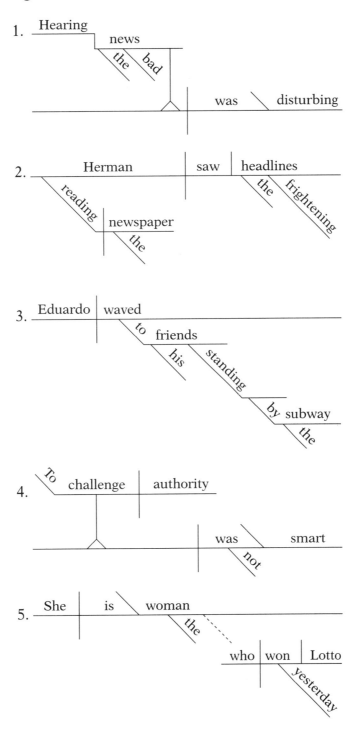

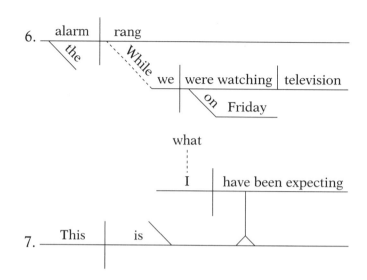

Review Activities

☒ Review Activity 1: Sentences by Structure

1. S	5. CPD	9. S
2. CPLX	6. CC	10. CPD
3. S	7. S	11. CC
4. CC	8. CPLX	12. CC

☒ Review Activity 2: A Part Here, a Part There, and Another Part There ... (Sentence Construction)

The seven sentences are arranged alphabetically.

A woman will be questioned about the incident that occurred at this intersection. (A-H-O)

All of the residents were directed out of the apartment building by the police searching for the robber. (B-L-P)

He is a former criminal defense attorney who has been called incompetent. (C-J-T)

Is this your watch that is here on the kitchen counter, Lyle? (D-M-R)

Most of the sandwiches had been distributed to the homeless men who live in this city neighborhood. (E-K-U)

They are looking through the videotapes to see if they can find the evidence. (F-N-S)

We were heading home along the lonely road in the dark. (G-I-Q)

☒ Review Activity 3: Combining Sentences

These are possible ways to combine each pair of sentences. There may be other methods.

1. My sister, who is twenty years old, will be getting married next June.

2. If you want concert tickets, I can buy them for you.

3. Babe Ruth pitched and played outfield for the Boston Red Sox, and he hit 60 home runs for the New York Yankees in 1927.

4. My uncle has a new car, which he purchased last Saturday morning.

5. Connecticut, the Nutmeg State, is one of the six New England States.

6. Eduardo, who has an A average and is an All-State pitcher, was selected for the Scholar-Athlete Award.

7. Stung by a bee, Denise immediately had to go to the hospital.

⊠ Review Activity 4: Let's Combine Some More Sentences

1. F		6. D	
2. G		7. B	
3. E		8. B	
4. A		9. A	
5. C		10. B and F	

Final Tests

⊠ Final Test 1: Complete and Incomplete Sentences

1. RO	5. S	9. S	13. F	17. S
2. F	6. F	10. RO	14. F	18. RO
3. RO	7. RO	11. RO	15. F	19. F
4. S	8. F	12. RO	16. S	20. S

⊠ Final Test 2: Sentences by Purpose

The declarative sentences are numbers 4, 8, 10, 12, 15, 17, and 20.

The interrogative sentences are numbers 1, 7, 9, 13, 14, 16, and 19.

The exclamatory sentences are numbers 3, 5, and 6.

The imperative sentences are numbers 2, 11, and 18.

⊠ Final Test 3: Sentences Classified According to Structure

1. CPLX	6. CC	11. CC	16. S
2. S	7. S	12. CPD	17. CPLX
3. CPLX	8. CPD	13. CPD	18. CPD
4. CPD	9. CPLX	14. CPLX	19. CPLX
5. CPLX	10. CC	15. S	20. CC

⊠ Final Test 4: Which Is the Best Sentence?

The reasons that the other four groups of words are incorrect are explained after the correct answer.

1. e
   a. The initial verb should be *are*; *less* should be *fewer*; *being that* is nonstandard and not permitted in formal writing.
   b. The initial verb should be *are*; *being that* is nonstandard.
   c. *Being that* is nonstandard.
   d. The initial verb should be *are*.

2. e
   a—c. This is a misplaced modifier problem. Mom was not dropped from her purse as the sentence suggests.
   d. This is an incomplete sentence.

3. b
   a. *They* is repetitive and unnecessary.
   c. This is a dangling modifier problem. The *dangerous jobs* were not *concerned about safety*; the coal miners were.
   d. This sentence is awkward and wordy.
   e. *Being that* is nonstandard.

4. c
   a—b. *Needs*, a singular verb, is required to agree with the singular subject *one*. In addition, *is* should be *are* since the adjective clause modifies *magazines*, a plural word.
   d. *Needs*, a singular verb, is required to agree with the singular subject *one*.
   e. The sentence is very awkward.

5. b
   a, e. A verb is in the subjunctive mood when it expresses a condition that is doubtful or not factual. The correct verb to use in this subjunctive mood situation is *were*, not *was*. Thus, if Lucy were taller (though she is not), she would have been able to change this ceiling light.
   c. *Had that* is not proper.
   d. The same subjunctive mood verb problem (as in "a") exists; *she* is unnecessary.

Section Four: Usage
Diagnostic Tests

⊠ Diagnostic Test 1: Agreement

All of the odd-numbered sentences illustrate correct agreement examples.

All of the even-numbered sentences illustrate incorrect agreement examples.

⊠ Diagnostic Test 2: Verb Tenses

Sentences 1, 6, 7, 11, 12, 15, 16, 18, 19, and 20 illustrate correct verb tense.

Sentences 2, 3, 4, 5, 8, 9, 10, 13, 14, and 17 illustrate incorrect verb tense.

⊠ Diagnostic Test 3: Cases

The underlined nominative case words are in sentences 5, 6, 8, 14, 15, 17, and 20.

The underlined possessive case words are in sentences 1, 2, 7, 9, 12, and 18.

The underlined objective case words are in sentences 3, 4, 10, 11, 13, 16, and 19.

⊠ Diagnostic Test 4: Words Often Confused

1. heard
2. counselor
3. advice
4. altogether
5. capital
6. break
7. Where
8. weather
9. morale
10. formerly
11. quiet
12. your
13. peace
14. course
15. principal
16. plane
17. too
18. already
19. bored
20. through

Lessons and Activities

⊠ 4.1A: What's Her Name? (Agreement of Subjects and Verbs)

The sentences that illustrate correct agreement are sentences I, L, O, and S. Unscrambled, these letters spell the name LOIS.

⊠ 4.2A: Let's Concur! (Agreement Involving Prepositional Phrases)

Here are the correct verbs followed by their subjects.

1. is—man
2. were—girls
3. was—game
4. wins—photograph
5. is—Los Angeles
6. were—aromas
7. is—one
8. were—noises
9. travels—employee
10. were—Both
11. have—Misspellings
12. seems—package
13. helps—anticipation
14. were—types
15. have—changes

⊠ 4.3A: Who Wins? (Indefinite Pronoun Agreement)

Group One	*Group Two*	*Group Three*
1. was	6. was	11. were
2. has	7. needs	12. needs
3. Were	8. is	13. were
4. have	9. travel	14. was
5. does	10. has	15. look
18 points	*19 points*	*20 points*

The winner is Group Three, with 20 points.

⊠ 4.4A: Two or More (Subjects) at a Time (Compound Subjects)

1. are	6. is	11. need
2. were	7. travel	12. stay
3. has	8. travels	13. forget
4. are	9. was	14. Have
5. are	10. were	15. are

⊠ 4.5A: Big and Small (Irregular Verbs)

1. ridden	6. went	11. wrote
2. shrink	7. begun	12. fell
3. stolen	8. rung	13. driven
4. did	9. swum	14. come
5. written	10. taken	15. seen

The correct letters spell the words *large, huge, massive, gigantic, colossal, puny,* and *miniature*.

⊠ 4.6A: It's All in the Numbers (Regular Verbs and Tense)

Group One	*Group Two*	*Group Three*
1. used	6. supposed	11. wondered
2. asked	7. reviewing	12. recall
3. walking	8. finished	13. collected
4. risked	9. landed	14. drowned
5. completed	10. experienced	15. carved

Group One's total number of letters is 31. Group Two's total number of letters is 42. Group Three's total number of letters is 36.

⊠ 4.7A: It's Better in the Active Voice (Active and Passive Voices)

These are possible answers. There could be other correct sentences.

1. My neighbor walked the dog last night.
2. All had a good time at the picnic.
3. Ray moved the hose in our backyard.
4. The manager cautioned the players.
5. The boss congratulated the hard-working assistants.
6. The top students in our class read these books.
7. Emma cleverly performed the challenging role.
8. The staff briefed the new president.
9. Pedro threw the teammate the ball.
10. All the students completed the math test on time.

⊠ 4.8A: College's Orange (Transitive and Intransitive Verbs)

The sentences that have transitive verbs are 2, 4, 6, 7, 10, 12, 13, and 15. The letters associated with those sentences spell out SYRACUSE, the college known as the ORANGE.

⊠ 4.9A: Looking for 29 (Nominative Case)

1. He	6. I	11. I
2. he	7. we	12. I
3. These	8. I	13. we
4. We	9. he	14. he
5. he	10. I	15. she

⊠ 4.10A: All Objects Should Be Located! (Object of the Preposition)

1. between Robert and Rania—sat
2. during the race—fell
3. aboard the ocean liner—were
4. for the playground—headed
5. to my parents—sold
6. with you—Take
7. by himself—jogged
8. into the closet—moved
9. beneath the dock—found
10. Under the eave—were
11. over time—decrease
12. near the shore—Were
13. off the charts—selling
14. throughout the movie—laughing
15. since last Tuesday—had

⊠ 4.11A: The Letter A (Objective Case Review)

1. DO	6. IO	11. DO
2. OP	7. IO	12. DO
3. OP	8. DO	13. OP
4. DO	9. OP	14. IO
5. IO	10. IO	15. OP

Direct objects: *llama, panda*
Indirect objects: *Alaska, gala*
Object of the preposition: *Canada, blah*

⊠ 4.12A: Three in a Row (Possessives)

your, mine, ours
my, his, hers
whose, anyone's, girls'

⊠ 4.13A: Ten Times (Who Versus Whom)

1. who	6. who	11. whom
2. whom	7. who	12. who
3. who	8. who	13. who
4. whom	9. who	14. whom
5. who	10. whom	15. who

⊠ 4.14A: Half and Half (Comparisons of Modifiers)

(A) The comparisons in sentences 1, 3, 5, 6, 7, 11, 14, 15, 18, and 20 are correct.

(B) Their code letters spell out the words *eerie, aardvark, loophole,* and *invisible.*

(C) The sentences containing the incorrect modifiers are below:

2. worse	10. more tightly	17. more quickly
4. most pleasant	12. wiser (no need for more)	19. more often
8. most	13. bumpier	
9. slowest	16. most eagerly	

(D) The words spelled out by these code letters are *bubble, giggled, lilies,* and *rearranged.*

⊠ 4.15A: Only Five (Dangling and Misplaced Modifiers)

The five sentences that do not appear here are correct. Here are possible corrected versions of the sentences that have dangling and misplaced modifiers.

1. Walking to the pitcher's mound, the coach kicked the grass.
2. Patty saw the beautiful new state flag attached to the flagpole.
4. The police officer found the mangy, panting, and hungry dog on the curb and handed the dog to its owner.
6. The owner washed his cat, who was licking its hind leg.
7. The doorbell rang three times after I washed the dishes.
9. Peeking into the closet, I saw my birthday presents.
10. I enjoyed the treat of sitting in the first-class section of the plane, which has comfortable seats and plenty of legroom.
12. After dirt-biking all day over this challenging course, I had sore muscles.
13. Looking down between the clouds, the pilot saw the Grand Canyon.
15. After lifting the heavy package, Richie placed it down on the platform.

⊠ 4.16A: Be Upbeat! (Usage Words)

1. beside	7. have	13. fewer
2. anywhere	8. teach	14. affect
3. like	9. doesn't	15. except
4. than	10. invented	16. among
5. unless	11. burst	17. Let
6. who	12. good	

The letters spell out the sentence, "A smile is just a frown turned upside down."

⊠ 4.16B: More Usage Words

A = 15	B = 6	C = 9	D = 4
E = 12	F = 1	G = 14	H = 7
I = 2	J = 11	K = 8	L = 13
M = 5	N = 16	O = 3	P = 10

⊠ 4.16C: Knowing When to Use What (Usage Words)

Sentences will vary.

⊠ 4.17A: Add Up the Points (Words Often Confused—Part One)

The correct answer and its point value are listed next to one another.

A. break (12)   F. effect (6)   K. board (9)

B. already (4)   G. bored (10)   L. capital (13)

C. choose (15)   H. capitol (14)   M. advise (2)

D. advice (1)   I. all ready (3)   N. affect (5)

E. altogether (8)   J. all together (7)   O. brake (11)

Each group's total is 40.

⊠ 4.18A: Parade of Animals (Words Often Confused—Part Two)

1. ze   6. ll   11. rl

2. br   7. am   12. io

3. ap   8. ac   13. nt

4. an   9. ou   14. ig

5. da   10. ga   15. er

The animals are the *zebra, panda, llama, cougar, lion,* and *tiger.*

☒ 4.19A: Shady Characters (Words Often Confused—Part Three)

1. peace (umb)
2. moral (rel)
3. quiet (law)
4. shone (eep)
5. plane (ing)
6. principle (wil)
7. passed (low)
8. morale (cra)
9. principal (yon)
10. quite (map)
11. plain (lep)
12. past (enc)
13. lose (ilp)
14. piece (ara)
15. shown (sol)

The shady characters are *umbrella, weeping willow, crayon, maple, pencil,* and *parasol.* They are shady characters because they all provide shade!

☒ 4.20A: A Balancing Act (Words Often Confused—Part Four)

1. al
2. lw
3. or
4. ka
5. nd
6. no
7. pl
8. ay
9. ma
10. ke
11. sj
12. ac
13. ka
14. du
15. ll
16. bo
17. yp
18. ro
19. ve
20. rb

The sentence is the well-known proverb, "All work and no play makes Jack a dull boy."

☒ 4.21A: This Can't Get No Harder! (Double Negatives)

These are possible answers. There may be others.

1. I don't have any friends.
2. He can't get any satisfaction from his job.
3. We can hardly hear the band from our distant seats.
4. There was no reason to stay around any longer waiting for our ride.
5. They only have three weeks to finalize the New York City Marathon plans.
6. How come she never did anything about it?
7. Julio never does anything wrong.
8. These directions from Dad make no sense to me.
9. I had scarcely enough money to afford the birthday gift.
10. We don't need any motivation.

Review Activity

⊠ Review Activity: Words Often Confused

A = 2	B = 15	C = 17	D = 23	E = 8
F = 10	G = 22	H = 1	I = 20	J = 12
K = 21	L = 19	M = 13	N = 7	O = 5
P = 14	Q = 6	R = 25	S = 4	T = 16
U = 18	V = 3	W = 9	X = 11	Y = 24

Final Tests

⊠ Final Test 1: Agreement

1. her	6. has	11. Have	16. Have
2. is	7. have	12. was	17. its
3. were	8. was	13. Were	18. are
4. are	9. have	14. were	19. were
5. is	10. are	15. her	20. seem

⊠ Final Test 2: Verb Tenses

1. reached	6. were	11. knew	16. amazed
2. preferred	7. had bought	12. fallen	17. Throw
3. laid	8. had been	13. had had	18. lie
4. swum	9. became	14. came	19. burst
5. leads	10. slept	15. broken	20. begun

✖ Final Test 3: Verb Tenses

The correct verb tense is in parentheses.

1. incorrect (flown)	8. incorrect (ridden)	15. incorrect (shrunk)
2. correct	9. correct	16. incorrect (rung)
3. correct	10. correct	17. incorrect (fallen)
4. incorrect (swim)	11. correct	18. incorrect (gave)
5. incorrect (blew)	12. correct	19. correct
6. incorrect (chosen)	13. incorrect (threw)	20. correct
7. correct	14. correct	

✖ Final Test 4: Cases

1. her	6. us	11. they	16. who
2. him	7. You and I	12. we	17. whom
3. We	8. they	13. her	18. whom
4. those	9. she	14. her and me	19. Who
5. us	10. he	15. she	20. us

✖ Final Test 5: Words Often Confused

1. shown	6. course	11. through	16. whose
2. dessert	7. passed	12. waste	17. week
3. lead	8. hear	13. stationary	18. here
4. complimented	9. formerly	14. morale	19. quite
5. bored	10. whether	15. lose	20. council

Section Five: Mechanics

Diagnostic Tests

⊠ Diagnostic Test 1: Capitalization

The letters that should be capitalized are in bold type.

1. **M**y sister, **N**ancy, owns a **T**oyota **C**amry.

2. **R**aised in **A**labama, this gentleman wrote many interesting stories.

3. **H**e does his shopping at **P**athways, the local supermarket.

4. **A**ndy **W**arhol's famous paintings of **C**ampbell's soup cans were part of our dinner conversation.

5. **W**e studied the **K**orean **W**ar in our history class last **N**ovember.

6. **D**id you drive to **J**ones **B**each last **M**emorial **D**ay?

7. **T**he play *Hello Dolly* will be performed tonight in **P**leasantville, **N**ew **Y**ork.

8. **S**he is a very popular **B**razilian dancer.

9. **W**e discussed the serious matters involving both the **U**nited **S**tates **C**ongress and the **H**ouse of **R**epresentatives.

10. **B**oth of my uncles attended the **U**niversity of **M**iami.

11. **T**his **H**oliday **I**nn will host a visit by **S**uperintendent **A**lston.

12. **T**he airport is near **S**hea **S**tadium in **Q**ueens.

13. **T**he woman asked her colleagues, "**A**re you going home for lunch?"

14. **M**y neighbor had been a colonel for seventeen years.

15. **S**ome of these tomatoes are unripe.

⊠ Diagnostic Test 2: Commas

1. Tomasita, is this the correct way to Jackson, Mississippi?

2. You need to carry the crate, the flag, and the two packages.

3. Having read the newspaper that morning, Georgia, a sophisticated and well-read editor, walked to her limo.

4. Since I do not have the correct change for the bus, could you lend me some coins, David?

5. John G. Loweret Jr., a college professor, would like to visit Madrid, Spain, in a few months.

6. When my sister was born on June 4, 1987, my aunt stayed over at our house for a few days and helped with the chores.

7. Rex would like to run for Congress, and many think that he, a charming, intelligent man, would make a good leader.

8. No, this is the wrong way to my cousin's cabin.

9. After the principal read the afternoon's announcements, the members of our club, the Brainstormers, met for practice.

10. This saleswoman, who is also a noted coin collector, will be visiting several of our town's stores next month.

⌧ 5.1A: Half and Half (Capitalization)

The correct answers are numbers 1, 2, 5, 6, 8, 12, 14, 16, 17, and 19.

⌧ 5.1B: Sporting Around (Capitalization)

1. re	6. et	11. ld
2. me	7. it	12. of
3. mb	8. an	13. dr
4. er	9. sf	14. ea
5. th	10. ie	15. ms

The two movies are *Remember the Titans* and *Field of Dreams*.

⌧ 5.1C: Ten Letters at a Time (Capitalization)

1. m	6. s	11. f	16. u
2. i	7. c	12. r	17. l
3. c	8. o	13. a	18. e
4. r	9. p	14. u	19. n
5. o	10. e	15. d	20. t

The two ten-letter words are *microscope* and *fraudulent*.

⌧ 5.2A: Finding the Missing Letters

The missing letter is in bold type.

1. accord**io**n	7. conven**i**ent	13. insu**r**ance
2. analy**si**s	8. describ**e**	14. leng**th**
3. analy**ze**	9. equivalen**t**	15. medi**c**ine
4. ben**e**fit	10. govern**or**	16. natura**ll**y
5. busi**n**ess	11. hypocri**t**e	17. omi**tt**ed
6. chang**e**able	12. impl**e**ment	18. over**r**un

19. perc**e**ive   22. psychology   25. thoro**ug**h

20. permi**tt**ed   23. quan**ti**ty

21. prepa**ra**tion   24. sub**t**le

⊠ 5.3A: Why We Use Commas (Part One)

1. C   6. H   11. H   16. G

2. B   7. F   12. B   17. H

3. A   8. F   13. C   18. C

4. E   9. D   14. A   19. D

5. G   10. A   15. E   20. D

⊠ 5.3B: Why We Use Commas (Part Two)

1. D   6. A   11. F

2. C   7. B   12. F

3. E   8. B   13. B

4. C   9. D   14. D

5. A   10. E   15. E

⊠ 5.4A: Showing Your Apostrophe Skills

1. He'd rather read last week's magazine.

2. My mother belongs to the women's club.

3. Can you estimate this box's weight?

4. We followed the mice's path.

5. A secretary's job is not an easy one!

6. Uncle Jack's, Grandpa Frank's, and Grandmother Anna's signatures are interesting.

7. She graduated with the Class of '05 from high school.

8. Is this somebody else's coat?

9. Have you painted the men's faculty bathroom yet?

10. How many too's did he misspell in the essay?

11. This is his father-in-law's radio.

12. Have you read the governor's new proposal?

13. the men's watches

14. fifty dollars' worth of equipment

15. Rich's medals

16. they'd

17. Chris' (or Chris's) stamp collection

18. Aunt Shelia and Uncle Tony's house

19. the wolves' lair

20. the children's fort

⊠ 5.5A: Quotation Marks in Every Sentence

1. I have read the short story, "The Story of an Hour," by Kate Chopin.

2. "I am not going to go home just yet," Lilly remarked.

3. "We will watch the television episode, 'The Rascals Are Here,' tonight," said Fern.

4. I really enjoyed the lecture, "The Way We Live," by Thomas Devlin.

5. Hymie asked, "Did Hamlet say, 'To be or not to be'?"

6. "I believe," said Hank, "that all people can better themselves."

7. Sandy said, "I enjoyed reading the short story, 'Bernice Bobs Her Hair,' by F. Scott Fitzgerald."

8. The director screamed, "I see a tornado in the distance!"

9. "Are they being sarcastic toward you?" I asked Vivian.

10. "The poem, 'Boy Wandering in Simms Valley,' is great," said Joey.

11. "Is 'Love Is All You Need' your mother's favorite Beatles song?" Ollie asked Stanley.

12. Tommy told us, "I know how much you are trying to do better."

⊠ 5.6A: Working with Punctuation

1. We could not believe that he ate two hamburgers, three helpings of macaroni salad, four hard rolls, twenty-six pretzels, six hot dogs, and a dozen olives.

2. Are you going to the prom with Maria Torres, Miguel?

3. We will have this window installed this Saturday; otherwise, we will have to wait until the spring.

4. My favorite novel by Ernest Hemingway is *A Farewell to Arms*.

5. May we go on a field trip to see the battleship, the USS *Intrepid*?

6. Where is Auguste Rodin's statue, *The Thinker*?

7. "What do you intend to do about our drinking water problem?" is the question to ask the politician at today's meeting.

8. I will meet you at the railroad station at 7:45 tomorrow morning.

9. Nadia remarked, "I am confused about this math problem."

10. Georgette reads the *New York Times* at least three days a week.

11. The movers intended to lift the piano by themselves; however, the home owner insisted on helping them.

12. Have you read F. Scott Fitzgerald's short story, "Bernice Bobs Her Hair"?

13. Both the Republicans and the Democrats bickered over Senator Larsen's remarks; moreover, neither side wanted to back off the issue.

14. He can bat from both the left and right side of the plate, slides well, and is very disciplined.

15. Tad is reading the article, "How to Succeed in High School," by Johnny Matzuka.

⊠ 5.6B: Using Semicolons, Colons, Italics, and Hyphens

1. Dear President Gavigan:

2. I read *The Great Gatsby* and *Julius Caesar* this summer. [or underline the titles]

3. My father has a subscription to *Games* magazine.

4. You will need to have the following items for the trip: tent, lantern, matches, and a compass.

5. There are between forty-seven and fifty-one tickets left to be sold for tonight's performance.

6. My best friend would like to attend college; however, he has to earn a scholarship in order to do so.

7. The newly appointed editor-in-chief is Millie Wilson.

8. Have you watched reruns of *Friends* lately?

9. Kent is a terrific company president; he will be honored for his business achievements at the banquet this evening.

10. We saw a film about the USS *Constitution* last evening.

11. I will pick you up at 6:45 tomorrow morning, Harry.

12. We attended the theater and saw *The Sound of Music* this past winter.

13. Our class studied the works of the following painters: Degas, Manet, Monet, Sisley, and Gauguin.

14. My thirty-two-year-old sister loves to discuss the articles from the *Boston Globe*.

15. Her favorite painting is Grant Wood's *American Gothic*.

⊠ 5.7A: Proper Punctuation, Please! (Brackets, Parentheses, Ellipsis Marks, and Dashes)

Answers will vary.

⊠ 5.8A: Putting the End Mark in Its Place

1. Hand me the hammer, Hank.

2. Is that your uncle sitting in the fourth row?

3. This is my final lap.

4. You have got to be kidding me!

5. Could you please pass the pepper, Peter?

6. She wished me well.

7. Will both workers be able to complete this job by tomorrow night?

8. He spotted his mother's car in the parking lot.

9. Stop talking now! *Or* Stop talking now.

10. What a relief that was!

11. What a great surprise!

12. We quietly resumed our conversation.

13. Please turn off that radio.

14. Catch that thief!

15. Congratulations!

16. Have you had enough to eat?

17. Where are you going to college, Jessica?

18. What a gorgeous dress!

19. Listen carefully to what I am going to tell you.

20. There were a few of the Madison High School students at the concert.

Review Activities

⊠ Review Activity 1: Traveling Along (Capitalization)

1. I took Tommy Alder and Linda Young to the Mets game last night.

2. Annual checkups with Doctor Richards should put your mind at ease.

3. Instantly David started talking to the Texans and Ohioans.

4. Peter studied English literature while he lived in Kansas.

5. Anyone who travels with Charley will book a room in this fancy hotel.

6. Harry loves India's landscape and the North American climate.

7. Surely Edward visited both Oklahoma and Utah last year.

8. Look at Sweden's culture for that inspiration.

9. Alan Levine was the recipient of this year's award.

10. Eventually the Martin family members will purchase a home in our town.

    The letters spell out *Italy, Madrid, Topeka, China, Seoul,* and *Salem.*

✠ Review Activity 2: Misspelled Words

1	2	3	4	5	6	7	8	9	10	11	12	13	14	15	16	17	18
	b		v					y						c			
f	a	m	i	l	i	a	r	o	c	c	a	s	i	o	n		
	l		l		n			u						l		h	
	l		l	t	e	c	h	n	i	q	u	e		u		a	
	o		a	r				g						m		p	
	o		g	o			h	g						n		p	
	n		e	d	e	f	e	r	r	e	d					i	
				u			i	a			e					l	
				c			g	m			s	a	f	e	t	y	
p	r	o	c	e	e	d	h	m			p						
	e						t	a			e						
m	a	i	n	t	a	i	n	r			r						
	l										a	b	s	e	n	c	e
	l	e	g	i	t	i	m	a	t	e	t						
	y									j	e	a	l	o	u	s	y

✠ Review Activity 3: Showing Your Comma Skills

Answers will vary.

✠ Review Activity 4: Inserting Commas

1. Cooking Thanksgiving dinner, Mom carried on several conversations with our relatives.
2. They talked, they laughed, and they danced during the reunion weekend.
3. In the span of two weeks in May, my brother bought and sold three houses.
4. When Stuart dieted, he lost more than twenty pounds.
5. Dr. Brown wanted to suspend the students, but she decided against it.
6. Yes, you should try to see that movie soon.
7. While she was reading the mail, Aretha talked with her friend on the telephone.
8. Hillary's three favorite colors are red, blue, and purple.

9. These scary, tall creatures are rather interesting.

10. Motivated by his coach's words, the quarterback worked hard during practice today.

11. The caustic, ill-tempered supervisor was immediately removed from this position.

12. No, I do not need any help.

13. After Aunt Dolly finished gardening, she went to see a movie.

14. Italy's capital city is Rome, and Spain's capital city is Madrid.

15. If you need an experienced carpenter, call Mike Barnes.

⊠ Review Activity 5: Writing and Punctuating

Here are sample answers.

1. Driven by a desire to succeed, the athlete trained very purposefully.

2. Carried into the museum, the painting is quite breathtaking.

3. These tickets, which the officer gave out, will be reviewed during the upcoming weeks.

4. Well, this is certainly not what I had expected!

5. Riley, can you please help me find my cell phone?

6. Our suggestions, in my opinion, are worth discussing.

7. Dear Sally,

8. These suitcases belong to James Donald Reimes, Ph.D., of Tacoma, Washington.

9. We visited my cousins at 1234 Friendly Street, Anywhere, NY, 00000.

10. This group of theater enthusiasts has already seen *Cats*, *Oliver*, *Rent*, and *Miss Saigon*.

Final Tests

⊠ Final Test 1: Capitalization

The letters that should be capitalized are in bold type.

1. **W**e read **H**omer's two major writings in **L**iterature 101 last fall.

2. **S**yracuse **U**niversity played against many good teams last season.

3. Listening to **P**rofessor **F**inkel lecture had been a treat for the **D**owling **C**ollege students.

4. **M**y parents enjoy going to hear **H**arry **R**eynolds do his comedy routine.

5. **T**he deliveryman drove up to the **M**anthas' house on **E**ast **L**inden **B**oulevard.

6. **H**e had formerly held an important position in the **U**.**S**. **D**epartment of **D**efense.

7. **O**ur **S**panish and **F**rench friends took us to an **I**talian restaurant called **M**ario's.

8. **T**om **G**lavine pitched for several **N**ational **L**eague teams.

9. **T**he **P**laza is a major hotel.

10. **W**e enjoy looking at photographs in *National Geographic* magazine.

11. **Y**ou should speak to **D**ean **J**ones about your troubling situation.

12. **W**ill you help to promote this new album?

13. **H**as your class studied the **D**eclaration of **I**ndependence this semester?

14. **C**ongresswoman **M**arla **J**ensen felt that this was a very complex issue.

15. **T**he principal of our school greeted the new students from **C**hina and **I**ndia.

⊠ Final Test 2: Commas

1. Bobby, do you still live in Spokane, Washington?

2. Running after the city bus, Geraldine, a college student, was late for school.

3. The deliveryman brought pickles, olives, celery, and apricots.

4. The speaker, who has already won several awards, will be appearing at another location on July 28.

5. Yes, I did hire you on August 15, 2004, Steve.

6. She grabbed the pillow, and then she threw it at her tall, pretty sister.

7. To tell you the truth, I do not remember that incident.

8. Since Kendra has not filled out the required application, we cannot be admitted to the festival.

9. After the song was over, all the dancers headed toward the long refreshments tables.

10. Henrietta, is this the way to the festival in Boston, Massachusetts?

11. The man who caused the disturbance went home, and the authorities started their investigation that night.

12. After he read the motion picture's reviews, Larry, a computer sales representative, decided to take his friendly, older neighbor to the movies with him.

Section Six: Meeting the Tests Head-On

⊠ **6.1: The Past Participles of Irregular Verbs**

⊠ **6.2: Pairing the Prepositions**

Answers will vary.

⊠ 6.3: Clauses and Verbal Phrases

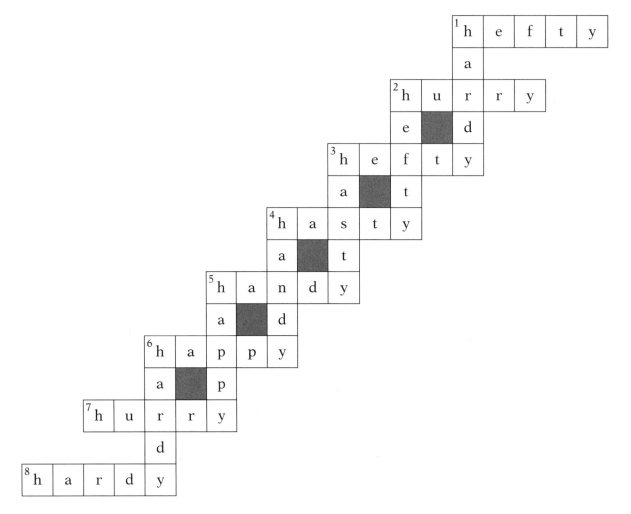

⊠ 6.4: Phrasing It the Correct Way

Here are sample answers.

1. In the morning, Christine, a mother of two, does her stretching.
2. To win the election is the goal.
3. Walking home from school, Leroy saw a deer.
4. The comedian opened her act with some humorous observations.
5. A cartoonist accepted the prize for his work.
6. Jimmy Carter, a former U.S. president, is known for his philanthropy.
7. She desperately wanted to win the election.
8. In the winter the family loves to ski.
9. See the ball rolling down the hill.
10. Looking carefully, the detective spotted the evidence.

⊠ 6.5: Placing the Words in Their Proper Places

1. I <u>wanted</u> to fix my <u>car's</u> noise, <u>but</u> I could <u>not</u>.

2. <u>Since</u> the deer entered our backyard, we <u>have</u> fed <u>it</u> twice a day.

3. <u>Take</u> the book <u>and</u> the wallet to the lost-and-found <u>department</u>.

4. <u>Should</u> they remove the <u>debris</u> from the road <u>or</u> wait <u>for</u> the police to arrive?

5. The <u>mountaineers</u> climbed the <u>very</u> tallest mountain <u>in</u> that <u>range</u>.

6. <u>Trying</u> to secure the boat, the <u>mate</u> tied the rope <u>securely</u> to the dock.

7. The financial planner had <u>attempted</u> to select <u>different</u> types of <u>investments</u> for his <u>loyal</u> clients.

8. <u>May</u> we assist <u>you</u> in moving the packages <u>down</u> <u>into</u> the basement?

9. <u>Several</u> of these couches <u>will</u> be on <u>sale</u> starting tomorrow.

10. <u>If</u> you believe <u>that</u> you can settle the dispute, let us <u>call</u> the two parties <u>together</u>.

⊠ 6.6: Placing the Phrases and Clauses as Directed

These are sample answers.

A. In the middle of the night, we heard a strange noise in our basement.

B. We heard a strange noise in our basement in the middle of the night.

C. That strange noise in the middle of the night awakened us.

D. Trying to lift the heavy stationary bicycle, the older man strained himself.

E. The older man trying to lift the heavy stationary bicycle strained himself.

F. We saw the older man trying to lift the heavy stationary bicycle.

G. While the rain continued to fall, the streets became flooded.

H. The streets became flooded while the rain continued to fall.

I. To win the lottery was Hector's dream.

J. Hector's dream was to win the lottery.

K. Hector wanted to win the lottery.

L. Lance Armstrong, who won the Tour de France bicycle race, also ran the New York City Marathon.

M. We waved to Lance Armstrong, who won the Tour de France bicycle race.

N. Accepting her party's nomination excited Phyllis.

O. Phyllis enjoyed accepting her party's nomination.

P. Phyllis earned our admiration by accepting her party's nomination.

Q. Phyllis's most recent political achievement was accepting her party's nomination.

⊠ 6.7: Picking Apart the Sentences

1. slowly
2. down
3. walked
4. street
5. the
6. He
7. he has improved his act
8. so much
9. Since
10. act
11. his
12. has
13. Since the magician practices so much
14. and
15. day
16. in
17. last
18. will be married
19. will
20. my brother

⊠ 6.8: Let's Pick Apart Another Sentence

1. Hank was a policman and a very good friend of mine
2. and
3. that
4. that he had
5. policeman
6. Hank
7. good
8. had
9. was
10. very
11. adjective
12. mine
13. of
14. he
15. adverb
16. Hank
17. past
18. but
19. four (Hank, policeman, friend, opinion)
20. four (mine, I, that, he)

⊠ 6.9: Putting It All Together

1. ADVC
2. ADJC
3. PP
4. ADJC
5. GP
6. ADVC
7. IF
8. NC
9. ADJC
10. ADVC

⊠ 6.10: Putting the Sentences Together—Bit by Bit

Here are the sentences and the numbers of the items used to compose these sentences.

He hardly ever goes a day without exercising. (7–15–3)

We listen to that radio station almost four hours a day. (16–8–18)

I travel frequently throughout the year. (2–9)

She experimented with mascara as a young teen. (17–19–10)

An experienced doctor treated the ailing child. (13–1)

Mariah is a full-time graduate student at Michigan State University. (5–20–4)

This company decided to create the richest, most delicious candy possible. (6–11–12–14)

⊠ 6.11: Putting the Sentences Together Again—Bit by Bit

Here are the sentences and the numbers of the items used to compose these sentences.

Reserve a special section in your notebook for your new vocabulary words. (12–6–13)

Although Charley has tried to change his eating habits, it has been a struggle for him. (3–9–14)

After memorizing our lines for the play, we performed a dress rehearsal. (17–5–20)

My mother always bought wonderful books for her grandchildren. (8–4)

If you need tickets for the Super Bowl, you will probably pay dearly for them. (2–15–18–16)

May I please borrow that book from you? (7–10)

We looked out the front window of the car and saw the deer crossing the road. (11–1–19)

⊠ 6.12: Is There an Error? (Part One)

1. D

2. A. Since *losing* is a gerund, it needs a possessive adjective to modify it. Thus, use *His* instead of *Him*.

3. B. The past participle is needed here. Use *done* instead of *did*.

4. B. Use *fewer* since you can count the number of cartoons. Use *less* when you cannot count specific items, such as *less* enthusiasm or *less* intelligence.

5. C. *Had* is the correct verb for this sentence.

6. C. *Anywheres* is not a word. Use *anywhere*.

7. A. The pronoun subject needs to be in the nominative case. Use *she* (nominative case word) instead of *her* (objective or possessive case word).

8. A. There is no such word as *spended*. Use *spent*, the past-tense form of the verb *spend*.

✖ 6.13: Is There an Error? (Part Two)

1. D

2. A. Delete *here* because it serves no purpose.

3. D

4. A. Use *Since* because *Being as* is not used in formal writing.

5. B. The past participle form of *fall* is *fallen*. Use *fallen* since it is required by the inclusion of the helping verb *has*.

6. A. *Let* means "to allow." Use *let* instead of *leave*.

7. A. *Of* is never correct if you want to use it as a helping verb. Use *have* instead.

8. C. *Into* implies that one has gone from one location and crossed over to another location. *In* implies that one is within the boundaries of a specific place. Use *into* here.

✖ 6.14: Can You Find the Two Errors?

1. Use *he* instead of *him*; use *chose* or *choose* instead of *chosen*.

2. Use *fewer* instead of *less*; use *than* instead of *then*.

3. Use *Whom* instead of *Who*; use *have* instead of *of*.

4. Use *as if* instead of *like*; use *more intelligent* instead of *intelligenter*.

5. Use *has* instead of *have*; use *frequent* instead of *frequently*.

6. Use *did not* instead of *didn't*; use *discovered* instead of *invented*.

7. Use *effects* instead of *affects*; use *fewer* instead of *less*.

8. Use *were* instead of *was*; use *too* instead of *to*.

9. Use *seems* instead of *seem*; use *exception* instead of *acception*.

10. Use *were* instead of *was*; use *him* instead of *he*.

✖ 6.15: What's Wrong Here?

1. *Good*, an adjective, is incorrect. The adverb *well* is the correct word.

2. *Items* is the plural subject. Thus, *are*, a plural verb, and not *is*, a singular verb, should be used.

3. The subject of each clause must be consistent. *You* and *one* are not consistent. Either change both subjects to *you* or both subjects to *one*.

4. There is a verb tense problem here. *Passed*, the past-tense verb of the subordinate clause, is not consistent with *ride*, the present-tense verb of the main clause. Either change *passed* to *passes*, and leave *ride* as it is, or add *will*, or change *ride* to *rode* and leave *passed* as it is.

5. The compound subject needs a plural verb. Thus, use *plan*, not *plans*.

6. The compound subject needs a plural verb. Thus, use *want*, not *wants*.

7. *Went*, a past-tense verb, should be used in place of *gone*, the past participle verb that needs *has, had,* or *have* with it.

8. This is a misplaced modifier problem. The lemon seeds were not looking into the bottom of the bottle; Dad was. Thus, the sentence should read, "Looking into the bottom of the bottle, Dad spotted the lemon seeds."

9. The correct word is *morale* (spirit), not *moral* (right or wrong).

10. *I* is not an objective case word. Use *me*.

11. This is an idiom problem. Use *than* instead of *from*.

12. This is a verb tense problem. Change *finish* (present tense) to *finished* (past tense) since *took* in the main clause is in the past tense.

⊠ 6.16: Which Is the Best Sentence?

Here are the correct answers with an explanation of why the other sentences are incorrect.

Group 1: d

    a. *Being that* is nonstandard and incorrect in formal writing.

    b. *Since that* is incorrect in formal writing.

    c. The adverb should be *easily,* not *easy.*

    e. *Being* does not introduce the sentence smoothly.

Group 2: c

    a. *She,* following the appositive phrase, is unnecessary.

    b, d, e. These are not complete sentences.

Group 3: a

    b. The relative pronoun, *who,* does not refer to things, only people.

    c, e. These sentences do not make sense.

    d. The sentence does not have fluency, and the predicate nominative is incorrectly written in the objective case.

Group 4: d

    a. The sentence compares a lawyer's salary with a lawyer.

    b. *Workers'* is not the required singular possessive form of *worker*; the sentence compares a lawyer's salary with a lawyer.

    c. *Workers'* is not the singular possessive adjective that is needed here.

    e. *Lawyers'* is not the singular possessive adjective that is needed here.

Group 5: e

    a. The pronouns *they* and *them* are vague.

    b. *In order that* is awkward.

    c. The sentence is both vague and awkward.

    d. The latter part of the sentence is both awkward and in the passive voice.

Index